No Ordinary Life

No Ordinary Life

The Biography of
Elizabeth J. McCormack

Charles Kenney

PublicAffairs

NEW YORK

Published in the United States by PublicAffairs™,
a Member of the Perseus Books Group

PublicAffairs books are available at special discounts for bulk purchases in the U.S. by corporations, institutions, and other organizations. For more information, please contact the
Special Markets Department at the Perseus Books Group, 2300 Chestnut Street, Suite 200,
Philadelphia, PA 19103, call (800) 810-4145, ext. 5000,
or e-mail special.markets@perseusbooks.com.

Book Design by Jenny Dossin

Produced by Della R. Mancuso Associates, Inc., Geneva, NY

Cataloging in Publication data is on file with the Library of Congress

ISBN 978-1-61039-201-3

First Edition

1 3 5 7 9 10 8 6 4 2

To the memory of Jerome I. Aron

Contents

Foreword by Joel L. Fleishman   *ix*

Prologue   *xiii*

1   Called by God   *1*

2   Never Laugh Again   *21*

3   Living with an Illusion   *47*

4   A Difficult Time   *67*

5   Firing Line   *89*

6   A New Life   *105*

7   The Love of Her Life   *121*

8   Light of Reason   *135*

9   Rebirth   *153*

10   Rockefellers   *173*

11   The Fine Art of Philanthropy   *199*

12   Today   *219*

Index   *231*

Foreword

IT IS A PRIVILEGE and a pleasure to introduce to you this compelling, fascinating story of Elizabeth McCormack's remarkable career, which we expect will be an inspiration to all who read these pages.

What makes Elizabeth's story so compelling is her unerring internal compass, which led her to overcome the limitations that existed for a young Catholic girl growing up in the suburbs of New York City in the 1930s. After graduating from Manhattanville College, she was called to the Society of the Sacred Heart, where she became a nun. With hard work, significant talents, and an entrepreneurial spirit, she returned to Manhattanville as its president a few years later. There she quickly set about pushing through greatly needed educational reforms, often meeting stiff resistance along the way. After several years in that role she left the Society, married, and assumed leadership positions with some of the most important foundations and philanthropic families in the country. She has always pushed boundaries, becoming a force of nature in the field of philanthropy, a pioneer as a woman in fields dominated by men, and a catalyst for change to improve institutions so as to make them vibrant, relevant, and effective.

Elizabeth McCormack is now well known in the world of philanthropy, business, and higher education. She is revered by both those who hold powerful positions and those who don't. This biography provides a comprehensive picture of her personal and professional life in an intimate way that will inform even those who already know her well. By observing the arc of her life that has touched so many and even had a profound impact on so many others, one comes quickly to understand why her advice is sought in person as well as the more public settings of boards and committees.

To me, the overriding picture that emerges in this story, the secret to Elizabeth McCormack's success, is her ever-ready frankness. She honestly and clearly expresses her views, and she can even be blunt if necessary. She offers advice without regard to any personal self-interest and with a genuineness, vision, consistency, and gutsiness that provide a fulfilling dynamism to those who follow it in their own decision making. All of this is always done in a respectful and balanced manner, with humility, gentleness, and grace. She is wise; never self-righteous.

This biography was written by Charles Kenney based on important preliminary work by the late Rod Gander and Tom Mathews. It is fortunate that Peter Osnos, the founder and now Editor-at-Large of Public-Affairs, was able to recruit Mr. Kenney, who has worked hard to bring this work to completion in time for the recognition of Elizabeth's ninetieth birthday. In addition to Elizabeth's involvement in the process, there were many who willingly participated in interviews, research, and fact checking to make this book such a fine read. And of equal importance, there were several donors who made significant financial contributions, but who have asked to remain anonymous.

The origin of this work, however, goes back some years and was catalyzed by Harvey P. Dale, who had sought the advice of Elizabeth

McCormack when he helped Charles Feeney shape the structure and policies of Atlantic Philanthropies. After Atlantic was launched and after Elizabeth served on the board for a number of years, Mr. Dale broached the idea of a biography, but Elizabeth would have none of it! She did not consider herself worthy of the time and effort for such a project. But Dale was persistent. And Nan Aron, the daughter of Elizabeth's late husband, Jerry Aron, kept the pressure on the development of the book and served as a critically important bridge between Elizabeth and Charles Kenney. The wise counsel, expertise, and heroic exertions of Susan Weinberg, Peter Osnos, and Robert Kimzey of PublicAffairs, combined to enable this biography to be completed in record time.

So, there were many angels, but in many ways, the life and work of Elizabeth McCormack "speaks for itself." Enjoy the story, learn from it, and be inspired to contribute to the world in ways that Elizabeth's life points us.

Joel L. Fleishman
Professor of Law and Public Policy
Faculty Chair
Center for Strategic Philanthropy and Civil Society
Duke University

Prologue

AT AGE EIGHTY-NINE, Elizabeth McCormack is noticeably hunched over and stands an inch or two shy of five feet. She has a shock of gray/ white hair hastily combed and her eyes are bright and penetrating—the eyes of a much younger woman. Her crisp, authoritative voice tends toward a higher register. She carries herself with a seasoned self-assurance. Her diminutive stature notwithstanding, she is a *presence*. The tiny woman with piercing eyes, a mischievous grin, and a turbo-charged intellect effortlessly dominates a room.

Who is she? Who is this woman known by not a soul in the great breadth of the country but known by everyone in certain New York circles? Although it has not always been the case, she works now among the elite of the elite; among citizens of the world who are so well-educated, so successful, that they spend vastly more time and effort now giving away money than making it. But not just giving it away—doing it *well*, with intelligence and purpose and, it is their hope, with effect. They are people devoted both personally and professionally to trying to make the world a better place. They succeed in places, and too often fall flat— but they *try;* their effort is real.

The calendar is dotted through the years with events on glittering Manhattan evenings when men and women of exceptional achievement gather to honor Elizabeth Jane McCormack. She is lavished with praise by the likes of Richard Parsons, former CEO of Time-Warner, and Thornton Bradshaw, the former chair of the John D. and Catherine T. MacArthur Foundation; by Bill Moyers and David Rockefeller; and by a dozen other members of the Rockefellers in the third and fourth generations.

As the holder of a PhD in philosophy, she is one of the planet's few experts on the somewhat obscure, but influential British philosopher F. H. Bradley. When she was twenty-one, she committed herself to God as a nun in the Society of the Sacred Heart. At twenty-two, she donned a beautiful lace wedding dress and engaged in a Roman Catholic ceremony where she gave herself as a bride of Christ. As a nun she committed to detachment from the world, purity of intention; to absolute and total obedience; to an entire surrender of self to the service of God. She shaved her head so it might more comfortably fit under the habit that covered her from head to toe. She owned *nothing*—had no money, no bank account, not a share of stock. She came of age in a time when opportunities for women were rarer than rare and yet she found a route to leadership and influence. She sailed into the eye of the storm of the 1960s and 1970s as president of Manhattanville College, where so much of what she stood for was under fire; where so much of *everything* was under fire. There was turmoil over race and gender, war and peace. A nun—a woman—committed to chastity, was surrounded by the sexual revolution.

In the 1970s, 1980s, 1990s, and into the twenty-first century, she became one of the most important actors in the world of philanthropy. She helped guide some of the leading foundations in the world—and, eventually, some of the leading corporations, as well. She would serve on dozens of boards of organizations and companies, including the John D. and Catherine T. MacArthur Foundation, the Memorial Sloan-Kettering Cancer Center, the Juilliard School, the American Academy in Rome, the Asian Cultural Council, Atlantic Philanthropies, Conservation International, the Trust for Mutual Understanding, Alliance Capital, United Healthcare, Champion International, and General Foods. She is a member of the American Academy of Arts and Sciences and the Council on Foreign Relations. A corporate leader gave her a small replica of a tank to acknowledge her fierceness.

But she is also a thinker, a conscience, a dissident, a strategist, a fighter, a mentor, a guide. Eventually, she became a wife and stepmother. She was a Roman Catholic nun for three decades who married a Jewish lawyer.

On a balmy June evening in 1997, many of Manhattan's elites gathered for a tribute to Elizabeth McCormack and her role in an environmental organization called Scenic Hudson. Before she was presented with an award from her friend Steven Rockefeller, a professor at Middlebury College, she was introduced by Bill Moyers, another friend. Moyers spoke from the heart about Elizabeth:

> I've come to cherish her as a friend and exemplar. She is an archetype, if you will, of how to live a life when, as Gabriel says in *The Green Pastures,* "Everything that's tied down is coming loose." Just think of the tumult of her times. She's lived through the Depression, the Second World War, wars in Korea and Vietnam, the revolution in civil rights, the feminist revolution, the atomic age, and the Cold War. She's outlasted the boogie-woogie, Elvis and the Beatles, Chubby Checker and the Andrew sisters. . . . Popes have come and gone, and presidents, too. She's survived Harding, Coolidge, Hoover, Roosevelt, Truman, Eisenhower, Kennedy, Johnson, Nixon, Ford, Carter, Reagan, and Bush . . .

and I'll wager you that Bill Clinton will be back in Hot Springs before Elizabeth even reaches her prime.

What's the secret of her long consistency of principle through the upheavals of the time? How to explain her leadership in education, organization, and philanthropy? Well, there are certain people for whom the world is as fresh as it was the first day, whose eyes never dim to its novelty, who see life as "wonderful, inscrutable, magical, and more" . . . because they move in the world with faith, and hope, and charity: charity as caritas, the benevolence of God and the caring we owe each other.

How else to explain the touch she brings to her work? . . .

To Elizabeth, any surplus of riches is a trust, and owners of great wealth are but agents and trustees for society. Albert Einstein thought it impossible for wealth to help move humanity forward. Can anyone . . . he asked . . . can anyone imagine Moses, Jesus, or Gandhi armed with the money-bags of an Andrew Carnegie? Well, yes—if Elizabeth had been their advisor. She would have seen to it that the fervors of the followers who organized religions in their wake would have been suffused not by the rivalry and competition which provoke crusades and jihads, create Beiruts and Belfasts, and cause bombs to explode in holy cities . . . but by the ethic of cooperation and the values of collaboration.

For this woman, our friend, knows that civilization is an unnatural act. It doesn't just happen. It's something we do together; we make it happen. For all the chest-thumping about rugged individualism and the self-made man, the building of America was a social, not a solitary, endeavor; individual initiative succeeded only when it led to strong systems of mutual support, and we moved beyond the laissez-faire philosophy of "live and let live" to the active and affirmative commitment to "live and help live." This is Elizabeth's way, the inspiration for us all to remember that "thou must live for thy neighbor if thou wouldst live for thyself" (Seneca).

She's a work of nature, our friend Elizabeth . . . just like the Hudson River. And like our river she reminds us of things that last, that transcend the tumult of the hour and the news of the day. Her life is about connections and continuities between past and present, between now and the future, between the natural world and the world we make together.

(1)

Called by God

WHEN THEY WERE children in Larchmont, New York, in the late 1920s, Betty McCormack and her younger brother George would ride in the backseat of their father's Ford sedan for the Sunday morning drive to Mass. Their route meandered through town, taking them past a Presbyterian church.

"Betty and I would always hold our breath as we passed it because, you know, you might get contaminated," recalls George. Elizabeth Jane McCormack—or, Betty, as she was called then—is dubious about the reliability of her brother's memory. Yet there is no doubt that they occupied a thoroughly Roman Catholic universe. Elizabeth and George attended weekly Mass with their parents, who were traditional Catholics. The family was culturally more comfortable in a Catholic world of Catholic friends and Catholic schools. Elizabeth describes her parents as "good Roman Catholics, but they were not the go-to-Mass-every-day kind."

Elizabeth Jane McCormack was born on March 7, 1922, in New York City, to Natalie (née Duffy) and George Henry McCormack. George was born nearly three years later on January 24, 1925. When she was four, her family moved to the affluent Westchester suburb of Larchmont. Elizabeth grew up in the 1920s and 1930s without television, computers, or other sources to connect a young girl with the world outside her small, Catholic circle. "All my friends were Catholics, and your friends all thought the way you did," she recalls. "I met a few people who were not Catholics because we had a summer house in Lake Placid and the Lake Placid Club was a very Protestant place, but you didn't think out of the box while you were growing up."

Elizabeth was a petite girl with crackling energy. Her sharp mind was evident early on. In the second grade at nearby St. Augustine's Academy, run by nuns of the Dominican order, Elizabeth was distressed by the idea of Hell. Her teacher described it as a place ruled by Satan, where sinners suffered for *eternity*. Elizabeth raised her hand.

"Do I have to believe in Hell?" she asked Sister Helen Vincent.

"Yes, you do," replied the nun.

Betty considered this, then asked, "Well, sister, do I have to believe that there are *people* in hell?"

Sister Helen Vincent answered wisely, "No, Elizabeth, you do not have to believe there is anyone there."

"Then I believe in Hell—but that it's empty," replied the child.

After grade school, the plan was for Elizabeth to attend the Ursuline School, a high school in nearby New Rochelle, where Ursuline nuns served as the faculty. But she was concerned. "Friends of mine had gone there and what I heard about it made me really not want to go," she recalls.

During the summer before tenth grade, she told her father she didn't want to attend Ursuline. He asked, "Well, where *would* you like to go?" She had heard good things about another school, Maplehurst, which had higher academic standards. It was an all-girl, five-day boarding school. The teachers belonged to the Society of the Sacred Heart, and the students were from not just Westchester County but also New Jersey and Connecticut. "What about Maplehurst?" she asked. The Society of the Sacred Heart was a distinguished congregation of teaching nuns. It was perhaps the Society's academic and intellectual rigor as well as the quality of religious instruction that persuaded Elizabeth's father that she and Maplehurst were a good fit.

And so, on a summery day, Elizabeth and her father went to the Maplehurst campus at 181st Street and University Avenue in the Bronx. The visit convinced Elizabeth that it was the right school for her. It would mean a major change in her life, since Maplehurst required five-day boarding; she would be home only on weekends. But this rule only added to the sense of adventure, and now she was sure she wanted to go.

In the fall of 1936, Elizabeth entered the tenth grade at Maplehurst. It turned out to be an awkward and disappointing transition for her. The great majority of the girls had started at Maplehurst in the ninth grade, when they established friendships. Elizabeth was an outsider, a newcomer, and teenage girls with their cliques are not always famously kind to outsiders and newcomers.

Elizabeth had never been as lonely as she was at Maplehurst. During the weekends, she told her parents she hated the school and wanted out. Her parents' reply was always the same: This was your choice, and you are going back. So back she went each Monday morning. And then as the season changed and the holidays came, Elizabeth had gotten to know some of the girls, and even made friends. Suddenly she was content in her new school.

She loved the Sacred Heart nuns who taught her. They were all college graduates, unlike nuns in some other religious orders. Many were women with powerful intellects who took great joy in discovery and learning—and the greatest joy in sharing their knowledge with students. Elizabeth studied ancient then medieval history and literature. She was happy to take on the most challenging material, and it soon became evident that she was an exceptional intellect. She had a joyful, inquisitive learning style and became a favorite with the faculty. A voracious reader, she developed a passion for the Romantic poets, Shelley, Keats, and Coleridge.

While she took the work quite seriously, Elizabeth had a sense of playfulness. She lived in a small dorm room right next to the door leading into the convent where the nuns lived. Just beyond her room, at the convent entrance, was a sign: "If you need a mistress during the night, ring this bell." She thought this was hilarious. "I was sixteen and these were cloistered nuns, and they didn't know how funny that sign was." She shared the joke with her parents, who had a good laugh too.

Her brother, George, recalls that during the summer after her junior year at Maplehurst, Elizabeth was tutored in math at Lake Placid by a teacher named Herbert Howard. The McCormack home in Lake Placid was near a boarding school, and some of the faculty lived there, including Mr. Howard. Elizabeth developed a mad crush on him. "Mr. Howard was a very good-looking guy," recalls George, "and she was nuts about him."

The tutoring was needed because Elizabeth had failed an exam in intermediate algebra. The unfortunate irony was that, near the end of the school year, the faculty had already nominated Elizabeth for a prize as best student in algebra. "I blanked on the test and failed," she says, "and my parents made me have tutoring and I retook the test in the fall, aced it, but it was too late to win a prize!"

.   .   .

Elizabeth's mother, Natalie, had graduated from high school, and taught for a while. But then Natalie's mother, who was still in her forties, suffered a debilitating stroke. Natalie quit working and devoted herself to her mother's care. She had all but decided that, because of her mother, she would never marry.

"When my father wanted to marry my mother, she said she couldn't because she could not leave her mother," says Elizabeth. "My father said, 'You don't have to. They will come and live with us.'"

So George and Natalie were married and moved into a large house at 10 Center Avenue in Larchmont. And Natalie's parents came with them. The home had four bedrooms on the second floor and an additional bedroom and bath in the attic.

George McCormack was president of the architectural firm of Halsey, McCormack and Helmer, which specialized in designing banks. Their most famous building is a great landmark in Brooklyn, the second tallest edifice in that borough, the Williamsburgh Savings Bank, which opened in 1927, next to the Brooklyn Academy of Music. The business was quite successful and enabled the McCormacks to enjoy an affluent lifestyle. On some Sundays after Mass, Elizabeth's father would play golf at the prestigious Winged Foot Golf Club in Mamaroneck, New York. The McCormacks' cook lived in the attic bedroom. One cook was with the family for some time until one of the McCormacks saw her making the Heil Hitler salute. They dismissed her.

When Elizabeth was a very young girl, her mother would read stories to her. But sometimes she stopped in mid-story to go off to prepare dinner or perform another household chore. Frustrated, Elizabeth felt she had to learn to read so she wouldn't have to depend on her mother to learn how a story ended.

Elizabeth's grandmother could do little on her own. Over time, glaucoma deprived her grandfather of his vision. As a girl, Elizabeth would read the *New York Herald Tribune* to him each day. She would begin by reading headlines, and he would select which stories and editorials he wanted to hear. "I became a Democrat at age seven or eight from reading the *Herald Tribune*," she says. When Elizabeth was in the seventh grade, her maternal grandmother died, and a few years later, her maternal grandfather died.

Elizabeth's paternal grandmother also lived in Larchmont. Each day her son would walk to the Larchmont train station for the commute to the Manhattan offices of Halsey, McCormack and Helmer. Each evening, on his way home, he would stop at her house for a visit.

After the death of her parents, Natalie suggested to her husband that his mother should come live with them. She thought this would make life easier for all concerned. When Grandmother McCormack moved in, however, quite the opposite happened. Elizabeth's maternal grandparents were sweet and kind, but Grandmother McCormack was demanding and difficult. "She thought she could run the house," says Elizabeth.

Before Grandmother McCormack moved in, Elizabeth and her brother had alternated weeks where they would have Sunday lunch at her apartment. Elizabeth remembers her grandmother listening to Father Charles Coughlin on the radio. The nature of his ugly message, which included a virulent anti-Semitism, escaped her at that time, but Elizabeth's grandmother liked what he had to say. Later, Elizabeth realized the nature of his hate-filled message.

Her grandmother McCormack was accustomed to running her own household and tried to dominate the family in every way. Elizabeth, now in her teens, would say to her mother, "The only one who can stop Grandma McCormack is Dad. You have got to tell him what is going on here." Her mother answered, "He deals with his business. This is my responsibility. I am not telling him."

.   .   .

In 1940, Elizabeth began to think about college. She was among Maplehurst's brightest students, and she knew she could get into just about any college. She knew about Wellesley, Smith, and Mount Holyoke, but Radcliffe appealed the most to her. Because it was connected to Harvard, Radcliffe was not an all-female environment.

And so at the dinner table one evening, Elizabeth raised the possibility of Radcliffe. Her father, quite calmly, said he found that very interesting. "Who do you think is going to pay the tuition?" he asked. And, with that, the discussion was over. Elizabeth would go to a Catholic college, and the most logical choice was Manhattanville, which was the first choice of many intelligent, affluent Catholic girls in greater New York.

"It was thought to be the strongest of the Catholic colleges for women," recalls Elizabeth. "That and Trinity College in Washington were considered the best. Manhattanville had also been founded by the same nuns—the Religious of the Sacred Heart—who ran Maplehurst."

.   .   .

Her father, George McCormack, had not attended college and, in fact, never finished high school. His father and brother had died when he was a teenager, so he left school to go to work to support his mother. Through the years, George educated himself, becoming, like his daughter, an insatiable reader. But the fact that he had not gone to college always bothered him.

In 1940, during Elizabeth's senior year at Maplehurst, she and her father visited Manhattanville, which was at that time in upper Manhattan, and met with the president of the college, Mother Grace Dammann. When father and daughter entered her office, Elizabeth noticed a picture on the wall of Jacques Maritain, the Catholic philosopher she knew from her studies.

In the early part of the twentieth century, Maritain was so highly regarded among Church leaders that he was asked by French bishops to write textbooks for Catholic colleges and seminaries. His work, *Introduction to Philosophy*, published in 1920, has been widely studied by countless Catholic students and seminarians through the years. This passage from the book is quintessential Maritain, bridging philosophy and religion:

Finally, I would say that, if the philosophy of Aristotle, as revived and enriched by St. Thomas and his school, may rightly be called *the Christian philosophy,* both because the church is never weary of putting it forward as the only true philosophy and because it harmonizes perfectly with the truths of faith, nevertheless it is proposed here for the reader's acceptance not because it is Christian, but because it is demonstrably true. This agreement between a philosophic system founded by a pagan and the dogmas of revelation is no doubt an external sign, an extra-philosophic guarantee of its truth; but it is not from its agreement with Faith, but from its own rational evidence, that it derives its authority as a philosophy.

Elizabeth mentioned to Mother Dammann that she had studied Maritain, and the nun was clearly pleased to hear this. Mother Dammann was a fan of Maritain's, too, and said she had attended some of his lectures.

The interview went well, and father and daughter left the building, but outside, George McCormack seemed agitated. Inside their car, he said, "I'm hearing you talk about Jacques Maritain-this and Jacques Maritain-that. *Who the hell is Jacques Maritain?"*

Elizabeth says, "If it had been Plato or Aristotle or St. Thomas Aquinas, he would have known of course. He thought he had failed some kind of test. He felt he should have known this guy." She did not want to hurt his feelings, so she replied that Maritain was "an unimportant Catholic philosopher from France."

What neither Mother Dammann nor Elizabeth nor George McCormack could have known at the time was that Maritain would soon move to New York and work throughout the war for the rescue and safe passage of Jewish intellectuals to the United States. After the war, he persuaded senior Church officials, including the pope, to speak out on the issues of anti-Semitism and the Nazi Holocaust.

. . .

Manhattanville was the only college to which Elizabeth applied. She was admitted and was quite excited about going there. The transition from Maplehurst to Manhattanville was a smooth one. Elizabeth continued studying English literature with a sense of joy and purpose. Her agile mind was well-suited to the rigors of philosophy, and she took as many philosophy courses as she could. On her own, she studied Old English, which she learned fairly quickly, and applied it to her study of *Beowulf* and other texts. Her social life at Manhattanville was quite rich as well, and she made many friends among other bright young undergraduates.

During her four years at Manhattanville she developed a profound respect, even a reverence, for the nuns of the Society of the Sacred Heart. She felt challenged and engaged by her course work, and she could see that her teachers were exceptional. "It was a very good education, a very broad education," she recalls. "It was not narrowly sectarian. Of course about half your teachers would be nuns. The other half would be Catholic, Protestant, Jewish. There were great teachers, and I made great friends. The college was always known for being very open. It was not a doctrinaire place."

At Manhattanville, Elizabeth developed her quick, powerful mind and her deep interest in intellectual life. As a senior, she wrote a paper, "The Role of Love in the Liberation of the Will," based on the book *The Mystical Theology of St. Bernard* by Etienne Gilson. The paper reveals the clarity of her thinking and the seriousness with which she took on religious topics. She wrote:

God made man "to His image and likeness." This image of God is in the mind of man and St. Bernard puts it rather in the will than in the intellect and very especially in freedom. He speaks of this free will as the "dignitas" in man because it is free will that raises man above all other living things, giving him power to rule them and to use them for the attainment of his ends.

This gift of liberty really implies three liberties. The first of them is "freedom from necessity" by which a person is able to accept or refuse a thing, to say yes or no. This "natural liberty" belongs to all reasonable creatures whether good or bad. It can be degraded but it can never be lost without the creature thereby ceasing to exist. And that is why this inalienable freedom is that whereby we are chiefly made to the image of God. However, as a result of original sin, man has no longer the liberty of choosing which would set him free from sin or that of acting in accordance with his choice which would set him free from the misery of an impotent will. Through the abuse of "libertas a necessitate" he has lost "libertas a peccato" and "libertas a miseria." Freedom from sin and from misery constituted the Divine Likeness in man so when man lost them he lost that Likeness.

Thus the soul's "greatness" consists in bearing the image of God and in its capability to participate in the Divine Life—it's by way of a gift and not affected by sin. St. Bernard describes the soul as "upright" when it desires this participation. However, it can cease to be to his likeness by loss of virtue. Demanding temporal things instead of those of God, it loses its "upright stature." Man turns away from heaven to which God had erected him, to bow down to earth to which his animal nature attracts him.

The soul is then disfigured by an "earthward curvature." It no longer has a love for eternal things but it still remains capable of that love; because it is the image of God it can receive His Likeness anew. Servitude to sin has not destroyed our natural freedom. Love has not been annihilated.

Her professor gave her an A for the paper and wrote, "I think this paper is excellent—I have no adverse criticism. It shows penetration, understanding and deep spiritual appreciation. The exposition is logical, extremely clear, and very thorough."

Elizabeth's Manhattanville yearbook photograph shows a serious young woman with stylish dark hair. She wears a single strand of pearls and lipstick. She looks serious, calm, confident, and intelligent. And it is clear in the yearbook that she was well-liked, for the editorial comment is: "McCorm is everything; every nice adjective, every good thought."

.　　　.　　　.

While at Manhattanville, she would often go home on weekends. And then on Monday mornings she would ride the train into the city with her father. She would get off at 125th Street—not far from Manhattanville, then located at 133rd Street and Convent Avenue—and her father would proceed on to Grand Central. Before they left the house or when they were on the train, he would give her an allowance for the week. Invariably, as the train drew closer to 125th Street, he would say, "I'd feel better if you had more money this week," and he would double her allowance.

Elizabeth and her mother had their own tradition during those years. They would regularly attend Broadway shows, usually a Wednesday matinee. Elizabeth would first go to the box office and buy tickets in advance, her mother would come into the city by train, and they would meet at the theater. Before the show, they would often have lunch at Schrafft's at 46th Street and Fifth Avenue.

"My mother was devoted to the theater and she taught me a love of the theater," says Elizabeth. "She would always phone beforehand and say, 'Are you sure you wouldn't want to go with a friend?' And I am happy to say I always said I wanted to go with her. I loved going with her."

Elizabeth made a point of never scheduling a Wednesday afternoon class so that she would be able to attend matinees. "We saw Katharine

Cornell, Helen Hayes, all of the great plays of those days." They would read about the plays in advance so they would always have an understanding of what they were about to see. If she and her mother had no plans to go, Elizabeth would often attend a show with several classmates and purchase inexpensive standing-room tickets.

.   .   .

Summers were spent at the McCormacks' vacation home in Lake Placid. For as long as she could remember, they would move to Lake Placid as soon as school ended only to return after Labor Day. Elizabeth's father came on weekends and for several weeks during the summer. Summer life was centered on the Lake Placid Club, next to the McCormacks' house. Elizabeth's days were filled with swimming, tennis, and other activities. The club was dry—no alcohol at all—and in the evening adults would often head into the village nearby for drinks. Elizabeth had long wanted to go on one of those excursions; it seemed so exciting. But her parents would not permit it until she was older. When she finally was allowed to go, at eighteen, she went into town and saw the drinking and thought, "Is this all there is to it?" Going into the village for drinks had carried such an allure for her for years, and now she saw that the reality of it was unappealing. In fact, their father promised Elizabeth and her brother, George, $10,000 in cash if they would refrain from drinking and smoking until age twenty-one. Both collected the ten thousand, according to George.

One summer during her college years was an exception to the Lake Placid routine. Elizabeth had signed up for typing lessons in Lake Placid at the start of summer, and, after she had done so, she had an opportunity to spend a couple of months working at the Woodstock summer theater upstate. It was something she very much wanted to do. When she asked her father's permission to go, he said he had already paid for the typing lessons, and he thought it was important that she follow through and learn that skill. The start of the summer theater season was still three weeks away. Elizabeth asked her father, "What if I learn to type in the next three weeks?" He considered it and agreed that if she did, she could go to Woodstock.

Elizabeth immediately got a typing instruction book and started learning. Three weeks later she was a proficient typist, and she was off to Woodstock. She and other college students worked as stagehands and had small roles in plays by Tennessee Williams, among others. It was wartime, and, due to gas rationing, Elizabeth and her friends had to husband what fuel they could get. The theater was at the top of a hill, and when she and her friends would go into town, they would set their car at the peak of the hill, then release the brake and roll into town without turning on the engine.

.   .   .

Inevitably, as she worked her way through the undergraduate years at Manhattanville, Elizabeth began thinking about what she might do after graduation. The more she thought about it, the more claustrophobic her options felt. She would describe it sixty years later as the *Revolutionary Road* option after the Richard Yates novel and the film made from it. "You marry a Catholic quickly after college and you have five children, maybe three and you live in suburbia and that is what your life is." She was not yet sure exactly what she wanted to do, but she was sure she didn't want that.

"It was World War II, and all these guys wanted to get married first, and you didn't even know them before they went overseas, and it was not for me," she recalls. Perhaps if she had met the right man it could have been possible, but she never did. And her father made it clear that he certainly did not think any of the men in her life were good enough for her. She found the men she met "very rapidly becoming boring and not all that intelligent and very self-satisfied. I can remember saying to one, 'You know, you are only interesting when you talk about yourself. You have nothing else to talk about . . .' What a hit I must have been with these guys!"

"She had very little in the way of male attention," recalls her brother. There was one young man, however, who pursued her. Bill Schreiber was a few years older than Elizabeth, a handsome skier and a businessman. Says Elizabeth: "He was fun, but his only topic on which he was very good was himself and his business and he was quite articulate about himself."

Elizabeth's brother says that when it appeared that "Bill Schreiber and Betty were getting serious—and surely he was, I'm not sure how she thought about him—Dad asked John Donovan, the former U.S. attorney, to get the FBI to check on this man, and discovered that Schreiber was Jewish and had previously been married and divorced." It would have been unthinkable to Elizabeth's father that she married someone who had been divorced. And if going to anything but a Catholic college was out of the question, marrying someone who was not Catholic was doubly so.

There was another young man whose company she enjoyed in Lake Placid. During a winter vacation week they skied together each day. "I loved cross-country skiing and he was a great skier," she recalls. "When you got to a steep hill which I couldn't maneuver he would just put his arm around me and lift me up and it was great. So I had a great time and phoned my family and said I think I will stay an extra few days and my father said 'Why?' and I said, 'I am having a great time.' And he said, 'With whom?' And I said, 'There's a guy here and he's a great skier and we're having a lot of fun and I like him.' And my father said, 'You better come home.'"

For a while Elizabeth considered applying to Columbia's graduate journalism program and becoming a journalist. Then, at the end of her junior year at Manhattanville, her thinking shifted. Perhaps to a certain extent she was influenced by Elizabeth Cavanagh, a nun who had taught her at Maplehurst. She had taught Elizabeth in English and history classes, but it wasn't so much the teaching as her presence. "Many times when people join a religious Society and become a priest or become a nun someone influenced them as a kind of ideal and she was that to me," says Elizabeth. "She was fun. She was smart. She was a great teacher. She was wonderful."

The model of Sister Elizabeth Cavanagh was deeply appealing to Elizabeth. Also, of course, young Elizabeth was a devout Catholic. At Manhattanville she went to Mass every day. Although she had never considered herself a particularly pious individual, she now decided that she had a vocation, a calling.

"I was called by God to be a nun," she says. "It was something I had to do with my life."

.   .   .

During the fall term of her senior year at Manhattanville, Elizabeth made her decision. She would join the Society of the Sacred Heart. She discussed this decision with Elizabeth Cavanagh and no one else—not her friends or teachers or family. And she made another decision: She would enjoy her final year of college. "I was not going to let that difficult decision ruin my senior year."

In February of her senior year, Elizabeth took the train from New York City to Albany to attend a ceremony marking the final vows for Betty Cavanagh. Final vows were customarily taken in Rome, but, due to the war, the ceremony was in Albany.

Before the trip, Elizabeth told Betty Cavanagh that she planned to tell Mother Superior Gertrude Bodkin that she was seriously considering entering the Society. Later that day, Betty Cavanagh pulled Elizabeth aside and asked whether she had spoken with Mother Bodkin. Elizabeth said she had not.

"Betty said to me, 'You told me you were going to meet with

Reverend Mother Bodkin.' And I said, 'I just may not do it.' And Betty Cavanagh replied, 'You said you were going to do it and I think you better do it. Talk to her.'" Betty Cavanagh said she would arrange a time for Elizabeth to do so.

Was this a meaningful hesitation? "I don't think it was meaningful in the sense that I was changing my mind," says Elizabeth. "But every step you take toward doing something like that makes it more real, and becoming a nun was not some romantic ideal of mine that I couldn't wait to accomplish. It was something I knew I should do and would do, but I wasn't looking forward to it with enthusiasm."

Elizabeth did, in fact, meet with Mother Bodkin that day for an informal discussion. Elizabeth was wearing a beaver hat, and Mother Bodkin, thinking it was Elizabeth's hair, asked whether she had gray hair. ("Gray hair! I was twenty-one!") Their conversation was informal. As they talked, Mother Bodkin, perhaps to gauge Elizabeth's level of interest, suggested that she might want to consider first getting an advanced degree at Columbia. Mother Bodkin did not push Elizabeth at all. She emphasized that there was no rush. Elizabeth later learned that was the standard approach—to try and make sure it was what the young woman truly wanted.

Elizabeth said to Mother Bodkin, "You know, this is something I should do and every month or year that I don't do it there is more of a chance that I never will. I think I should do it right away."

And she committed to do it. Her commitment came from her belief that she was being called by God. She had no doubt of this, no doubt that this was exactly what God wanted her to do. It was not as though she approached it with an overriding sense of mission or excitement. It was much more from a sense of duty. "I wasn't enthusiastic about it," she recalls. "It wasn't something I liked. I *had* to do it."

Thus was she committed to enter the Sacred Heart convent, known as Kenwood, in Albany in September 1944. As she rode the train back to New York, she was comfortable with her decision. She was fully committed to it. And it was her decision. Apart from Mothers Cavanagh and Bodkin, she had never discussed it with friends or teachers or her brother or her parents.

She did, however, have one very brief conversation about her decision with a cousin who was a Jesuit. While she had a deep admiration for the Sacred Heart nuns, she also admired, although from a distance, the Maryknoll sisters, whose mission was to work throughout the world as missionaries. The Maryknolls were also much more modern and did not impose the severe traditions embraced by the Society of the Sacred Heart. Importantly, the Maryknolls were not a cloistered order and were quite open in embracing the modern world. She told her Jesuit cousin that she was considering entering the convent and was unsure whether it should be the Society of the Sacred Heart or the Maryknolls.

"He said, 'That's easy—Sacred Heart.'" He knew Elizabeth was smart and committed to education, and that was the essential identity of the Sacred Heart nuns.

. . .

There was no question the Sacred Heart Society was right for her. She knew about the history and mission of the Society. It was founded in November 1800 by a Frenchwoman, Madeleine Sophie Barat, when she was barely twenty years old. Mother Barat's vision was that the nuns of the Society of the Sacred Heart would devote their lives to prayer and the education of Catholic girls. She viewed education as the means of transforming society and strengthening the social fabric. Her ambition was an order of nuns committed to "detachment from the world, purity of intention for the glory of the Sacred Heart, gentleness, zeal, and obedience; this means, for the religious, the training of the novitiate, and spiritual exercises, for others, boarding schools for the upper classes, free schools for the poor, and spiritual retreats."

At age twenty-six, Mother Barat became the Order's first Superior

General, succeeding a priest, Father Varin, who had helped start and guide the Order. During the nineteenth century the Order spread across Europe to Egypt, Japan, and South and North America. It arrived in the United States in 1818, and by 1910, there were twenty-seven U.S. Sacred Heart convents with 1,100 nuns.

According to the Society's website,

> The society aims at a twofold spirit—contemplative and active. . . . In addition to the indication of a true religious vocation there is required respectable parentage, unblemished reputation, a good or at least sufficient education with some aptitude for completing it, a sound judgment, and above all a generous determination to make an entire surrender of self to the service of God through the hands of superiors. The candidate is not allowed to make any conditions as to place of residence or employment, but must be ready to be sent by obedience to any part of the world, even the privilege of going on foreign missions is not definitely promised in the beginning to those who aspire to it.
>
> An essential element of the Society's mission is "Education of the upper classes in the boarding schools and of late years in day schools." The Society also provides tuition-free schools for the poor in a variety of countries.

.   .   .

During the summer before she entered Kenwood, Elizabeth began attending daily early morning Mass at Lake Placid. "I thought if I'm going to enter the convent in September I better get used to going to Mass every day. I would drive over to the other side of the lake to the church, go to Mass, come back, go back to bed and nobody would ever know that I was there."

At one point that summer Elizabeth went to Saint Augustine parish in Larchmont to get a copy of her baptismal certificate, which she would need upon entering the convent in September. At the rectory she asked the priest for a copy. He went into a file room and retrieved the document, and when he returned it became clear that he was wondering why she needed it. Are you getting married, he asked her.

When Elizabeth told him she needed it because she was becoming a nun, he paused. He said she seemed reluctant. And he added, "Remember that there is a front door into the convent and there is a back door out."

Elizabeth replied, "The reason I am reluctant is I know that for me there is no back door out."

This is a telling moment. She did not say, "Oh, no, Father, I feel no reluctance." She confirmed that, in fact, she was reluctant. When she was asked about this many years later, she replied, "Sure I was reluctant. It is a huge change. I mean you are giving up your life, your independence. I knew what it was. I think some people become nuns in some kind of a romantic thing."

But for Elizabeth, it was not a romance or a passion—it was a calling. *I was called by God to do this.* "I really believed that this is what God wanted me to do, and I hoped that I'd be like Betty Cavanagh."

The commitment was staggering in its dimensions, in its pledge to devote a lifetime to sacrifice.

Detachment from the world.
Purity of intention.
Obedience.
An entire surrender of self to the service of God.

(2)

Never Laugh Again

I N J U N E 1944, Elizabeth's brother, George, was about to travel by
night train from Lake Placid to New York City, where he would start
medical school at Columbia. "A lot of friends came and saw me off,"
George recalls, "and my sister was with them. And she said, I remember
it so vividly, she said, 'Walk down the platform with me because I have
something I want to tell you,' and I thought she was going to say, 'Bill
Schreiber and I are getting married.' And what she said was 'I am going
to join the Sacred Heart Society in September.'"

George was stunned. There had been no hint, no inkling, nothing.
And he experienced an almost immediate sense of regret that he had
not spent more time with his sister. "So many times during that time I
was there, I spent, I don't know, a month there, between college and
starting medical school, and she asked me to do stuff with her like go
canoeing, and I always found a reason not to, and of course I was beating my breast that I hadn't, and here she was going in the convent."

In July, Elizabeth and her parents were vacationing in Canada and she told them of her plans. And how did they take the news? "They were okay," she recalls. "They were okay. It was a surprise to them."

In reality, though, they weren't all that okay. George came home to Larchmont from Columbia one weekend, and he was chatting with his father and asked him what he thought about Elizabeth's entering the convent. And their father broke down and wept. "He didn't want her to do it," says George. "She never knew that."

Elizabeth did not know about her father's crying until more than six decades later. An interviewer told her. He had read about it in the transcript of a conversation with George. Elizabeth speculated: "He wasn't weeping because I was going to be a nun. He liked that. But he was weeping because it meant I joined an order where the rules were that I would never go home again."

.　　.　　.

Elizabeth felt an obligation to tell Bill Schreiber of her plans. He was sick at home in New York City, and she went to visit him. He was lying in bed with covers pulled up to his chin when she explained that she would soon be entering the convent. "He was handsome in his bed with his sheets up to here. He sat up and he said, 'Oh, my God, let's go get married right now!'"

She laughs at the recollection. "He thought what I was going to do was a fate worse than death and he would save me from it!"

.　　.　　.

On September 7, 1944, Elizabeth Jane McCormack, age twenty-two, rode the train from New York City to Albany with her good friend Maggie Sheehan along to keep her company. En route, Elizabeth realized she had some money with her but would no longer need it. She gave it to Maggie.

Elizabeth traveled from the train station to the Sacred Heart's Kenwood Academy. The campus was where young nuns would spend their months as postulants, in training for monastery life. Arriving at Kenwood, Elizabeth was warmly greeted at the convent door by the Mistress of Novices, Mother Agnes Barry. They walked together across the grounds to the section of the campus where the novices were housed. During the walk, Elizabeth remarked to Mother Barry, "Well, I am reconciled to the fact that I may never laugh again."

"Of course you will laugh again," Mother Barry replied.

But Elizabeth was not so sure. The internal conflict was there, even as she walked through the door. As she reflects upon it, she believes that it was such a huge thing to do that *not* to feel some sense of conflict or trepidation would have meant that she wasn't thinking it through or was somehow numb. Yes, she says, some young women entering the convent do so with a highly romanticized notion of what is to come. "But it never was that for me," she says. "I guess Mother Elizabeth Cavanagh was a kind of ideal for me, but I don't think it was a romanticized thing." As she later told her family's oral biographer: "I recognized that from then on I would be doing what I was told to do rather than what I wanted to do."

Forty-seven years after joining the Society, she told an interviewer from an Indiana University Oral History Research Project her reason for joining: "I think that early on I decided that the most important thing one could do for the rest of mankind was in the field of education and therefore when I entered a religious order I entered an educational one where, in that order, every one of the religious of the Sacred Heart was involved in one way or another in education. I think that if one really wants to 'change the world,' in quotation marks, the best way to do it is by educating people so that they *can* change the world."

. . .

A postulant's life involved meditation and prayer. It involved the daily chanting of the Office, a collection of holy texts. It involved spiritual instruction but also cleaning and doing dishes.

The road ahead was straightforward. If all went according to plan, Elizabeth would spend six months at Kenwood as a postulant. During this period she and the other aspiring nuns wore civilian clothes. They would not earn the right to wear a habit until later. She would then spend two years as a novice studying, praying, and meditating. And if all went well, she would make her initial vows. She would then become an aspirant, a five-year process. If that was successful, she would make her final vows in Rome.

The Kenwood campus was an inviting location in which to begin her journey. It was set on a beautiful thirty-acre wooded tract of land that was ideal for walks, for reflection, meditation, and prayer. The grounds included well-kept flower gardens as well as carefully cultivated vegetable gardens and chickens. The postulants and novices did much of the work in the gardens and tended to the chickens as well. Elizabeth couldn't quite handle killing the chickens (breaking their necks), so she volunteered instead to clean them afterward.

There were a few buildings on the campus. A large, four-story brick structure from the 1860s housed the convent, where the classrooms were, and it had an attached chapel. Attached to this was a plain building of more recent construction where the novices lived. There were another small building for priests and a few small structures for gardening equipment. There was also a cemetery for Sacred Heart nuns.

During the two years of her novice period, Elizabeth would rise each morning at 5:30. An hour-long period of meditation began at six. "Meditation was on some scene from the Gospel," she recalls. "Thinking about it. The night before in the noviceship room at night prayers, someone was called on to read the notes that they had taken in preparation for the next morning's meditation, and I was good at that because I could have no notes at all and if they called on me I could make up a good thing about the marriage feast of Cana or what-ever it was."

The meditation was followed by a fifteen-minute period when the novices would chant the Office. The chanting was done in Latin, and the book used was known as the *Little Office of Our Lady* to distinguish it from the Divine Office used by monks. Chanting the Office was important and performed three times a day—in the morning, after lunch for thirty minutes, and again in the evening. Breakfast was taken in silence, but during lunch and dinner someone would read aloud to the assembled nuns.

In the morning, novices would engage in some sort of manual labor, cleaning typically, and then receive spiritual instruction until lunch. In the afternoon novices and postulants would walk through the grounds in threesomes discussing a particular spiritual issue. "It was always three," Elizabeth recalls. The rule was, "You're friendly with everyone but you don't have special friends. This was protection against lesbian relationships." During Elizabeth's nearly thirty years as a nun "only once did I have that problem and the other nun was my superior."

In the evening, novices took turns reading from the lives of the members of the Society. The book was in French and told the stories of many nuns through the years. Every nun who was a member of the Society would be commemorated in some way within the book.

Novices were taught to waste nothing and were specifically instructed that when a bar of soap dwindled down to a thin sliver that it should be pressed into a new bar rather than thrown away.

This was a period during which the novices were, in effect, learning the basics about convent life, learning how to be nuns. Early on, it was announced that an office for the new mistress/surveillant of novices needed to be redone—to be cleaned and painted with floors and furniture waxed. The novices were asked whether they would like to help, and Elizabeth immediately volunteered. She believed that it was God's will that she was there, and she therefore was committed to doing everything it took to live the life fully and completely, to be the best nun she could be. Right from the start she found herself quite comfortable with the mixture of study and reflection, of prayer and manual labor. Perhaps above all, there was a sense of obedience, a belief that having been called by God, Elizabeth would do whatever she was asked to do, and she would do it to the best of her ability.

Early on, she was discussing with another nun, Margaret Howe, how much she liked and respected Mother Barry. They talked about a nun they had known at Manhattanville, Mother Schroen, whom Elizabeth had particularly disliked. Mother Marie Louise Schroen was very smart, but just as difficult as she was bright, recalled Elizabeth.

"I remember saying to Margaret Howe, 'What would I ever do if Mother Schroen became the Mistress of Novices?' She said, 'Well, she won't.' Well, *she did.* I only had Mother Barry as my superior for a short time and then Mother Schroen replaced her."

Elizabeth was not pleased. She had certainly not liked having Mother Schroen as class warden at Manhattanville. But Elizabeth accepted the fact that it was her job to accept Mother Schroen completely, and not to complain about her in any way.

"You took everything," she recalls. "This was God's will. In for a penny, in for a pound. She was going to be the Mistress of Novices. This was God's will. It is a good way to live. You can take almost anything if you believe that."

Sometimes in the evening the young nuns would sit around the Superior in a semi-circle and discuss a variety of matters. "All conversation was directed to the Superior," she recalls. "We didn't talk to one another. It was all a very, very formal thing." This was considered a form of recreation.

Elizabeth and the other novices lived in a large dorm area where each woman had a bed with a water basin and pitcher. The women would fetch hot water with their pitchers, pour it into their bowls, and wash with it. Like the others, Elizabeth had what amounted to a small cubicle with walls, although they did not reach the ceiling. Everyone could hear everyone else. At the end of the large dorm area were lockers where they kept what few items of clothes they had.

By chance, Elizabeth's cubicle was located near a window allowing her to see the spire atop the chapel. While she quickly became accustomed to her surroundings, she did not get to know the other postulants very well because the women were so rarely permitted to speak to one another. Even in the dorm area at night, talking was forbidden. In fact, the time between night prayers—signaling the official end of the day—and the end of Mass the following morning was known as "the greater silence." During this period of approximately ten hours, no one spoke. Instead, they meditated and prayed silently. In the early morning, before the women reported to the meditation and prayer session, Elizabeth would make a quick visit to the chapel for a few moments of prayer. She liked praying in the chapel choir loft and fell into the habit of going there to start each day. This was a level of piety she was committed to and that she thought was expected of her.

For postulants, and nuns generally, prayer sessions tended more toward reflection and meditation than the more typical prayers of petition offered by lay people. "Prayer was thinking and meditating," says Elizabeth. Their meditations focused for the most part on the Gospel.

Each evening, novices participated in night prayers. There was a special room where they gathered, and the Mistress of Novices would call on someone to talk about the meditation that was assigned for the next day. She would ask general questions: What do you think about it? What are you going to pray about?

Elizabeth found herself somewhat impatient with these exercises. Without really giving it much thought she would come up with something quickly that would satisfy the mistresses' questions.

"A few words were more helpful, a phrase, for instance: 'My God, why have you forsaken me?' It is a pretty good thing to think about, and there are lots of sentences like that. There is also what is called the

'Jesus prayer,' which I think began in Russia. You simply think about, meditate on, empty your mind, accept the thought, *Jesus*. That can be a prayer."She considered prayer "a very mysterious thing." She recognized the elemental forms—prayer of petition—a personal plea to God to intervene on one's behalf—a cry for help on matters ranging from health to finances to love. There was the kind of repetitive prayers children recited. And then there was the sort of meditative and reflective prayers favored within the Society of the Sacred Heart.

.   .   .

Elizabeth enjoyed the rhythm of each day, the structure and certainty of each block of time, the commitment to chanting, prayer, work, and study. It was a structure, she says, that "helped us to pray and to be prayerful. From the time we rose at 5:30 a.m. until we went to bed at 10:00 p.m., our time was totally regulated, with three hours devoted to Mass and our prayer life each day."

Elizabeth found some of the psalms and prayers comforting and inspiring—such as "The Lord is my shepherd, I shall not want." But others, upon translation into English, revealed violent messages—to smite your enemy, for example.

The usual meditation was taking a scene from the Gospel and reflecting upon it, thinking carefully and deeply about it, imagining it and then applying it to one's own life. "I wasn't all that good at it," says Elizabeth.

An essential part of spiritual instruction focused on learning and understanding the Rule of the Religious of the Sacred Heart. This was adapted from the Jesuit Rule, and once a month a portion of the Rule was read aloud. A central tenet of the Rule was obedience.

"If you are asked by your superior to water a dry stick, you water it," says Elizabeth. "You don't make a judgment about what you're asked to do, you just do it. Obedience is a very literal thing. It's unquestioning." However, she was never asked to do anything she felt was unreasonable.

On a regular basis, the Mistress of Novices would appear before the novices and explain a particular rule. Typically, she did so by providing the reason and history behind it. In the years to come this instruction would continue through Elizabeth's time as a postulant and novice and even later in Rome before she took her final vows.

The first six months were not an unpleasant time for Elizabeth. She adapted to the routine quickly and enjoyed the intellectual aspects of reading and meditation. And she was perfectly content performing whatever she was asked to do. Additionally, she had no difficulty with the ascetic nature of her new life. But the discipline and silence were exceedingly difficult for some of the young women, and quite a few decided to leave the convent during that initial phase.

Barbara Carter, who had been a student at Kenwood, years later recalled school as "very strict. It was medieval, monastic. . . . You couldn't talk unless they rang a bell in the dining room. You had to stand on line to get into class. . . . We were back in the 19th century."

She recalled that the nuns' cemetery was on the Kenwood grounds. "The first dead person I ever saw was a nun. They must have had an open casket. It was Mother Green and she was green . . . They did the funeral and the whole procession and the burial . . . was up by our playing fields, so we had to go past it every day to get to the hockey field."

During Elizabeth's first months at Kenwood, time was set aside each Sunday afternoon for visits from families. Elizabeth's parents would travel to Albany on Saturday and stay at a hotel before visiting her from mid to late afternoon. George and Natalie McCormack would sit with Elizabeth in the Kenwood convent parlor and talk. In good weather they would stroll the campus. Conversation was quite general and specifically avoided discussion of what Elizabeth's life or routine was like within the convent. "You weren't supposed to give them details," she recalls.

A particular rule about parental visits precluded giving any sort of gift to an individual postulant. "They couldn't bring anything—candy, food, anything," says Elizabeth. "If they brought you anything, you had to leave it at the door of the Mistress of Novices. You had nothing."

At one point Elizabeth developed a problem with her foot and required surgery. She was hospitalized at Saint Agnes Hospital in White Plains, where she was cared for by nuns of a different order.

"The nun said to me in the hospital, 'Get them to bring in your bedroom slippers,' and I said, 'I don't have bedroom slippers.' And she said, 'You don't have bedroom slippers?' And I said, 'No, we don't have bedroom slippers.' You just put on your shoes in the morning. So this nun of some other order brought me one of her slippers because I couldn't put a shoe on."

She does not know for sure because she never discussed it with them, but she assumes that it was a difficult period for her mother and father. Their daughter had been close to them, and except for her years at Maplehurst and Manhattanville had never lived anywhere but home. And now she was gone, as gone as she could possibly be, in a way.

.   .   .

Six months after Elizabeth McCormack arrived at Kenwood, she took the habit. The ceremony was an important symbolic milestone for postulants. They had made it through the brief initial phase. But before donning a coarse, black woolen habit, the postulates engaged in a ceremony where they became symbolic brides, complete with wedding dresses.

The previous June, Elizabeth had attended the wedding of her college friend Margaret Slaughter at the Saranac Inn. Margaret wore a beautiful dress of white satin and delicate lace around the neck. It was a long dress, but without a train. Margaret, like Elizabeth, was petite, and it was Margaret's wedding dress that Elizabeth borrowed for the ceremony. There were eight or ten postulants in the ceremony that day. Family members were invited, and Elizabeth's parents came. A professional photographer took pictures. The young women who were dressed as brides proceeded to the chapel for prayers. When the ceremony was completed and pictures had been taken, Elizabeth and the other postulants went into a room where their hair was cut short and they donned their new habit—the garment they would wear for the rest of their lives. Short hair was a practical necessity. Nuns wore a tightly fitting white cap, a black band over the forehead which was tied on, and a veil over all.

"For years I shaved my head with an electric razor," recalls Elizabeth.

In addition, the women were outfitted with white veils, which signified their progression from postulant to novice. Wearing their new habits and white veils, the women returned to chapel for Mass with their families. Afterward, Elizabeth's mother was given a lock of her hair as a memento.

The novice period was a time for reflection, prayer, and, ultimately, decision. The young women seriously focused on whether this was the life for them, whether their calling from God was clear and true. Elizabeth's view was that young women who entered with some sort of romanticized view of what life in the convent would be like were much more likely to be disappointed, and to leave the Society, than women without such a view.

The novices wore their black habit every day. One habit was for use six days a week, and a second, identical to the first in every detail, was for Sunday or feast days. The habits were thick wool and in the heat of an Albany summer, they were terribly uncomfortable.

Elizabeth recalls, "It never occurred to me to think, *Why do I have to wear this in this hundred degree temperature?* You had nothing else to wear! So you were unquestioning and one of the things that remains with me and I think that remains with anyone who lived that life is that you are pretty uncomplaining for the rest of your life. I am often with people whom I know when I have gotten to know the husbands through some board or something and then I meet the wives and they are demanding women: 'It is too hot, it is too cold, this wine isn't all that good.' I mean, that never even now occurs to me. I just learned not to complain."

While Elizabeth enjoyed life as a novice, she found that certain aspects of convent life were not immune to the kind of competitiveness that she regarded as quite silly. After she became a novice, there was a Thanksgiving field hockey game organized pitting the novices against the nuns—white veils versus black. Elizabeth was never much of an athlete, but she wanted to participate in the spirit of fun. The Mistress of Novices approached it quite seriously, however.

"The Mistress of Novices was a very intelligent person, but it was important to her that the novices win this game!" says Elizabeth. "So we are all there. We are all young—even the black veils are young—in their thirties probably. And this mistress of novices was saying 'Get in there! Win! Win!' I was thinking, 'What is going on here? Here we are. We have given our lives to this and what difference does it make who wins this game? And it struck me then and still does that unimportant things matter to people. This was an extremely intelligent Mistress of Novices to whom the fact that the novices win a Thanksgiving game against other young nuns mattered! I think that is a lesson for everyone. Is the wine the best that you ever had, is this restaurant disappointing? What do you mean it is disappointing? What difference does it make?"

·   ·   ·

A year and a half after the Bride of Christ ceremony, Elizabeth was assigned to teach at Kenwood. It was rare for novices to receive teaching assignments, yet it was an early indication that her superiors recognized Elizabeth's intellect and abilities. There were not many perks for novices at Kenwood, but there was one: When a novice became a teacher she got her own room. It was small, ascetic, but it had a door that closed and a window that opened. Sheer luxury!

She was assigned an eighth-grade class of about fifteen to twenty students, and as eighth graders, these girls were typically away from home for the first time and sometimes homesick or uncertain about how to handle their new environment. It was not an entirely happy group of girls, and Elizabeth found with a fair number there were problems in the family, such as divorce and alcoholism. The student body included a number of international students, typically girls from wealthy families in Latin American countries such as Brazil, Bolivia, and Colombia, where a high-quality Catholic education was unavailable.

The Sacred Heart schools measured students' progress via tests given at all the Sacred Heart schools in the United States. These tests were considered significant educational markers and were taken very seriously by the nuns, students, and parents.

Elizabeth's first days in the classroom did not go smoothly. The girls were unruly and assumed they could behave as they wished with this diminutive, twenty-three-year-old teacher who barely looked to be out of her teens.

"They knew they were going to have to take these tests and that it was important to pass, but they were unruly, totally unruly," she says. "Talking, writing letters, not paying attention. I had no training in teaching at all. After a couple of days I said, 'I want to tell you something. I don't have to take tests. You do. I am only going to teach you when I have absolute attention from everyone. Any one of you not paying attention, all of you will know it because I will just stop teaching.'"

This captured their attention. After stopping teaching about three times, her approach worked. The students would immediately identify the guilty party and get her to behave. "Stop it," they would say to the particular girl, "or she won't teach us."

Says Elizabeth: "It worked like a charm."

It was an important learning experience for a young teacher. "You don't win by getting angry at the children," she says. "Another time, one of the class was reading a letter and I took it, saying, 'I will give it back to you but give it to me now.' She brought the letter up to me. She was Princess Nadia Romanov and I thought, 'Well, if I am going to take someone's letter I may as well take a Romanov's letter.'"

While nuns engaged closely with groups of students in a classroom setting, Elizabeth and her colleagues were strongly discouraged from forming any sort of close bond with an individual student. Girls with personal or family problems and in need of emotional support or counseling were directed to the Mistress General. Individual nuns were not supposed to deal with such issues. And in light of the widespread sexual crimes of priests revealed later, this was an exceptionally wise policy.

"I remember one child and I don't even remember her name, but I was in charge of the 'play closet' where all of the costumes were. It was a mess so I was cleaning it and there was one of the children who began wanting to be with me all of the time, wanting to help whatever I did and wanting to just be with me."

The girl was probably in ninth grade, and "she had a crush on me. And I remember saying to her, 'You know you are annoying me. You are really annoying. Why are you always around?'" Elizabeth's intent was to put the girl off, to create distance between them and head off a potentially unhealthy dependence. "It was a smart thing to do."

Most of the girls at Kenwood were quite happy and well-adjusted, but there were some during the long frigid Albany winters who grew homesick, particularly girls from Latin America. In the Society of the Sacred Heart the rule was that the Mistress General was the one person designated to deal with the girls' problems. "So you were really not supposed to get involved in their personal lives but you couldn't avoid getting involved in them," says Elizabeth. "I tried not to get really close to them and again when you were young they could have crushes on the nuns. There were dangers that the Society realized and so you had to be careful."

One of Elizabeth's students, Barbara Carter, remembered "Mother McCormack's class" as a kind of sanctuary. "Once you were in her classroom it was a different world. She was amazing. It seemed like she taught us everything during those two years—History, English, humanities, Latin."

.   .   .

As a novice, Elizabeth taught at Kenwood for approximately six months, and then, in 1945, she was transferred to the Convent of the Sacred Heart in Greenwich, Connecticut, another Sacred Heart school for girls, where she would teach for the next five years. She adapted to the Greenwich environment quickly and loved teaching there.

It was a plum of sorts for her to be teaching as an aspirant; that was atypical within the Society. Being assigned to Greenwich was an honor as well since it was "a very good school, a relatively new school. It was a small religious community, and therefore everyone in it had a great deal of responsibility. Right away I had responsibility for one of the cottages where the children lived. I don't think that the degree of responsibility that I was given was typical. Now that doesn't mean that nobody else was given it, but it wasn't typical."

The Convent of the Sacred Heart, Greenwich, attracted affluent, smart, Catholic girls from Westchester and Connecticut, mostly Fairfield County. The high school students boarded during the week, while the lower grades were composed entirely of day students. Elizabeth lived in a small house on campus where she supervised a dozen or so girls. It was known as the Farmhouse and contained a small room for Elizabeth and six or seven dorm rooms, each of which housed two girls. Elizabeth's room was quite small and sparse, so small, in fact, that her bed was a foldaway. At the start of one school year Elizabeth's mother came to visit her. During the course of the tour in the Farmhouse, a student's mother arrived and said she was upset with how small her daughter's room was. When the mother said she was going to complain about this, Elizabeth's mother said: "Should I show her *my* daughter's room?" Elizabeth intervened and requested that her mother stay out of the fray.

Teaching at Greenwich was hard work, but she loved everything about it. "I loved teaching. It is the thing I like better then anything. Not disciplining children but teaching them. I taught history, literature, and Latin. I was teaching Caesar and the teacher who was teaching Cicero couldn't control her class and so suddenly I was told that I was going to teach Cicero instead. I said, 'I don't know enough Latin to teach Cicero' and the nun who was the Mistress of Studies said to me, 'Well, learn it. Teach it.' So whatever we were going to translate I did it the night before and I learned it with the children."

This was no simple matter. She had taken Latin at Maplehurst but had only one year of it at Manhattanville. "It wasn't until I was assigned to teach Caesar that I really taught myself Latin," she recalls. "And then because I was teaching Caesar and I had a very good class, I said most of them could come right into Cicero with me. Which they did and we learned it together. We faced the required common exams together, which were prepared each year at the Vicariate House in Albany. When I passed out the test, the children all began laughing."

It turned out that one of the passages on the test was from a particularly difficult letter of Cicero's that the class had laboriously translated and every student knew cold.

Elizabeth also enjoyed her role as house mother and found the girls generally bright and inquisitive. Each day started with the same ritual. "When I woke up the children in the morning I took a little bottle of holy water and each child dipped her hand in the holy water and blessed herself. And I was frequently going to the sacristy to get new holy water until I realized how ridiculous it was"—particularly on cold winter mornings when she ran out and had to go across campus to the chapel for a resupply.

"I mean some priest prays over the water. It is like kosher chicken. Some rabbi says some kind of prayers. Some priest said a prayer." Her solution: Tap water.

.   .   .

It was a strict environment, of course, but Elizabeth felt great respect and affection for the Superior, Reverend Mother Theresa Hill. While Elizabeth was teaching in Greenwich, her brother, George, attending medical school at the time, fell ill with tuberculosis. Elizabeth told Mother Hill about this, and Mother Hill suggested that Elizabeth phone home to check on George's condition. This was, of course, against the rules, but Mother Hill insisted. She told Elizabeth that her parents needed her at that time and that it was important for Elizabeth to know how her brother was progressing. "I mean, you never phoned home," says Elizabeth. "*Never*. But during that time she said, 'Phone every day. This is very hard on them that your brother is sick.' She was wonderful."

On another occasion, Elizabeth had a growth on her foot that had to be removed surgically. She was admitted to the hospital the night before the procedure, and early the next morning Mother Hill visited her at the hospital. "And I said, 'What are you here for? This is nothing.' And she said, 'Your foot is going to be operated on so I am here.'"

Not all of the nuns were as thoughtful as Mother Hill, of course, but Elizabeth found that most were warm and kind and cared deeply about their students and about other nuns. This caring created a comforting, secure environment, and she was happy.

Not long thereafter, word came that Mother Hill would be leaving Greenwich for a new assignment. Elizabeth was heartbroken. Around that time Elizabeth's parents came to visit her one Sunday afternoon "and I was reduced to tears losing this woman who was just wonderful to me, and my father said, 'When you left *us* you didn't cry.'"

.   .   .

Seven years after she entered the convent in Albany, Elizabeth Mc-Cormack was ready to take her final vows. She was twenty-nine years old, and she was absolutely, totally committed to her life as a nun.

She traveled with a group of seven or eight other nuns from the United States and Canada to Rome in 1952 for final vows. They stayed at the Mother House, an elegant old structure on the Via Nomentana. The six months in Rome were considered a probationary period during which young nuns meditated and prayed and focused on preparing for their final vows. There was religious instruction, of course, but there was also an opportunity to spend some time enjoying Rome. Elizabeth was one of forty-four nuns from all over the world. She felt part of something truly special, truly significant, something that was a force for good throughout the world.

One thing about Rome in particular surprised her. The people there struck her as "anti-clerical." It was in sharp contrast to life in the United States. "If you had a habit on you were extremely well treated in the U.S. Old ladies would try to give you a seat on the bus. Everyone was nice here. In Rome I think they had too much of it so they would almost knock you down just as if you were anybody else."

Unfortunately, her father was quite ill when the ceremony was performed in Rome, so neither of her parents was able to attend. The ceremony itself was simple. There was a Mass, of course, and then the commitment from each nun that she would remain a nun forever.

As part of the ceremony, she was awarded a stylized silver cross, not a crucifix, which she wore with her habit. After the ceremony, she left Rome having vowed that she would spend the rest of her life as a member of the Society of the Sacred Heart; that she would do whatever was asked of her; that she would die a nun.

After Rome, Elizabeth returned to Albany, where she was assigned the position of Mistress of Discipline at Kenwood.

"It was a terrible job," she says. "It was an extraordinarily hard job, seven days a week, on call twenty-four hours a day with many children who were there because of problems in their homes. It was a very difficult, exhausting job. I didn't like it at all because you had to control the children and the discipline did not recognize their individual needs. Those two years at Kenwood were the hardest years I ever had."

Though it was an unpleasant job—and certainly far from her first choice of what she wanted to do with her life—Elizabeth spent two years devoted to doing the finest job she possibly could. This was her calling, after all. This was what God wanted her to do and she would do it to the very best of her ability and she would never complain about it. She believed that the difficulty of it was part of what she was "meant to do. It's a philosophy that in many ways keeps people from tension, nervous breakdowns.

"As Surveillant General I was responsible for these kids and the rigor of their lives. There was no talking before classes. After night prayers they went up to their dormitories and there was no talking and many of them were very lonely and unhappy kids. I lived in the dormitory there—a little place with a bed and then maybe fifty kids and each of them in their little cubicle—and I remember one night we are all in bed and some child brought with her a whole bag of marbles and when it got dead quiet she emptied the marbles and they rolled all over the dormitory floor. Everyone was laughing."

This was a moment when Elizabeth was required to make a quick decision. Essentially, she had two choices: She could be angry and severe or kind and forgiving. She could demand that the guilty party come forward. She could upbraid the girl for interrupting everyone's time of rest. She could do what so many nuns have done in so many situations for generations—scare the children and make them feel guilty. She chose the alternate route, however, because she knew that anger and severity usually did nothing but send children into a resentful shell.

"So I get dressed fast and go out and say, 'This is kind of fun isn't it?' It was the middle of the night. I said, 'Why don't we all get up and pick up the marbles?' So fifty kids are going around picking up marbles. I did not say, 'Will the person who is responsible for this please come here and tell me. You have ruined everyone's night sleep.' Instead, I made a joke of it. We all remember the night with pleasure."

.   .   .

In 1954, after two years as Surveillant General at Kenwood, Elizabeth was ordered to return to the convent of the Sacred Heart in Greenwich. This time, though, she would not be teaching. She had been promoted to the role of Mistress General. She was thus returning as headmistress of the school at which she had taught, a place she loved. This was a pivotal moment, for it was a tangible recognition by the Sacred Heart Society that Elizabeth was a particularly capable educator and leader; that she was among the elite. The Sacred Heart schools were the jewels of the Society's teaching mission, and being asked to lead one of them was a great honor. She was just thirty-two years old and somewhat surprised by the assignment.

"I said to Reverend Mother Helen Fitzgerald, '*Me?* The Mistress General of the Convent of the Sacred Heart in Greenwich?' And she said, 'Frankly, I have no one else.'"

If she had loved her time teaching there, she loved being headmistress even more. It was a role for which she was ideally suited. She was an educator at heart, but she also knew how to bring out the best in girls. The marble incident at Kenwood spoke volumes about her understanding of girls and the kindness and generosity of her heart, not to mention her spirit of fun.

"Of all the jobs I had I enjoyed it most," she says. "It was a manageable-size school, about three hundred children. I enjoyed the work, I think I did it well, and it was the first time since 1944 where I was in a position to make really important decisions. One of the most interesting things to me at that moment was that I learned by what I did that I had really not approved of what some other people were doing. I found myself making decisions in the school which were very different from those that I had been implementing that other people had made and I had implemented without question.

"When I was teaching at Greenwich as a young nun under a woman called Mother Helen Bourke, and then back in charge of the discipline under another nun called Anna Boyle, I was just amazed to realize when I was in the position myself how differently I acted from the way they had. When I was working for them I seemingly approved of their decisions. And I can remember thinking when I was in a position to make decisions, 'My goodness, I must not have liked what they were doing because look how differently I am doing it.'"

Under Elizabeth's leadership, discipline generally was less rigorous—and much less emphasized. She set a much less formal tone throughout the school and afforded children a greater degree of freedom. "In other words," she says, "it was a far more liberal approach to education. I didn't do anything so revolutionary that it caused concern. It was more an attitude, a way of dealing with people."

Each year, for example, there was a feast day for the headmistress of the school, which featured a performance by students. Some children participated in a play while others sang or gave readings. "A few days before this first feast I saw one of the young nuns and said, 'You look exhausted. What's the matter with you?' And she said, 'The children don't know their parts in the play. And you know how important that is. If they don't know the parts it's dreadful and I am very worried about it.'

"And I said, 'Who is the play for?' And she said, 'It's for you. It's your feast.' And I said, 'Do you really think I care whether they know their parts? Forget it, these are little children, I don't care how well they do the play. I don't care what they do—relax.'

"Now that means that the person I replaced—Mother Helen Bourke—cared *very much* how well they knew their parts and how perfect the feast wishes, as they were called, were for the head of the school. So little things like that made me know that I had a different set of priorities. I guess that's the way to say it, and incidentally they were priorities that made it a lot easier to work for me. It took a lot of the strain out. Mother Bourke was a very difficult, gifted woman and it was wonderful to be able in that job to make life easier for the young nuns than she had."

Very soon after taking over the headmistress role, it was evident that Elizabeth was extremely comfortable as a leader and decision maker. "I had taught for seven years before that, and in the classroom the decisions were always mine—how I taught, what I demanded of the children, what happened in the classroom. But I felt that where my values could be influential on an institution rather than simply in a classroom didn't come until I was put in charge. Maybe it's the reason I enjoyed it as much as I did."

As soon as Elizabeth assumed the job, she began getting calls from parents seeking her advice. Elizabeth was just thirty-two, had never before been a headmistress, but it did not matter. In 1950s America, parents believed in the inherent wisdom of a nun who had been chosen to lead an elite school.

"They were calling for my advice and it didn't matter who I was," she said. "I was amazed at it because one day I am nobody, one of the young nuns, then I am the Mistress General and parents are calling for my advice."

Parents called seeking counsel about their daughters, though some asked for marital advice. Elizabeth's overriding rule when parents asked for advice was, "Don't make a big issue over non-important things. The way they want their hair cut or dyed. What difference does it make? It is going to grow out. There *are* things you have to make an issue about."

Elizabeth was very young to serve as Mistress General, and she anticipated that the much older, highly experienced head of the lower school, Mother Miriam Schuman, might be concerned that Elizabeth did not know enough about educating younger children. At her first meeting with the heads of the lower, middle, and upper schools, she tried to forestall any problem. She said, "You know, Sister Schuman, I don't know anything about teaching younger children. Nothing. I am going to be no help to you. If you think at any moment I might be helpful, let me know but in the meantime you run the lower school which is something I don't know about." They got along famously after that.

Elizabeth's predecessor at Greenwich had been quite demanding of the staff, and many faculty members seemed anxious and upset. "My challenge initially was to make the people who worked there relax," she says. "So my challenge was pretty easy—be nice and don't care about the unimportant things. I didn't have to pretend. I *didn't* care."

At this time two senior nuns who served as her superiors were positive role models for her. Mother Gertrude Bodkin had been vicar when Elizabeth was a novice, and when Elizabeth arrived at Greenwich as headmistress Mother Bodkin was serving as the local Superior. Mother Helen Fitzgerald at the time served as the Reverend Mother Vicar, essentially the head of the nuns.

"They were very intelligent, strong women with a dedication to religious life, a vision of what they believed the Society should be," she recalls. "They had fine minds. Neither of them was very warm, but when you got to know them they turned out to be very human. And they were very pleased, each of them in her own way, to be recognized as human beings, which I always did, because many people were very much in awe of them, and if one began treating them far more normally, you got close to them."

There were also students who sought her advice on how to deal with their parents. One girl had just discovered inadvertently that she was adopted. "I heard my mother on the telephone talking to a friend about this that I was adopted and she has never told me," the girl said. "I said, 'Well, if I were your mother, I would have told you but she is trying to spare you by not telling you. She is thinking this would be upsetting to you.'" And the girl said that would not be as upsetting as hearing it the way she did.

"And she had a brother who was not adopted, and I said, 'About your brother, your parents had no choice, but they *chose* you.'" They talked a while, and Elizabeth suggested the girl should go to her mother and explain exactly what happened and how terrible it made her feel. "And she did that and she told me afterwards that her mother apologized and it was a wonderful conversation."

Another girl, who was sixteen, came to her to speak privately. "The girl had a deformed foot, and she said, 'I went on my own to a doctor and I learned that the condition is hereditary and I can never marry.' I said, 'Now think about this. This foot hasn't hurt your life. It's not an awful thing. Obviously if you found someone you wanted to marry, you would have to talk it over with him, but I don't think it should be an obstacle. Maybe you decide it is, but you shouldn't at sixteen say because you have to have a special shoe, you can never marry.'"

.   .   .

While headmistress at Greenwich, Elizabeth was instructed by her superiors to enroll in a program leading to a master's degree in religion at Providence College. This would enable her to earn an advanced degree while continuing to teach at Greenwich. For four summers, starting in 1954, she went to Providence. There she lived in a Sacred Heart convent and traveled a short distance to the college campus, where she attended graduate-level courses in Thomistic Theology. "It was considered a very good thing to do, and several of the nuns had already done it, and some of us were told that we'd been chosen to have this opportunity."

It was clear that Elizabeth was being groomed for advancement within the Society. She didn't think about that at the time, but "looking back on it that must have been what was going on. I must have been chosen as someone the superiors saw as having potential of some kind. I don't think I thought about it at the time. I suppose, looking back on it, that the choice of people for that program implied that those chosen had the qualities for leadership within the Society. Because my superiors looked on the program as very good."

Elizabeth did not see it as a particularly good program, however. In fact, she found it narrow and intellectually stifling. "It was very doctrinaire, very narrow," she says. "It was training rather than education. I had gone to Manhattanville College, which was a very open, liberal intellectual setting . . . *Very.* Faculty, some nuns, some lay people, some Catholic, some Protestant, some Jews." Providence College, on the other hand, "was extremely rigorous orthodox conservative, and it was a shock to me. I only really understood what a broad liberal education I had received at Manhattanville when I was sent to Providence." But Elizabeth knew that her superiors within the Society thought this was a good thing for her to do and, of course, she obeyed. But she did not have to believe what she was taught—and she did not.

Much of the coursework centered on Thomistic philosophy as enunciated by St. Thomas Aquinas, the thirteenth-century Dominican priest and theologian. Aquinas sought to explain the foundations of the Catholic religion and is perhaps best known for his work *Five Ways of Proving the Existence of God.* At Providence, there was deep devotion to the writings and teachings of Aquinas since he was perhaps the most revered figure in the history of the Dominican Order.

It was a particularly compelling topic for Elizabeth, for it centered to some extent on the clash between faith and reason. Aquinas preached that such a clash was nonexistent because both were derived from God. He argued that by relying upon either faith or reason, a man would come to the inescapable conclusion that God did, in fact, exist. (It is ironic that, much later on, when Elizabeth began to reexamine her life as a nun, the conflict between faith and reason became central to her thinking.)

"I had to answer an oral examination on Thomistic theology. When I was subjected to this oral examination by four Dominican priests, the president of the college came in, Father Slavin. . . . It was the fifties. . . . The priests were showing off. They knew I knew the answers so they asked me all the tough questions. Predestination and all the particularly controversial questions I answered saying: 'I have been taught at Providence College'—and I gave them the answers. And the president called me over after the examination and asked me: 'When you said you had been taught, does that mean you don't believe what you were saying?'

"I said, 'That is right, Father, I don't.' And he said—and I will never forget it—he said, 'Well, you are honest but you are wrong.'"

But there was kindness too at Providence, a sense of caring for her from at least one priest. When Elizabeth's father died on July 22, 1954, she was not permitted, under the rules of the Society of the Sacred Heart, to go home and be with her family to grieve. A Dominican priest teaching one of her courses informed the class that Elizabeth's father had died and asked the students to pray for him and for Elizabeth as well.

"At the end of the class I went up to him, and I said, 'Thank you very much for that, Father,' and he said, 'What are you doing here? You should be at the funeral.'"

Elizabeth explained that as a member of a semi-cloistered Society, she was not permitted to go to her father's funeral. In fact, the Sacred Heart rule was that nuns were permitted to leave their convents only for education and medical reasons. In retrospect, of course, it seems a monstrously inhuman policy, but at the time, Elizabeth accepted it.

Elizabeth adapted easily to her new life. Part of that was due to an innate adaptability she would display throughout her life. But more than that, having been called by God, she was entirely comfortable with whatever she was asked to do.

(3)

Living with an Illusion

M ANHATTANVILLE WAS A STAR in the constellation of Catholic universities. It was founded as the Academy of the Sacred Heart in 1841 by the Society of the Sacred Heart, and it possessed a strong and enduring Catholic heritage. Originally, it was a boarding school for Catholic girls located on the Lower East Side of Manhattan. In 1847, with the school growing, the nuns moved the academy to Manhattanville, a neighborhood in the northern part of the borough. The Academy of the Sacred Heart became Manhattanville College in 1917, when it was licensed by New York State to award both undergraduate and advanced degrees.

Manhattanville was a place with a special vision for its students, a vision of service to those in need. An ethos pervaded the college in the 1930s and beyond that students should engage with the community outside the campus walls in a variety of productive ways. The essential lesson, taught over the decades by Grace Dammann, a Sacred Heart nun and Manhattanville president from 1930 to 1945, was of service to others. It was a foundational element of the Christian message, and she integrated it into the daily lives of her students. Mother Dammann did this in a practical way by making certain that Manhattanville women were acutely aware of a wide variety of social ills within their own communities. For many years, Manhattanville students volunteered substantial blocks of their time to work with children in the Bowery and East Harlem. A widely published speech by Mother Dammann, "Principles vs. Prejudice," served as an inspiration to leaders at other colleges to break down racial barriers.

The essential Christian mission of the college, as well as rigorous discipline and high academic standards, drew a select group of young women generally from the northeastern United States. Many of these girls were from affluent Catholic families. Among Manhattanville students through the years were Rose Kennedy and several of her daughters and daughters-in-law, including Ethel Skakel Kennedy, wife of Senator Robert Kennedy, and Joan Bennett Kennedy, first wife of Senator Edward Kennedy. Manhattanville also included a number of bright girls from working-class Irish and Italian Catholic families.

In her book *Changing Habits: A Memoir of the Society of the Sacred Heart,* Manhattanville alumna V. V. Harrison writes that "although it ranked below colleges like Vassar, Smith, and Radcliffe in prestige and social standing, Manhattanville represented the best the Sacred Heart had to offer, and for many [first-generation] Irish and Italian families that was enough." She quotes author Phyllis Theroux as writing that Manhattanville was "almost a breeder station of beautiful, appropriate Catholic women who would presumably lead beautiful, appropriate Catholic lives."

In 1958, Elizabeth McCormack was assigned to work at Manhattanville College as assistant to the president, another sign she was being groomed for bigger things within the Society. Nonetheless, she was deeply disappointed. Leaving Greenwich was terribly difficult—she had loved the job—and she dearly missed it when she left.

"I loved that job so much that I wept when I had to leave," she says. It did not help when she discovered at Manhattanville that the job she was assigned to do essentially had no meaningful duties. It was, she thought, "an incredible waste of time." She found that the president, Mother Eleanor O'Byrne, did not know how to use an assistant.

"When I arrive, I have nothing to do," says Elizabeth. "I don't teach. And the president says one weekend, 'Would you go to the alumni office and be sure that the alumni file cards are in alphabetical order?' *Okaaay.* So I go and I do it and while I'm manually sorting through all those many cards, I think, 'Wouldn't it be good to get a PhD?'"

She requested and received permission to pursue a doctorate at Fordham, a Catholic university in the Bronx. Naturally, she attacked the work with a feverish intensity, and by 1962, she had completed a significant amount of work. At this time, the dean of Manhattanville fell ill and Elizabeth was promoted to a position that required a good deal of her time and energy. But she was determined to earn the PhD, and she received permission from the department chair at Fordham, Father James Somerville, S.J., to take the comprehensive exams during the summer rather than the fall. She completed these successfully.

At Fordham University she studied under Professor Robert Pollock, a scholar and philosopher. She would later say that during the time she studied with Professor Pollock, "My own view of the universe altered. He had a much more complex notion of reality and the realization that everything that is real is related to everything else. That you can't think of yourself as just an individual. To *be* is to be related. Therefore it's not God-then-man-then-the-universe. It's one and each part of it is what it is because of the rest of it."

Oddly, Professor Pollock never returned her tests or papers to her. But when she had completed her written comprehensives and had also completed her study of the German language—a prerequisite for the PhD—he phoned her with a suggestion. He said he had just reread all of her papers and was struck by how similar her thinking was to a

British philosopher named F. H. Bradley (1846–1924). "Do your dissertation on him," Professor Pollock suggested. "You will find it very easy."

F. H. Bradley was born and grew up outside London, the son of an evangelical preacher. He studied at University College, Oxford, and was a professor at Merton College, Oxford, for most of his life. According to the Stanford Encyclopedia of Philosophy, Bradley

> was the most famous, original and philosophically influential of the British Idealists. These philosophers came to prominence in the closing decades of the nineteenth century, but their effect on British philosophy and society at large—and, through the positions of power attained by some of their pupils in the institutions of the British Empire, on much of the world—persisted well into the first half of the twentieth. They stood out amongst their peers in consciously rejecting some main aspects of the tradition of their earlier compatriots, such as Hume and Mill . . .
>
> It is for his metaphysics that Bradley has become best known. He argued that our everyday conceptions of the world (as well as those more refined ones common among his philosophical predecessors) contain hidden contradictions which appear, fatally, when we try to think out their consequences. In particular, Bradley rejected on these grounds the view that reality can be understood as consisting of many objects existing independently of each other (pluralism) and of our experience of them (realism). Consistently, his own view combined substance monism—the claim that reality is one, that there are no real separate things—with metaphysical idealism—the claim that reality consists solely of idea or experience. This vision of the world had a profound effect on the verse of T. S. Eliot, who studied philosophy at Harvard and wrote a Ph.D. thesis on Bradley.
>
> On later generations of philosophers, however, Bradley's contributions to moral philosophy and the philosophy of logic were

far more influential than his metaphysics. His critical examination of hedonism—the view that the goal of morality is the maximization of general pleasure—was seminal and stands as a permanent contribution to the subject, which can still be read with profit today. Some of the doctrines of his logic have become standard and unnoticed assumptions through their acceptance by Bertrand Russell, an acceptance which survived Russell's subsequent repudiation of idealist logic and metaphysics.

In pursuit of her thesis, Elizabeth traveled to Oxford for two consecutive summers. There, she lived in a small Sacred Heart convent on Norham Gardens. It was a different kind of convent from the norm within the Society of the Sacred Heart because it was not affiliated with a school—not a convent where nuns teaching in a particular school lived. Rather, it was a place for nuns from all over the world to stay while they were pursuing advanced degrees at Oxford. Thus, it was a place that drew some of the brightest nuns within the Society.

"It was an intellectual community," says Elizabeth. "It was wonderful. We talked about the world, politics, what people were studying at that moment. It was a stimulating environment with very bright women. The conversations were very good."

It was damp and cold that summer in Oxford, and each day Elizabeth would walk from the convent to Merton College and work in the very room that had served as Bradley's study. The room afforded Elizabeth a rich array of works in philosophy that had influenced Bradley and each book had been annotated by the man himself.

"It was wonderful and fun and easy," she says of the work those two summers. "I mean a scholar's life is a nice life. And every day a young guy came and we worked together and we never spoke. He was a young graduate student and I guess he was made nervous by this nun. The first thing he did every day was take off his coat even though it was very cold often. One day after we had been working together for at least a month he got up and put his jacket on and I said to him, 'Thank God you are human.' And we became great friends."

.   .   .

Elizabeth had a broad vision of a liberal arts education before earning her PhD and an even broader view afterward. Back at Manhattanville, as academic dean, she was afforded a good deal of independence, and she became committed to hiring the finest-quality faculty regardless of their religious affiliation. Rather than focusing searches for faculty on candidates from Fordham, Catholic University, and Notre Dame, for example, she looked across the academic spectrum. Gradually, during Elizabeth's years as academic dean, from 1962 to 1966, the faculty grew increasingly diverse.

"I had come to believe that the idea of Catholic—capital C—liberal arts college was a kind of contradiction," she says, "because when one says 'Catholic' in that sense one is admitting a whole series of beliefs or dogmas, and the whole notion of a liberal arts institution where liberal learning takes place is that there *aren't* answers and you don't say, 'We're going to think and we're going to inquire in all these areas but in these areas of our belief—they're not open to question.' I guess by then I thought and still think, that inasmuch as an institution of higher education is sectarian, it is less what's meant to be a liberal arts institution or an institution of higher education. So that if a place is doctrinaire, it is less an educational institution."

Thus, from the start, Elizabeth's instinct was to lead Manhattanville in a secular direction. She saw that the old cultural norm where Catholic families wanted their bright young daughters to have a Catholic education was rapidly drawing to a close. The world was changing. Old norms were falling everywhere. Girls who would typically have come to Manhattanville in the past were heading off to Mount Holyoke, Wellesley, and Smith.

The challenge was obvious to Elizabeth: If Manhattanville could no longer rely upon a large pool of applicants from smart Catholic girls, who would populate the student body? How would the college remain vibrant and alive? How would it even stay in business? The answer was clear: appeal to an applicant pool much broader than Catholic women.

.   .   .

Elizabeth McCormack became the sixth president of Manhattanville College of the Sacred Heart in the summer of 1966. This would prove to be the most difficult time perhaps in the nation's history to lead a college. It was a time of cultural, social, and political upheaval. Issues of war and peace, race, gender equity, religion, and the role of Catholic education in society—all exploded in a violent collision during her watch. In her book *Changing Habits,* V. V. Harrison describes Elizabeth as "the most controversial president" of the college. She notes, as well, that Elizabeth was the last nun to hold that position.

Elizabeth began as president fully aware of the controversies of the day and many of the challenges she would face in leading Manhattanville. She started her inaugural address by posing a series of questions, including "Can we who wish to be both Christians and educators realistically aspire to carry on such an enterprise? Can a Christian college be in fact a center of independent thinking and a community of concern? Can it be dedicated at once to open inquiry and to social responsibility, to learning and to man?" And she answered her own question "Must faith forever shun inquiry and Christians flee the world?" with "a mighty 'No!'" She emphasized that "the college *must* change. . . . Ours is an age of wide and rapid change, an age of crisis and danger, an age of hard questions." Referring to the many human problems facing Manhattanville's students in a wider world, Elizabeth closed with a warning, "The Catholic college of today will be judged by the role its graduates play in helping solve them."

It was a brutally difficult job. She had loved being the head at Greenwich, but she described being president of Manhattanville as "hell. Everything you had to do, displeased some constituency."

.   .   .

But Elizabeth had been president for barely a year when she was instructed to travel to Rome for a critically important meeting. It was known as a General Chapter, where Sacred Heart nuns from all over the world would make important decisions about the future of the Society. The expectation was that she would be back leading Manhattanville in a month or two. Elizabeth prepared diligently for the General Chapter. All meetings in Rome would be conducted in French, and since her ability with the language was rusty, she enrolled in a Berlitz immersion program—100 intense hours in just ten days.

The General Chapter convened in Rome in September 1967. Every religious society within the Roman Catholic Church convenes at regular intervals to review the state of the society and make recommendations for change—and that was the purpose of this gathering. It was an opportunity to examine the Society and its practices in light of the many changes wrought by the Second Vatican Council of 1962 to 1965, inaugurated by Pope John XXIII. Eighty-five nuns from all over the world convened on the Society's Mother House on Via Nomentana. The nuns held their meetings there, and stayed there as well in small, comfortable rooms called cells. The Mother House was a stately, ancient stone structure with a long, wide interior corridor and a chapel off to one side. Chapter meetings and discussions were held in a large meeting room.

Elizabeth was honored to be among such select company for the mission to Rome. Superiors from the Society worldwide were chosen automatically while an additional group, Elizabeth among them, was selected by vote. There were many Sacred Heart nuns in the New York area—so many that the New York delegation numbered three: Elizabeth and Mother Margaret Coakley, who was also selected by vote, and the Provincial Superior (the head of the Society's U.S. branch or province), Mother Helen Fitzgerald.

Early on, Elizabeth was chosen to serve on the General Chapter's coordinating committee, which included Mother Jacobs (Congo), Mother Chu (Korea), Mother Espadaler (Mexico), Mother Belon (Peru), and Mother Guizard (France). They held differing viewpoints on various issues yet worked diligently together for the good of the Society. "We have grown very close to one another due to our common work—it is up to us to keep this Chapter moving," Elizabeth wrote at one point. This small operating group met frequently to help set the agenda for each day's meetings.

A major theme of the sessions focused on how best to liberalize some of the rules governing the Society. For example, the prohibition against nuns visiting their families at home was a topic in which many of the delegates were keenly interested. "From the time I entered in 1944 to 1967, I had never been into my own home," says Elizabeth. "There was a cloister which was only lifted for reasons of one's job. One could go to get educated. One could go to an educational meeting. I very strongly urged that many of those restrictions be lifted, not in Society to make life easier but in Society to make the people who were Religious of the Sacred Heart more able to do the work that they were doing. There was a kind of austerity. One never went to a concert. One very rarely went to a lecture and then it had to be very clearly identified with the work one was doing. One wasn't a cultivated educator because one wasn't allowed to be. So I pushed for those changes."

Elizabeth arrived in Rome in mid-September and was a reliable correspondent back to her colleagues at Manhattanville, who, in turn, shared Elizabeth's missives with other nuns within the Society in North America and perhaps even in the United Kingdom. That September, she wrote to Manhattanville—addressing her letter, as she would nearly all the others—to "Dear Reverend Mother," and reporting that although they had been there a fortnight nothing had yet been accomplished. "The two weeks have been *long* indeed," she writes. "Now we are all anxious to begin." She noted in her direct, pull-no-punches style, that a priest had spoken to the group that day, a Father Louis Renard, S.J. "Some like him," Elizabeth writes. "He is not my type."

"I am more sure each day," she writes in closing her letter, "that if this job is to be done, God must do it. It is beyond our power. Now it is a question of *faith* that He will in fact do what needs to be done." The subtext here—what was in her mind at the time—was unsettling. She fully expected upon arriving in Rome to be among a group of very smart, forceful, visionary women. She believed she was part of an elite group of thinkers and leaders. Very quickly, however, to her crushing disappointment, she found that was not the case. This was not the intellectual firepower of those women who gathered at Norham Gardens in Oxford. These were administrators and others—women in the middle of the road. Women too timid by half. Women who would do anything to avoid conflict—for whom the status quo was perfectly acceptable. She was stung by this—and disillusioned.

"This was the leadership and I quickly recognized that they really hadn't a clue what needed to be done," she says, and what needed to be done was difficult, challenging—and would require a deft touch and a real sense of vision. "What needed to be done was some updating, bringing the Society into the modern world, but doing so *without destroying it.*"

She writes on October 1 that she had "just returned from the opening Mass and I must write—at least begin this letter before the official opening of the Chapter at 11:00. I cannot begin to tell you how I felt at Mass—so very near to each one at home—nearer to you than to the person in the stall next to me!"

Yet a sense of frustration is clearly there early on. "It is my hope that now we will get a certain feeling of doing something which up to this point I certainly have not had." A similar frustration was evident three days later on October 4, when she writes: "Alas, many do not know how to *press* forward. Everything stops at supper time. No one seems to work after supper! Except the Americans. We may be here for the Easter Vigil!"

She writes on October 6, "We meet and meet and meet and between meetings little groups get together to talk about what has happened, will happen, may happen, should happen. It is *something*. I *know* now that it cannot go more quickly. Ideas are so new to so many that it takes time for the first *horror* to wear off and then, with some, a little light begins to dawn."

When she had arrived in Rome she had hoped to be back in New York by mid-October, but on the seventh she writes that "now I pray for mid-November. Please, pray with me, and for me. I love you all *so* much."

On October 16 she complained that "we move oh so very slowly! I wonder sometimes if we move at all. I just think that something is really fixed and then minds and hearts change and it isn't fixed at all. It is good for me—perhaps I shall learn real patience." She notes in the same letter that there is "much anti-American feeling due to Viet Nam. Alas, this is everywhere even on Via Nomentana. Some of us understand why."

She closes her letter of October 16: "Father du Lubac spoke to the Chapter from 9:30 this a.m. until 12:00. He answered questions. All the old thinking, so alas we must begin again on several subjects. I think that he gave us re authority and obedience the thoughts that helped him 20 years ago. He is a *holy* man, but he has not kept up with the thinking of the Church in some areas. I wish he had been given a subject other than Authority in Religious Life. We are all for it, but not all of us think that it is absolute. He said for example—'Dialogue, yes, if the superior wishes it—otherwise no' . . . . I'm off to a meeting—PRAY— I lose heart from time to time."

She was discouraged because by the middle of October, nothing had really happened. Yet she seems more hopeful on October 18 writing that "a General Chapter is a *process*, a kind of experience for each one— an experience that cannot really be described. It is painful, but I believe that it will bear fruit—if not immediately then in the future . . .

"It is wonderful to see the spirit and end of the Society 'emerge' as we hoped it would during these days. Each day a few more of us are aware that all that we say is in reality talking about our life of consecration and Devotion to the Sacred Heart. This becomes more clear during each discussion. For example, our apostolate, whatever its form, is in reality the giving of the human love of God to men. Surely that is Devotion to the Sacred Heart. Pray that all our ideas may come into *focus*. When they do, we will have the beginning of renewal and adaptation."

On the last day of October she wrote that "I know that you are all praying very much for the Chapter. I have one thing that needs very special prayers. Will you say them? Storm heaven that God will show His will."

.   .   .

In addition to Elizabeth's sense of surprise and disappointment at the lack of strength and leadership among her colleagues, she was disturbed by what she perceived as erratic behavior by the Mother General, Mother deValon. As a member of the coordinating committee, Elizabeth had much more face-to-face contact with her than 90 percent of those at the meeting. And Elizabeth could clearly see that there was something very wrong with the worldwide leader of the Society. She had been elected for life and was barely sixty years old when the Rome sessions began.

"Her behavior at our meetings was clearly erratic," says Elizabeth. "We would meet to set the agenda for the meetings and on some days when we met she seemed fine. Other days she was inconsistent, erratic. She was psychotic, sick. She was very different some times from other times." She was unpredictable and not even close to the kind of strong, steady leader the Society needed at this critical moment in its history. "I *knew* this woman could not remain as the Superior General of our Society," she says. Elizabeth's fellow members of the coordinating committee agreed. "And it became clear to me that our major responsibility during that Chapter wasn't changing this rule or that rule—it was getting that particular woman out of that position because she had final responsibility for maybe seven thousand people all over the world."

But deposing the Mother General could not be done easily. No one knew of a time when a Mother General was turned out of office. And very few of the nuns there had any intention of raising the issue directly. Of the eighty-five women in the room, there were essentially three groups. The first consisted of women who saw no real problem with the Mother General. The second group—quite a large group, in fact—could clearly see she had serious emotional problems, but they nonetheless believed that loyalty demanded that the Mother General remain in office until death. They suggested that she could be surrounded by a strong staff and continue to function. And then there was a very small group, including Elizabeth, who believed that the Mother General's deterioration was a threat to the Society, that she was a sick woman who should not have the responsibility for leading an organization of seven thousand devoted, hard-working woman around the world.

It was the first time in her life—but absolutely not the last time—that Elizabeth McCormack would demonstrate determination and unusual courage in the face of a personnel issue. She was not afraid of making a difficult change for the sake of the larger organization—not in Rome in 1967, not in New York and other places in the 1970s, 1980s, 1990s, and beyond. "I found myself in the position," she says, "with two or three others, of organizing that small group of people to see to it that she was no longer Mother General before we left Rome."

Elizabeth knew the rules—that when the nuns convened in the way they had in Rome, as a General Chapter, that they were the Society's governing body and thus could make changes. But there was a strategic challenge that Elizabeth recognized right away. If a vote of all the delegates was held, Mother deValon would surely win easily. Elizabeth could see that a large number of delegates were committed to abiding by the Mother General's lifetime appointment. In addition, there were quite a few delegates, Elizabeth could see, who saw no problem with her leadership. It was only a relative handful of nuns who clearly saw the problem. Elizabeth was in a very small minority, and yet she saw clearly that the problem was a serious one—a threat to the very Society to which she had devoted her life. She thought carefully about what strategy might work. Since she was certain a vote of the delegates would go the wrong way, she set upon a very different approach.

"Every religious society of the kind I belonged to had a person who was called a Cardinal Protector," she says. "So I identified three of the major superiors—Holland, Great Britain, one from this country—and I got them together and I said, 'We have a problem and I cannot deal with it and I haven't the age or position to do it in this group but you must deal with it. How do we deal with it?' I said, 'You go to the Cardinal Protector because we must not vote. If this group voted they would vote to keep her.'"

The three nuns Elizabeth had recruited went on a private mission to talk with the Cardinal Protector. He listened carefully and was persuaded. Several days later he appeared at a gathering of all eighty-five nuns and sat next to the Mother General on a stage. The nuns in the audience were hushed. Something historic was happening before their eyes; something few other Sacred Heart nuns had ever witnessed.

In French, the Cardinal Protector praised the Mother General and her piety. Then he turned to her and said, "It is time for you to retire, to resign."

In a remarkable tribute to the sense of discipline built into the Society, the Mother General did not hesitate. *"Oui, mon père,"* she replied.

As Elizabeth looked back upon it years later, the strict sense of immediate and unquestioned obedience did not surprise her at all. The cardinal "represented the church and the church represented God and you obeyed."

·   ·   ·

On November 14, 1967, she wrote about the remarkable events she had witnessed. She noted that the past week involved

> the first *sub secrete* week of the Chapter. Clearly it was wise not to send word home until the whole event could be sent. What a week!
> . . . We worked on the Treasury as a kind of distraction. Our Mother gave her resignation on Tuesday, November 7 at the 9:30 a.m. session. [The Cardinal] accepted the resignation in the name of the Church on Friday at 5:00 p.m. Between those days you can guess the *suffering*. We did not know whether we would have to vote whether or not to accept the resignation. I have never been so grateful to Holy *Mother* the Church. Our Mother was acting in the spirit of Vatican II and it was fitting that the Church, not the Society, make the decision.

Three days later, on November 17, she wrote about what a "strange week" it had been.

> It is hard to realize that our Mother General has really gone. She is still at Naples, but she leaves Monday for Egypt. She wants to be there in the missions—for how long has not been said. . . .
> We have had difficult days. I believe that this is easy to explain. Many are finding problems in the policy documents (known as schemas) that they would not have found had Our Mother been with us. Their sorrow concerning her resignation is manifested in disapproval concerning the most liberal points in

the papers, a kind of transfer of problems! It has been hard going
. . . resistance to change . . . all too clear.

On November 21 she reports that she hopes to be home by December 8, and she notes: "Our Mother flew to Egypt yesterday."

On Thanksgiving Day, November 24, she is a bit wistful about having missed more than half the first semester at Manhattanville. She briefly discusses the Mother General's resignation and observes that "I never thought I would appreciate the bureaucratic side of the Church, but I did—very much. All our triumphalism should be dead; I hope it is."

What she meant by "triumphalism," in this context, was the essentially arrogant attitude of the Roman Catholic Church that, as she puts it, "We've got it. We've got the answers. We've got a direct line to God. Our Pope is infallible. No matter what we go through we will win. We will triumph in the end."

Near the end of the letter she is unable to resist a jab, noting that her committee on governance consulted with "a canon lawyer last evening. . . . He was just what you would expect a canon lawyer to be like. Enough said . . ." Asked years later what she meant exactly, she says, "Rigorous, unyielding, without nuance, letter-of-the law, inhuman."

On November 28, she mentions a particular schema and writes that "it is probably the most imaginative schema in the lot. (Remember we are *not* an imaginative group, so be grateful for any sign of imagination which you find in the papers!)"

"When is the faculty-staff Christmas party? Dec. 17th???" she asks on December 4. In the letter she mentions a Jesuit who gave a sermon: "He has been good, but somehow sermons do not speak to me anymore." What she meant by this was that she was influenced more by discussion, analysis, interpretation—by an honest back-and-forth debate or conversation in which those involved were honestly searching for the truth.

In her final missive home, on December 11, 1967, she writes that she had "the happy(?) task of explaining the final modifications to the Assembly before the vote yesterday!" Then she noted that she would be arriving home December 19, "BOAC 505—arrives Kennedy at 3:40 p.m. ALLELUIA."

.   .   .

A new Mother General was elected, a Spanish nun Elizabeth greatly admired and respected. She agreed to serve for a term of three years as an interim. Then new rules would limit subsequent Mothers General to a maximum of two consecutive six-year terms.

While Elizabeth felt she had done something important for her Society, she also felt a sense of disillusionment she had never before experienced. She was disillusioned by the weakness of her colleagues, by the failure of so many of them to see clearly the problem with the Mother General, and by their failure to have the courage and conviction to act. She was disillusioned that they put a kind of petty politics ahead of the overall good of the Society.

"It was incredibly disillusioning," says Elizabeth. "I had been living with a kind of illusion. I thought that the leadership within this group was probably really strong and intelligent."

After the new Mother General's election, Elizabeth went to her privately. She said, "You know this Chapter shows me the incredible needs of the Society and what you've taken on is a very difficult situation. If you would like me to, I could go home, get out of the job I'm doing, and come back and help you do this. If that's what you want I'm ready to do it. But I can't do both. I mean I've been away far longer than I should have been." But the Mother General said that what Elizabeth was doing at Manhattanville was too important to give up. Elizabeth was disappointed in a way. "I thought I might be able to make a difference," she says.

That was late in 1967. Elizabeth McCormack was forty-five and had been a member of the Society of the Sacred Heart for twenty-three years, more than half her life. She had just participated in—led, in a way—a coup against the leader of the Society. She had played a crucial and constructive role. Yet she left Rome disillusioned. She was surprised by the weakness of her colleagues from around the world. She loved her Society and was committed to it. But in Rome at that time, a seed of discontent had been planted within Elizabeth.

But changes emerged from the sessions in Rome. Among them, nuns were now allowed to go home and visit their families. But given the rigor of the Society, the strict rigor that was at the heart of the life she had led since entering the convent, Elizabeth was concerned that too much change was coming too rapidly. She worried not about the new rules—they were reasonable. She worried about how they would be interpreted as well as how—and at what speed—they would be implemented. "They had no idea of the consequences of the fast implementation and interpretation of change," she says. "By the end of the General Chapter we had made too many changes too fast."

The new Mother Superior was an impressive woman—Mother Josefa Bulto from Spain. Before heading back to Manhattanville, Elizabeth made a point of sitting down with her. "I said we made too many changes too fast. And she said, 'What do you mean?' I said, 'Let me give you an example. We were semi-cloistered. Now we are no longer semi-cloistered.' And she said, 'Do you mean that the Mother Superior should not be allowed to take the nuns to the park near the convent for a picnic lunch?' And I said, 'Reverend Mother, I don't mean that. But the nuns won't be there to go to the picnic lunch. They'll be at the movies.'"

Elizabeth has always been open-minded about ideas. But she recognized that the essential strength of the Sacred Heart Society lay in its rigor. "I don't think you can take something as rigorous as our life was and change it in significant ways without also mandating the ways in which it wouldn't change. We had something very strict and then you open a window to let in a breeze and a hurricane comes through. . . .

"After Vatican II religious life changed. Instead of living in large communities the nuns were assigned to small groups. The daily schedule was put in the hands of each individual. The time given to prayer was not mandated. It became the responsibility of each individual. There was no longer a common order of the day. The common work in the schools gradually disappeared. Therefore, since neither the common life nor the common mission remains, very few young people are attracted to the Society. What is there to join?

"Instead of having a mission on which everyone agreed and made their own, each one decided what she believed she was called upon to do. Judy Garson was a very bright woman, and I thought she should be the next president of Manhattanville. So she went and did a PhD at Columbia and when she had everything done but the dissertation this whole new thing . . . do what you are called on to do. So she stopped. She didn't get the PhD and she began working in Harlem."

The sudden shift in the Society's culture and structure alarmed Elizabeth. She had entered the convent with her eyes wide open. She knew about the discipline and restrictions and she bought into all of it. She knew that it was irrational that she could not visit her dying father but she accepted it as part of the discipline of the Society. By changing so radically, it lost its essence, she thought.

"Now the few postulants there are live right in the community, and the communities are little groups of four or five people. And the postulants can go with everyone else to the movies! The very fact that those years were rigorous and different and demanded a lot of each one of us I found made it worth doing."

.   .   .

Three years later a similar gathering was held, again in Rome, and

Elizabeth told the Mother General that she would not be able to attend because of her work at Manhattanville. The Mother General replied, "You were the only one then, in '67, who said what was going to happen."

"After '67, almost no one worked for a PhD again," Elizabeth says. "Because there are any number of reasons not to do it. And it's a very hard thing to do. I think that if one is living in the real world, outside of a convent or any other institution, just by that fact one has imposed upon one certain disciplines. Most people have to work for a living. Most people if they don't cook their meals don't eat. Most people have to worry what they're going to do when they retire. What are they going to live on? Most people have to worry that they have Blue Cross and Blue Shield and everything else, because they don't *dare* be without medical insurance. All those normal things nuns don't have. They absolutely know they have a roof over their heads. They have three meals a day. They have total care when they're old and sick as long as they stay in the cloister."

Elizabeth was shaken by the Rome experience. She had given her life to the work of this Society and now she had seen its leaders gathered and she had been truly unimpressed. As she reflected upon the inadequacy of the leadership, she thought back over her own career and commitment.

"I had entered the society in 1944 and twenty-three years later at that General Chapter in Rome was the first time I thought, 'Am I going to stay with this for the rest of my life?'"

(4)

A Difficult Time

MANHATTANVILLE WAS A VERY Catholic college in every way except its legal charter. Nearly 100 percent of the students were Catholics, and prayer and Mass, although not required, were essential elements of campus life. After the school moved from Manhattan to Purchase, New York, in 1952 (to the former estate of Whitelaw Reid), a large chapel was built, in 1963, near the center of campus, and religious symbols were set around the grounds and throughout nearly every room in every building on campus. The administration and faculty consisted overwhelmingly of Sacred Heart nuns. And there was a plot of land on campus dedicated to a graveyard exclusively for nuns.

But the world was changing. When Martin Luther King Jr. was assassinated in April 1968, Elizabeth McCormack felt a duty to travel to Atlanta for his funeral. She managed to hitch a ride on New York Governor Nelson Rockefeller's plane—well before she worked for the Rockefellers—as president of Manhattanville and still in her full habit. She walked to the church in a large procession, through some very poor black neighborhoods. "It was a scorching day and, along the way, in the poorest of neighborhoods, families had put out large basins with cool water and soup ladles. I walked with Robert Kennedy and we were both refreshed by drinking the cold water." In another nine weeks, Kennedy would be killed, too.

In this changing world, as president of Manhattanville, Elizabeth worried about the financial security of the nuns there and worried about the social turmoil that seemed likely to chip away at congregations like the Sacred Heart. Thus, as president, she put all of the nuns on real, though modest salaries. In addition, she made sure that all the nuns were contributing to Social Security, and she also enrolled them in the TIAA-CREF retirement plan specifically designed for people in the not-for-profit world.

"I got a lot of criticism for that. 'Where is your faith? Who is going to need that?' My answer was, 'I hope it will never be needed and if it isn't needed when the money comes in, it can be given to the poor.' But of course it became very much needed."

When Jerome I. Aron arrived as chief financial officer in October 1969, he saw that the college was not in the best possible financial condition. There was a deficit, and the situation was aggravated in the short run by the changes Elizabeth was making. These changes upset, angered, or infuriated many alumnae, so contributions declined.

Alumnae effectively "stopped giving because they disapproved of Elizabeth," Jerry later told an interviewer. "Their loyalty never ran to the college. It ran to the Society, although, the college, while a function of the Society, did not belong to the Society. The college was chartered by the regents of New York as a private, nonprofit college. Like Vassar. But the alumnae, all these girls were Sacred Heart girls and they went to Sacred Heart convent schools and then to a Catholic college. . . . They disapproved of Elizabeth fairly strenuously. Her intention was to give the college a future. And as a Catholic girls' college, she saw no future."

.   .   .

Elizabeth sought to bring a sense of historical perspective to the students and faculty. During an all-college address, on December 9, 1968, she said that "to gain perspective, we will look to the PAST, to the FUTURE, to the NOW. Let us look at 1918, 1948, and 1968. What paths link these dates to give them substance and meaning?"

> [In 1918], ten months had passed since the United States had, in fact, declared war on Germany; American soldiers were in Europe, American women were faced with new responsibilities and new opportunities. The establishment of a college for women where diverse and contradictory ideas were not only tolerated but encouraged, where liberal learning was offered, where women could be prepared for their new role, was a direct response to a national need.
>
> At Manhattanville in 1918 there were twelve students and eight faculty members (one of them teaching a course in Buddhism). By 1948, there were four hundred and seventy-two students, seventy-seven faculty members and eighteen major programs . . .

This was the year, 1948, when the college decided to move from the city to the beautiful property in Purchase. It was also the year, Elizabeth pointed out,

> of the Marshall Plan: "Our policy is not directed against any country or doctrine but is directed against hunger, poverty, desperation, and chaos"; it was the year of the Communist seizure of Czechoslovakia, of the blockade of Berlin, of Truman's campaign against Dewey, and [campaigns by] Henry Wallace, of the New Progressive Party, and the Dixiecrat, Governor of South Carolina, J. Strom Thurmond. It was the year when the horizons of the country were widened and rebuilding for the future became a national concern.

It was the year when this college determined to open its doors on a new campus to more students from the world community and to offer them an ever more varied curriculum.

Then she turned to the particular challenges she and the college faced in 1968.

The decision to begin a college and the decision to move to Purchase were undoubtedly difficult to make, but in retrospect the questions these decisions attempted to answer seem comparatively simple. Nineteen hundred sixty-eight's questions are not. The decisions made in response will *not* be clear cut or certain, but they must be made, if the future, with its new questions, is not to pass us by. Today's world, and Manhattanville in that world face an unknown future, but we face it with hope, with confidence and with a resolve to be equal to the task before us.

My final questions are less broad but no less important. Manhattanville will not hasten to join other institutions by announcing next week that it plans to be co-educational in the fall. To do so would be to give a simple answer to a complex question. Such an answer would be no answer at all; and it would be one arrived at hastily and without due deliberation. I ask you therefore: How can Manhattanville achieve the educational advantages of co-education without admitting under-graduate men directly to its degree programs?

The speech was interesting for many reasons, not the least of which was the nugget at the end where she informed the students and faculty that there would be no rush to coed education. Naturally, this was as disappointing to many undergraduates as it was thrilling to many alumnae. But it was not an issue that would go away, and it would not be long before Elizabeth felt she had no choice but to take it on.

There was another issue, more incendiary than any other she faced, which was on the horizon. She had done some fairly intensive research and discovered that what she had long assumed was true—that from its founding, when its charter was granted in 1917, the college was an educational institution, pointedly *not* a religious one. It was never a church college. It was never under the bishop. And the charter allowed the college to function under the Regents of the State of New York with a mixed board. This would come as a surprise to many, a shock to others. Thus, she believed that the name of the college was misleading—that it should really be called simply Manhattanville College, not Manhattanville College of the Sacred Heart. She thought that the name of the college carried the clear implication that the Society of the Sacred Heart owned the college, which it did not. And she knew that renaming the college would help broaden its appeal as a general liberal arts institution.

Elizabeth spoke privately with the Provincial Superior, Mother Helen Fitzgerald, who was a member of the Manhattanville board. "Mother Fitzgerald loved me and respected me and she was a wonderful woman," recalls Elizabeth. "I told her that it no longer made sense to have a Manhattanville College of the Sacred Heart and that we had to make changes and that it didn't mean that the values had to change, but the name did have to change." Elizabeth explained that she believed that changing the name would be "politically very sensitive." And Mother Fitzgerald asked whether Elizabeth wanted her to propose it at the board meeting. Elizabeth said yes, and Mother Fitzgerald did so. Her proposal was simple: Drop "of the Sacred Heart" from the college name.

"The College had changed before I became president, but my saying, 'This is not a Catholic College,' my changing it from Manhattanville College of the Sacred Heart to Manhattanville College, was very real to the alumnae. To the student body, which was a largely secularized group of Roman Catholics, the change was minimal. . . . The student body of Manhattanville, and the faculty, during those years, between

1958 and 1966, became an increasingly secular group—the nuns, after that Chapter in 1967, the lay Roman Catholics even before it, so that the kind of 'religious spirit' that had been typical of the college when I was there in the 1940s, was gone."

Besides, says Elizabeth, "'Of the Sacred Heart' is possessive genitive in Latin and indicates the college is 'owned by' the Society. Not true." The board, approximately twenty people, approved the name change overwhelmingly with only a single dissenting vote. And there was little pushback on the change from alumnae.

.   .   .

Changing the name required other changes as well, and one, in particular, was extraordinarily sensitive. Throughout the campus there were hundreds of Catholic symbols, including the central one, the crucifix, which hung in nearly every classroom on campus. And now, with the secularization of the college, these symbols would have to be removed. To many in the Manhattanville community, alumnae in particular, this bordered on the sacrilegious. It would be a move that would enrage many alumnae and prompt some to vilify Elizabeth at every opportunity.

Elizabeth took no joy in this, but she felt it was her duty to have the crucifixes removed. To do otherwise would have been to violate its declaration as a secular institution. She thought about how to go about it and gathered together a small, trusted unit of three young nuns—Cynthia Hettinger, Peggy Wallingford, and a third nun from the Philippines whose name is lost to history.

Once given the assignment, these young women went to work. They would go out late at night and remove a few crosses from a handful of classrooms. "We didn't want everybody in an uproar, so we would take down four or five every time," says Cynthia. They would store them in Cynthia's closet in her dorm room in Spellman Hall.

"One night we finally went to Elizabeth and said, 'Look, we're partially doing this because of you. We want you to have the experience of doing this because it is a very strange feeling.' We were certainly all three of us in agreement with her that the college had to be secular and that this was consistent with Vatican II and Pierre Teilhard de Chardin and all of those things . . . But it was still a very strange feeling to climb up on a chair and take these things down. So we made her do it one night. She admitted it was a strange feeling."

Cynthia and her two co-conspirators had one big problem: What were they to do with hundreds of crucifixes? "We found out sort of deviously what you were supposed to do with old crucifixes, not crucifixes that you stole . . . But we managed to ask this nice Irish priest, 'What happens to crucifixes that are damaged? What is the right thing to do with them?' He said, 'You either deep-six them in a lot of water, or you bury them.' We couldn't figure out how to deep-six them in water so on Good Friday, we thought there was something appropriate: We got a whole bunch of shovels from the grounds crew of the Manhattanville campus, who of course didn't have a clue what we were doing, and we went back out behind what was then the hockey field. We didn't bury them on the actual hockey field but sort of off the hockey field in this little wooded area. There we were with our little shovels digging away. . . . On Good Friday, when you are commemorating the burial of Christ, we thought it was an appropriate day."

Initially, there was very little reaction. For a time, people generally did not notice that the crucifixes were gone. And then people noticed—alums noticed and heard about it and word spread, and many people—alumnae in particular—were quite angry. Letters poured into Elizabeth's office letting her know in frank terms what they thought of her decisions.

"The letters were terrible," says Elizabeth, "but I never found them personally wounding because I never was in the position of doubting the decision, which was very nice. It made it easier. Secondly, they were so unkind, so really vicious." She felt there was an extremist or fundamentalist tone to some of the criticism. "The reaction of some people was a fundamentalist reaction," she says. "And fundamentalism, whether Muslim, Christian, or Jewish, is extremism and it takes over rational thought. And that's what happened with some people."

A lighter moment occurred as the hate mail poured in. Elizabeth asked her secretary, Elizabeth Porter, what she thought of it all. Ms. Porter replied: "Up to this moment in my life, I've always worked for respectable people."

The bitterness over Elizabeth's decision to make the college non-sectarian dissipated slowly over time but never went away. There were many people—nuns, former faculty and administrators, former board members and of course many former students—who were deeply disappointed and angry about it. "Many of them were very negative about it and it didn't fool any of them that Reverend Mother Fitzgerald proposed it," she says. "They knew who was behind it."

Some of the anger, Elizabeth believed, was a general sense of betrayal among fervent Roman Catholics that their church was changing too much too fast. "Many critics were angry at the changes within the Church and felt it's very hard to lash out against the whole Roman Catholic Church. The College was an easy victim of their anger. I think there were some who believed in the College as they remembered it—as a very Church-oriented, religious institution. These graduates would have rather seen it close its doors than make that change. Better dead than red. I would say many graduates of Manhattanville would say, 'Better not to be at all, than to be secular.'"

The tone of so many of the letters was strikingly nasty. "They were really just dreadful," she recalls. "I guess the one that symbolized all of them contained a picture of a medieval stained-glass window with Judas kissing Jesus, and the note said, 'This is you, Sister.' That was the kind of thing. Terrible. And too many of them, to be able to say, 'These are a few crazies, cranks.' Too many of them."

The experience scarred her in a way. She read the letters from women who had received a first-rate Catholic education, and she found the narrow-minded cruelty difficult to stomach. "If this is what one becomes, when one is 'religious' then who wants to be religious? If this is what a religious education does to people, should we continue educating people in religion? That's a very big question. I mean I guess religion, just taking it in general, has been the cause of some of the greatest inhumanities of man to man. That's a matter of record."

Elizabeth disagreed with her critics, but she understood their point of view. Many wanted the college to grow and prosper and still remain Catholic, but she could clearly see that was not going to happen. "The point is that I realized that the reason Manhattanville was as successful as it had been was because good Roman Catholics like my father believed that their children had to go to Catholic colleges. That disappeared. That built-in constituency was gone.

"The Catholic college was the institution to which Roman Catholics believed (because they were told by the Church) that they had to send their children. So if one was the strongest Catholic women's college, one could count on, for many years, a very intelligent group of Catholic women enrolling. Catholics have given up going to Catholic 'places.' If they go to them it's because they happen to want to go. The Church stopped requiring it eventually (after the fact in many ways) so that, for the college such as Manhattanville, the very small pool of applicants from which to draw resulted. So I think that, for two reasons, the financial one we spoke about, and the fact of the change in custom among Roman Catholics, not to mention my reason, which I believe (although one can always deceive oneself, about one's reason) was primarily an educational one. Take those three together, the Catholic women's college doesn't have a very bright future."

Elizabeth had no doubt she faced a stark choice—change or go out of business. And change meant competing for a much larger pool of students—male as well as female, Jewish and Protestant as well as Catholic. "I remember saying to a board member, Morris McLaughlin,

'You know we had to do this or we would have gone out of business.' He said, 'I would rather we went out of business.'"

.　　　.　　　.

Like other colleges across the country, Manhattanville struggled with how best to diversify its campus. In 1967 a new program, Project SHARE, was initiated in an effort to integrate the campus more effectively. Elizabeth says, "From the time of Mother Dammann's presidency there had always been African American students at Manhattanville. They had been accepted with the same standards as the other applicants. In 1969, I decided to continue to attract well-educated and gifted black young women, but to do more. The college would inaugurate the SHARE program. We would recruit African American students whose educational background was weak, but whose motivation and intelligence gave promise. These students would attend a summer of preparation for entrance into the freshman class.

"Sophomore students agreed to become roommates of the SHARE freshman. I will never forget a meeting in October with a sophomore roommate. She was disabled and depended on a wheelchair. 'How is it going?' I asked. She said, 'It is great. I help her with her homework and she lifts me into the bathtub.' Project SHARE at work!

"The college had an archeological dig in Majorca. Two SHARE students, Debbie Belcher Karim ('71) and Pamela Stewart Cassandra ('71), wanted to join it. My assistant told them that my schedule was full and to come back the next day. They waited until Elizabeth Porter had gone to lunch and then they knocked on my door. They explained that their grades were good and that there were two places left in the program. I asked: 'What's the problem?' 'Well,' they answered, 'we do not have money for the plane fare.' 'Is that all?' I said. I then said, 'The college will buy the tickets.' The trip was a great success for these two who had never left Manhattan Island before."

.   .   .

In the fall of 1969, America was gripped by social upheaval over the Vietnam War, gender equity, and the issue of race. Affirmative steps to integrate many institutions, including college and university campuses, were relatively new, at least on a broad scale, and did not always go smoothly.

In March 1967 the Manhattanville Association of Negroes was formed to sponsor speakers, arts exhibits, and other events. In the fall of 1968 it was renamed the Manhattanville Afro American Society. In May 1969, the group presented a series of proposals to Elizabeth including an increase in black enrollment, more black faculty members, the establishment of black studies curriculum, hiring a black counselor, and more. The group demanded action on these items within twelve days.

Elizabeth was sympathetic to the students' concerns. She knew that in the 1969–1970 academic year there were only forty-seven black students out of a total of 1,479 students at Manhattanville and she could clearly see the level of inequality and racism in America reflected in the college. But she was not about to respond to such suggestions in twelve days. She continued what had already begun in the administration, a discussion about how to create a more robust black presence and engagement on campus.

In the fall of 1969 there was a more palpable sense of racial tension on campus than ever before. Some of the black students wrote incendiary pamphlets that alienated many white students while firing up supporters of the black students. An October 1969 flyer from the head of the Manhattanville Afro American Society and others asserted that "black is absolute purity . . . pure beauty" and white minds are "bland." This sort of rhetoric was fairly common throughout the remainder of the semester as the divisions on campus grew deeper. Frustrations on both sides mounted.

At 6:30 on the evening of Monday, December 8, seventeen black students occupied Brownson Hall, which housed laboratories, classrooms, and art and music facilities. They entered the building supplied with food and blankets and chained the doors from inside using combination locks. Within an hour of the takeover, reporters and photographers from major New York newspapers and broadcast outlets were on the scene.

Once inside, the students issued a list of demands, including "admission of 150 non-white students. Seven Black teachers by September, 1970; Full time Black Counselor, Black Dean and Black Program Director," as well as a "position on the Admissions Staff to recruit Black students."

The students also demanded the payment of a monthly stipend between $40 and $60 for every black student and faculty member at Manhattanville. The amount would depend upon family income. The students also sought an office on campus for the Manhattanville Afro American Society, and another for the National Association of Black Students, and various other items.

The young women within Brownson noted in a flyer that "black students have to deal with overt racist professors, and this racism determines the professors' evaluation and perception of black students. Black students are further alienated in the classroom by the white students' racist remarks and racist attitudes." Paula Williams, president of the Afro American Society, told reporters the night of the takeover that "blacks get lower marks because they're black."

The events made the front page of local newspapers and were mentioned in the *New York Times* and other major dailies, and covered on CBS, NBC, and ABC television news.

Elizabeth was in Boston when the takeover occurred and prevented from returning that night by bad weather. In her absence that evening Manhattanville vice president Franklin Kneedler filled in. He told reporters, according to a Manhattanville summary of events, that he "did not consider the demands unusual and expected that [the administration] would meet with the students tomorrow." The *New York Times* quoted Mr. Kneedler inaccurately as having said the "the demands would be met tomorrow."

When Elizabeth got back to campus the following day, she instructed her secretary to "get Jerry Aron here." Jerry had been working at Manhattanville for just a few months, and yet Elizabeth knew enough that she wanted him nearby as she made decisions.

"I made a couple of rules right away," Elizabeth recalls. She would allow no police to enter the building or the campus. She would not capitulate to any demands. She would make sure that the building remained accessible to anyone and anything the students wanted inside—friends, food deliveries, and so on. She left the telephone lines operational so the students could make and receive calls. And she decided that she would talk with them—and, as she put it, "not be hard on them."

She issued a statement to the Manhattanville community:

Since I learned last evening of the occupation of Brownson Hall I have acted according to certain principles. I returned to the campus from Boston this morning as soon as the weather allowed me to do so. I believe that it is important for me to understand the entire situation as fully as possible before taking the action that it is my responsibility to take. I have therefore spoken with students, faculty (both individually and in executive committee), members of the administration, parents, and alumnae. My concern must be for all members of the College and I must therefore consider not only the demands of the Black students, but also the petition of a group of students who opposed the tactics used. Finally, I have met this evening in Brownson Hall with the students who are there. I shall continue discussions tomorrow. The basic validity of the struggle for racial justice, as well as the right of the entire community to pursue its daily life will continue to govern my actions.

The Administration was convinced that the occupation of Brownson Hall was a problem that should be solved within the Manhattanville community, according to the tradition of the College. In the past, students have never been dealt with summarily without a hearing so it was decided that the students in this incident would not be treated differently. In addition, if legal machinery were to have been put into motion to eject the students forcibly from the building, the matter would then have been taken out of the hands of the Administration. Finally, past experience with campus disruptions has shown that the arrival of outside authorities on a campus tends to foster two undesirable results—the rapid polarization of opinion without benefit of full discussion, and a potentially dangerous rise in emotion often leading to violence.

She told the *New York Times* that "the college recognizes the need to create a community which feels a greater responsibility to minority groups."

Elizabeth convened the faculty at 3:30 p.m. on Wednesday, December 10, and, as might be expected, debate was lengthy and heated. After more than five hours of often passionate give-and-take, the faculty, in a divided vote of 46–36, approved this statement: "We support the demands of the Black students in theory and in principle and will immediately assist the Administration in implementing those demands to the extent that it is possible." A milder, more generic statement of support for the students was then passed unanimously. It read: "The Faculty resolves actively to seek solutions to the problems of the Black students at Manhattanville and to assist the Administration in this regard."

Around the same time 275 students signed a petition supporting the building occupiers' efforts to eliminate racism "but not necessarily supporting the demands."

"These were our students and this was going on all over the country and what was happening was that people were capitulating," says Elizabeth. "Black students were saying, 'We need twice as many black students and three times as many black faculty.' I said no acquiescence to demands because we can't do it. It is a lie. If to make these kids leave the building I have to say, 'We'll do what they want'—it is a lie. We won't do that."

Jerry asked the college accountant to put a rough price tag on the students' demands and found that it would cost millions at a time when the college "didn't have two cents."

The reaction of Manhattanville alumnae varied, although those with negative views had some particularly nasty things to say. Some were vile and racist, others merely angry. In those days well before email, telegrams were the preferred route for those with an urgent message.

"Strongly urge immediate removal and suspension or expulsion," read one. Another wrote: "You should be ashamed of yourselves—you are disgusting and it will serve you right to be kicked out for a nigger president. It will come. *You bunch of dopes!*"

Many parents of students were upset as well. Some parents in New York and Baltimore got together and retained an attorney to represent their daughters. They told an administrator that their daughters "have been harassed. Negro men on campus forcing girls to sign petitions."

When Elizabeth met with the students in Brownson, she had to get into the building through a fairly narrow window—an awkward and somewhat dangerous maneuver. In fact, the whole situation was fraught with danger and Elizabeth was worried that an individual or a mob could so something tragic.

One student in particular stood out among those who took over the building. Ruby Sales was an undergraduate, a bit older than most. She was from Mississippi and quite radical in her views. "Ruby Sales was there to cause trouble and she did," says Elizabeth.

Prior to the building takeover, Elizabeth was walking through an underground passageway between buildings and Ruby and Marie, a friend, were passing through as well. "And one of the two said, 'Down here we could kill you.' And I said, 'I don't think you should. You will get in a lot of trouble if you do.'"

As commencement approached, the dean of students, Mother Ann Conroy, approached Elizabeth and expressed concern that Ruby might disrupt commencement. Elizabeth thought about this and suggested that Ann find out whether Ruby's mother would be coming in from Mississippi for the ceremony.

"If her mother is coming, she is not going to disrupt commencement," Elizabeth told Ann. And, in fact, Ruby's mother did arrive for commencement and Ruby did not disrupt it in any way.

Several years later, after Elizabeth had left Manhattanville, she was awarded an honorary degree at Princeton. The night before commencement, Princeton president William Bowen hosted a dinner for the honorary degree recipients. During dinner, seated next to Bowen, Elizabeth said she wanted to ask him about a particular student. "He said, 'I don't know any students. It is unfortunate but as president here, I don't.' I said, 'Well you may know the one I want to ask about.' He said, 'Yes, who?' I said, 'Ruby Sales.' He said, 'Oh my God. She took over my office. I came in and she is there with her feet on my desk!'"

.   .   .

As Elizabeth approached the building that first evening for her initial meeting with the students inside, she was apprehensive. "I thought, 'Are all their black men friends in there?' But there were not. As I went in I heard one say to another, 'Don't let her fall' and I thought if they are not going to let me fall then I'm safe. So we sat around a table and they abused me. Four-letter words which I had never heard before. *Awful.*"

The takeover happened on a Monday, and Elizabeth went into the building and met with the girls each day and, as Jerry recalled, each day it was "the same story: 'You have me under duress, I can't negotiate under duress and I'm not going to. You come out of this building, we can sit down and talk." But the students would not budge. Nonetheless, Elizabeth made sure they had continued access to incoming and outgoing telephone calls as well as food deliveries and visitors. She felt this helped lower the temperature.

Throughout the course of the building occupation—from Monday through Thursday night—Elizabeth got about ten hours of sleep. She and Jerry spent most of the time together in her office.

"People were phoning in and telling us what to do," recalled Jerry. "Amazing, these advice-givers. Some of these were pretty prominent people."

On Thursday, December 11, Elizabeth met with the students in Brownson for ninety minutes, yet little was resolved. That same day, Manhattanville records indicate that "students and Faculty discussion groups met in the Kennedy Building with those Black students not occupying Brownson Hall. Throughout the day they discussed their attitudes toward the campus situation, and in order to make the dialogues effective the expression of all points of view was encouraged. At the end of the day Larena Brown (a black student who was the liaison between the students in Brownson Hall and the College) chaired a meeting at which ad hoc committees were formed to raise funds for the establishment of scholarships and the development of a Black Studies Program."

Then came what seemed a dangerous moment. Jerry recalled that Mother Iona McLaughlin, the Manhattanville business manager, came running into Elizabeth's office and said, "Come quick, come quick, they are coming to kidnap you!"

Elizabeth, Mother McLaughlin, and Jerry ran from Elizabeth's office to the end of the chapel corridor where there were two large oak doors separating it from another building. Along the hallway there were also a number of nuns' cells. The three of them entered the first room, which contained a wooden bench, a cot, a chest of three drawers, and a telephone.

"Mother McLaughlin drags us in," Jerry recalls, "gives me the key, and says, 'Lock it behind me,' and she dashes out and so I lock it. And I take the key in. And by now Elizabeth is really pissed and knocked out and she is sitting on the bed and she calls the switchboard and she says, 'I don't know what extension I am calling you from, but can you tell from the board?' And the girl says, 'Sure I can.' And she hangs up, and I'm sitting on this cot with this key, looking at it, and I start to laugh. And she says, 'What are you laughing at?' I said, 'I am looking at this key. I'm sure you realize that I am the only Jew in America with a key to the convent!'"

.   .   .

Elizabeth was patient. She also understood why these girls were doing this. "It was the name of the game," she says. "It was what everybody was doing. It was not personal at all. These were kids taking over a building because they hated the Vietnam War and they were down on any kind of authority. I could understand that conflict and I could understand where those kids were coming from and I knew that when they took over buildings at other colleges, the administration got rid of the problem by acquiescing to demands which they never could really deliver on. This was going on all over the country and what was happening was that people were capitulating.

"So the conflict over issues was not what I suffered from. What I suffered from was, for instance, in that takeover of the building I can remember where I was standing and one faculty member whom I don't remember who he was said to me, 'You know you are holding firm and I have information that one of those black students is going to commit suicide.' I said, 'I can only hope you have inaccurate information.'

"But the fact that some students, whether in the building or out might be hurt during that time, that was my fear and when parents phoned and said, 'Is my daughter safe?' my answer was 'I hope so but I don't know. If you are worried you bring her home.'"

Meanwhile, Elizabeth was getting feedback and advice from many sources, including alumnae, who were generally quite harsh in their judgment of the students who had taken over the building. Elizabeth terms some of the letters "cruel" to the students who were "caught up in the movement of the times." Some wrote urging her to summon the police, shut off the students' water, prevent food from going into the building.

But she resisted that approach. On Friday, December 12, she issued an invitation to the Manhattanville community:

> Since December 9, when I last wrote to you, I have continued to act according to the principles which I then expressed: the validity of the struggle for racial justice and the right of the entire community to pursue its daily life. To act according to these two principles has been extremely difficult, if not impossible. Priorities had to be set, and I set them. Every member of the Manhattanville Community should know
>
>> That I deplore the taking of Brownson Hall and the consequent inability of the members of the College to carry on their academic life in the ordinary fashion;
>>
>> That I decided *not* to set in motion the procedures for dealing with campus disruption;
>>
>> That I believe that the problem we face is the problem of *this* Community so we have tried to solve it here;
>>
>> That I am convinced we have been educating one another in a profound sense;
>>
>> That the problem which the taking of Brownson Hall

symbolizes is nearer to solution on December 13 than it was
December 9 because we are more nearly a Community.

She wrote that she hoped for an all-college meeting that afternoon
at 2:30 in the chapel. She was seeking a "re-united Manhattanville, by
which I mean everyone on this campus wherever he or she may be at
this moment, so that I can make a proposal to the entire community."
But when the appointed time came and went and the students in
Brownson did not show up, Elizabeth canceled the meeting, saying as
long as some girls were in the building the campus was not reunited.

. . .

On Friday she decided enough was enough. She would meet with
the students in Brownson that night and she would object to whatever
they said. She would force some sort of showdown. That night, during
the meeting, one of the young women in Brownson said to Elizabeth:
"You come here so benevolently . . . ." And Elizabeth reacted. "I lifted
my hands and I banged the table so that it came up and I said, *'I won't
be called benevolent!'* And they said 'We're sorry.' It was the only good
thing they said all week. Benevolent is kind of a compliment. They
didn't mean it as such."

On Saturday morning, December 13, Elizabeth declared an "emer-
gency situation of a disruptive and obstructive nature." She issued a
terse two-line letter: "To the occupants of Brownson Hall: I demand
that you leave Brownson Hall which you have occupied since Monday,
December 8, 1969 forthwith."

That night, a radical black lawyer came to see the students. "And
he said to the girls, 'You know, you are lucky that nothing has been
done to you. You have taken the building, you have disrupted a college,
you better get out of here because if you don't she will call the police.'"

The next morning the students left the building.

. . .

A couple of months later, in February 1970, the board of trustees of the Manhattanville Alumnae Association printed and distributed a brochure that sought to calm the waters among angry alumnae. "Alumnae are Asking Fiction or Fact? Have you heard . . . 'Manhattanville is no longer a Catholic college.' 'The Society of the Sacred Heart is abandoning Manhattanville.' 'Manhattanville is losing its identity in order to get State [money].' 'Black student rebels force the College to close for six weeks.'"

The document stated that "each of these claims, while inaccurate, is linked with the very real problems and complexities of operating Manhattanville College today, 1970. But there is distortion, exaggeration, and a lack of comprehension. In short, these are rumors. . . . " The group sought to dispel these rumors by speaking with college leaders, including Elizabeth, and then by publishing the document.

A Manhattanville summary of the Brownson event raised the question of "why no disciplinary action?" The response was that "in the opinion of the Administration, the fact that this was the first such campus disturbance at Manhattanville and—far more compelling—that it dramatized a real problem on this campus—were factors that determined their decision. Although the means used by the students were not acceptable and did not succeed, the College has recognized the validity of their problems. It has chosen to focus its efforts on making this campus community one that is 'more responsive to the needs of all its members.'"

"And when it was all over they cleaned up the room," Elizabeth recalls with a laugh. "Our revolutionaries cleaned the room."

Years later, when Elizabeth had left Manhattanville and was working for the Rockefeller family, she was invited to speak at Yale. "All the students were interested in was talking about where they might get good jobs when they left and could the Rockefellers help them, and I remember thinking, 'I like my students who took over a building better. A student shouldn't be thinking only about jobs when he or she is twenty years old. Give me the students who took over the building.'"

(5)

Firing Line

I N THE LAST THIRD of the twentieth century, William F. Buckley Jr. was the most feared debater in the United States. As host of *Firing Line*, his weekly program on PBS, Buckley challenged hundreds of guests, most of them liberals, with his razor-sharp wit and intellect. Buckley was a product of Yale, where he captained the debate team, and later founded the conservative magazine *National Review*. He was also a staunch, and very conservative, Roman Catholic who was in the habit, post–Vatican II, of attending a traditional Latin mass.

On November 30, 1970, Elizabeth McCormack bravely dove head-first into the dangerous Buckley waters. She appeared on an episode of *Firing Line* to discuss the fraught subject of the future of Catholic higher education. Although she was exceptionally bright and verbally skillful, she had only a tiny fraction of Buckley's debating experience. His ardent Catholicism made him particularly formidable and an in-tense foe on the issue of Catholic higher education. Add to this the fact that his sister-in-law was an alumna of Manhattanville, and Buckley was as intensely focused on the subject as he could be.

It would have been difficult enough if Elizabeth had been taking on just William Buckley. But another guest on the program, Kenneth Baker, S.J., a very smart Jesuit priest, fully shared Buckley's point of view. It was two against one. It wasn't a fair fight.

Elizabeth's clash with Buckley came at a time when the country was deeply divided between liberals and conservatives. There seemed little common ground in America during the 1960s and early 1970s on issues involving the Vietnam War, race, social change, religion, or education. Buckley was deeply unhappy about Catholic colleges becoming secular. He viewed the trend as a kind of betrayal of important beliefs and values and he argued that it had been done, at Manhattanville and elsewhere, purely to secure eligibility for public funds.

Buckley introduced both guests, describing Elizabeth as having "had her troubles" as president of Manhattanville. Buckley described Father Baker as having "just concluded a stormy and very brief career as president of Seattle University," where he "sought to accomplish many things—among them the desecularization of Seattle University, his point being, if I understand it, that if you're going to have a Catholic college, you may as well make it distinguishably Catholic."

Buckley initiated discussion about the Blaine Amendment in New York State, a state law that prevented any state financial aid from going to a religious school. A number of schools in the state had gone from being religious to secular institutions, Manhattanville obviously included. This enabled these schools then to receive some state funding.

Elizabeth staked out her position: "there are two criteria, and these come from the Blaine Amendment: that the college may not be governed or controlled by a church or a religious community; and religion may not be taught in such a way as to proselytize . . . Those two requirements were fulfilled by Manhattanville College for many years. In fact, from the founding of the college, its governance and control were in the hands of an independent board of trustees. So we didn't have to do anything to become eligible, except answer a questionnaire which dealt with these questions."

Elizabeth explained that religion could be taught at Manhattanville just as it was at any state college. "I suppose the easiest way to make the distinction is to say that religion which can be taught in a state university—and is in many of them—must be taught as an academic discipline," said Elizabeth. "And if it's taught as an academic discipline, rather than in a pastoral sense . . ."

Buckley interrupted: "Would, say, Jonathan Edwards would have been qualified to teach in your college?"

Elizabeth: "I think he would."

Buckley: "And would Martin Luther?"

Elizabeth: "Martin Luther?"

Buckley: "Or was he too hortatory?"

Elizabeth's response, which prompted hearty laughter from Father Baker, was: "I was never in a class of his."

Then came an uncomfortable, and for Elizabeth, an unfortunate moment. "If Manhattanville does not stand for Catholicism," Father Baker asked her, "what does it stand for?"

An awkward silence. Then, from Elizabeth: "Well, that's a good question."

It was one of those defining moments in a debate where, because of her inexperience, Elizabeth wasn't quite ready with an answer to a crucial question. In the rapid-fire world of television, to hesitate at such a bedrock question was to appear somehow less than thoughtful.

Elizabeth replied: "First of all, I believe—in fact, I would rather speak of the nonsectarian college, rather than the secularized institution. It seems to me there when we speak of a sectarian college, that college is in some way controlled by the sect and exists to bring new members into that sect. Now, I think that if that's what you mean when you say a

Catholic college, sectarian in that sense, that adjective, Catholic, before the word, college, makes the institution less a college."

Father Baker: "Yes, but how many Catholic schools define themselves in the sense that they're set up to proselytize? I think you're setting up a straw man that you've knocked down. I reject that definition of the Catholic college completely."

Then it was Buckley's turn. He referred to the long history of Manhattanville as a Catholic college and asked: "Would you say then that a lot of people would have labored in vain over the years—people who had sacrificed and who had made contributions of material and other kinds to Manhattanville?"

Elizabeth: "I certainly think not."

Buckley: "Why not? If their interest was in helping Manhattanville to survive as a 'Catholic' institution, there would have been some form of historical treachery—or, if not historical treachery, at least historical neglect. . . ."

Elizabeth was getting her sea-legs, and her answer was a belated but pointed response to Father Baker about what Manhattanville stands for: "No, I don't agree with that at all. Father said, what does Manhattanville stand for? Manhattanville stands today for the *same* values that it has always stood for. These are human values, values of freedom, the value of the individual, the value of free inquiry. . . ."

Buckley abruptly steered the conversation to the subject of Jesus Christ and whether Elizabeth considered him an important historical figure.

Of course, replied Elizabeth.

Buckley: "Well, do you want your students to believe that?"

Elizabeth: "I imagine some of them leave the college believing it, yes. Perhaps *many* of them."

Buckley: "Did you urge them to believe it?"

Elizabeth: "Well, I don't think we urge them. You see, what you're doing is making me do, or trying to make me do exactly what I say we *don't* do, and that I believe we *shouldn't* do. Because, if we urge our students or if we push our students, if we take, so to speak, what we see as truth at this moment and hand it on—first of all, it's not going to be accepted."

Buckley: "Why? It depends upon how successfully you do it."

Elizabeth: "Not by the way you *talk,* it's not. You're never going to succeed in doing it, by speaking."

Buckley: "Why? Isn't this to deny the whole teaching function? Why can't people teach persuasively?"

Elizabeth: "People teach persuasively by what they are, much more than by what they say."

Buckley: "Oh, c'mon. Lots of scoundrels are very successful teachers. Don't you think that's true? . . . I mean, the point is that the teaching function is not necessarily a property of one's own behavior, is it?"

Elizabeth: "No, no, no. It isn't that but—I think we're talking more about life and values, and I think that they are communicated person to person much more than what is said in a classroom."

Buckley: "Well, what is it that makes—that will make the day after tomorrow Marymount different from, say, Mount Holyoke? . . . Or Bryn Mawr?"

Elizabeth: "I always believe that what makes one college or university different from another is the people who are there. And there are different people at Manhattanville than those at Mount Holyoke."

This came across as somehow mushy and ill-considered, and Father Baker commenced a lengthy attack. "I just can't buy that at all," he said. "I mean, there *has* to be some kind of view—you have to have some kind of ideology, some kind of view that you're trying to project in your school. And the way you described it, I don't see any difference between the type of school that you describe and any State University. And if that's so, I can't see why Catholic parents would want to send their children—or have sent them in the past—to Manhattanville; why not go to Radcliffe or N.Y.U., or something like that? Otherwise, you're not really offering anything distinctive. You've described a good, secular, humanist school. And it seems to me that the role of the Protestant and Jewish and Catholic schools is precisely in America, as a pluralistic society, to offer something different—so that there is really a choice between the types of schools that are available. It doesn't mean that everybody has to go to it; but, on the other hand, I don't see why every school should be dedicated to secular humanism."

Father Baker said he believed "that there is a Christian view of the world, and that there is truth that has been communicated to man by God that goes beyond what the human mind can acquire in the laboratory—and in the scientific approach to reality—there are various ways of achieving truth and through our Christian faith, we have received a much broader and a much nobler vision of man—what man is really destined to—and it's on the basis of this that you get the real dignity of man. The whole Christian perspective of man as a free person before a free God. And that his decisions that he makes in this life really do have consequences both for himself and for others—and both for this life and the next life. This is the whole dimension of the supernatural in man's life. . . . The various views of reality that you're talking about is a ready-made system to turn out skeptics and agnostics, and I don't think that a Catholic school should be established to turn out an endless series of skeptics; that is, they should be turned out with a particular Christian view of reality. There is a Christian view just as there is a Marxist view, there's a secular humanist view, there's a fully Christian view of man and reality—as I say, a free person before a free God. And we need types of schools where people who espouse that view can come and pursue it. . . . I think we need the kind of school where people want to *pursue* their faith . . ."

Buckley jumped in: "Sister McCormack, it may be, in a rather horrible way, that what Father Baker has said exactly justifies what you have said. He's talking about a crisis of faith, and it may be that that crisis of faith resulted from an inadequate performance of schools that were oriented ten, fifteen or twenty years ago in a way in which you disapprove, i.e., it may be that what you consider to be the typical pedagogical methods of the religious schools. In fact, they didn't produce Catholics who were willing to make sacrifices necessary during the seventies to sustain them so that their children could have equivalent experiences. . . . But, I want to ask you this, do I understand you to be saying that if, a few years from now, there is no more vestige of Catholicism in your school than there is of Congregationalism in Yale, you will not consider this to be much of a loss? . . . Presumably, the reason that you chose to teach as a nun, rather than as a non-nun, is because that which you set out to teach was going to be greatly influenced by the special training that you took. Right?"

"I believe that truth is one," replies Elizabeth. "And I don't mind what the truth is that I am communicating in a classroom—it does not have to be labeled, Christian, Catholic; it's all one. And any one truth that I'm able to communicate to anyone makes my life what it was always—"

Buckley interrupted: "Suppose it's untrue?"

"Well, if it's untrue," Elizabeth replied, "it is at *least* a groping for the truth. That's what I believe we're all doing in education."

.   .   .

When she left the television studio that day, Elizabeth did not feel good about the program. She had clearly been on the defensive and even somewhat overwhelmed. She was not at her sharpest. She felt that she couldn't really say what she had to say. "I had to be on the defensive, which is not pleasant." She reflects for a moment and then adds about Buckley: "He was a mean man. He wasn't a nice person." She vowed not to look at the program, and she stuck to that for forty years, finally watching a tape of it in 2010.

After the program, Elizabeth received some of the most scathingly negative responses she had ever experienced. A woman in California wrote: "What a ridiculous and disgraceful spectacle you made of yourself on the William Buckley show! You exposed, not only unattractive thighs but a warped sense of values and very nebulous thinking. It was embarrassing to have you even utter the word Catholic . . . thirty pieces of silver from the state of New York seem a small price tag for the prostitution of your spiritual heritage." From Omaha a woman wrote that she was "embarrassed for you" by the "display of knees and plenty above."

Some modest relief came in a genteel letter from a woman in Louisville, Tennessee. She wrote in a pleasing, respectful tone and expressed a number of positive thoughts. On page two of her missive, however, she wrote: "I was distressed by one thing about your television appearance—your skirt was too short to present a ladylike appearance. I rather imagine that in this detail of your otherwise attractive dress you were misguided by a laywoman and your own better judgment was overruled! When one sits down, these awkward too-short skirts do all of us a disservice in being too revealing."

A woman in California was not nearly as restrained: "I must say, I was absolutely shocked to see a so-called Catholic nun (and who would ever know it from your attire?) sitting up on a stage with your dress ABOVE THE KNEES; Shame on you . . . and if you are not ashamed, then I am ashamed for you. In all my years as a Catholic (I became a Catholic when I married many years ago). . . . I have never regretted my choice. But when I saw you on national television in civilian clothes . . . and immodest ones at that. . . . I was thoroughly disgusted. The very idea of a woman your age and a Catholic nun, appearing in public like that." Elizabeth responded that she was "most grateful to hear your concerns and reactions. As you must know, many religious are wearing secular dress in an effort to bring Christ to our world. That was my very sincere intention and I believe that as the habit once gave witness, so too can this."

A priest in Fort Lauderdale wrote to Elizabeth that he was "quite appalled last night to hear you defend a secularized philosophy of education which, as Father Baker said, can only lead to producing generations of skeptics and agnostics."

Truth is not learned through "the meeting of many minds" on the secular campus. All the Hindus, Muslims and Buddhists in the world could not formulate the Apostles Creed. Man with unaided reason could never come to an adequate understanding of life. That is why God sent His Son into the world to save by teaching as well as by atonement.

The Catholic Church is the Divinely appointed teacher of men. Failure to accept this truth as a basic principle is failure to understand the basic truths of Christianity. It is a betrayal of Christ.

The Catholic college is the Church teaching in the field of higher education. That teaching must be done not merely by the good example of its members but by the bold, explicit, and unabashed profession of the teachings of Christ as preserved and transmitted by an infallible Church.

"Woe to me," says St. Paul, "if I preach not the gospel." And woe to every other professed Catholic who fails to profess Christ and His teachings openly. What a day of reckoning will be laid up for Sister McCormack and her religious superiors if, as Father Baker and I both believe, Manhattanville soon, and probably is already, graduating each year, in ever increasing numbers, skeptics and agnostics with little or no love of God in their heart, rather than the kind of Catholics who would lay down their lives for the faith. Ask yourself this question: "Would today's students at Manhattanville, if they lived in Elizabethan England, live up to their faith under persecution as did these brave men and women who were canonized only last year by Holy Mother Church?

When Elizabeth watched the tape in 2010, her first thought was "that skirt is too short but it's not awful."

While many letters were scathing, some were quite supportive. A woman in Elmira, New York, wrote: "If ever I were proud of being a Catholic college graduate, it was tonight after listening to you on *Firing Line*." A man in California wrote, "I thought that Mr. Buckley gave you a rather hard time and was unfairly critical of your views on education. . . . I agree with your idea that students should be exposed to a variety of points of view and that they should be allowed to choose freely among them. Very often, I find myself in agreement with Mr. Buckley but not this time."

"Hearty congratulations" came from Sister Mary Ann Miller, president of St. Thomas Aquinas College in Sparkill, New York: "I found it personally encouraging to hear my own view on catholic higher education expressed so well. Buckley's barrage of questions was done in extremely poor taste." Sister Biller wrote that Elizabeth deserved "credit for your valiant perseverance and composure throughout." John T. Green, chairman of the Religion Department at Marymount School in Manhattan, wrote: "The girls thought your position was much more appealing than father's or Mr. Buckley's." And Father James Michael Sullivan, a Maryknoll priest, wrote that "Mr. Buckley would surely be in a catatonic stupor if he knew the freedom of expression and plurality of vision [that exist] not only in our Catholic colleges but in our seminaries as well."

.   .   .

It was a frustrating experience. She would have welcomed an opportunity to go on television and explain—in a non-confrontational environment—her views on higher education. She believes—and has always believed—that the primary function of a college or university is not to impart knowledge, but to train students to analyze carefully, to judge critically. "A college," she says, "is not a place to proselytize.

"Catholic parents often sent and some still send their sons and daughters to Catholic institutions to learn to be Roman Catholics. I do not think that a college is the place to do that."

She was frustrated by the way her answer about the faculty came across. "Students are influenced by their teachers and when I was at Manhattanville in the forties and then president in the sixties and seventies, there were people from all religions on the faculty. When I used to visit alums all over the U.S. their questions were *always* about the nuns."

The nuns literally devoted their lives to their teaching mission and therefore had a huge impact on many students. "It wasn't that they preached, but *they lived a Christian life*," and that was evident to every student every day.

. . .

William F. Buckley Jr. was not done with Elizabeth, however. Nine months after the television program was originally aired, Buckley again criticized Elizabeth in the August 21, 1971, issue of *The New Yorker*. In a long piece on various topics, Buckley again objected to Manhattanville's decision to become a secular institution. He saw it as giving up its precious attachment to the church and suggested, as he had on the television program, that Elizabeth's motivation was to be able to secure public funds as a non-religious institution of higher education. Since the Blaine Amendment prohibited the state from providing funds to any college with a religious affiliation, Buckley's view was that the move toward secularization was all about the potential for state funding.

A few days later, on August 25, 1971, Elizabeth wrote to *The New Yorker*'s editor William Shawn asking whether he would grant her space for a letter to respond to Buckley. Six weeks later, on October 4, 1971, Shawn got around to responding to Elizabeth writing that he would be happy to "consider publishing a letter you write amplifying William Buckley's article."

In a letter published in the December 8, 1971 issue of *The New Yorker,* Elizabeth responded:

Dear Sirs:

William F. Buckley, Jr., in his August 21st article "Cruising Speed," further obscures already muddy waters in respect to the controversial Blaine Amendment to the New York State Constitution. Social trends toward secularism, religious and moral judgments on such trends, and educational quality are indiscriminately intermingled in his discussion. Mr. Buckley does accurately report the gist of the Blaine Amendment itself: That it forbids state aid to a religious educational institution. But his statements misrepresent the successful effort of Manhattanville College to prove its eligibility for state aid. It is important to clarify his misrepresentations, not just for the sake of Manhattanville but because they confuse the public understanding of the relationship between institutions of higher education and society at large. These institutions, public and private alike, exist in the public interest. Thus, to some extent they must serve the interests and needs of all sectors of society. . . .

The real question, which Mr. Buckley avoids, is an educational one. I strongly believe that a college committed to the mind cannot be closed. We must think of it, rather, as a vicinity. A vicinity is not a completed entity; rather, it is an openness, it is a process that evolves in an environment of universality. Our colleges must be places where the deep questions of mankind are asked—questions that will not go away. Students no longer come to the liberal arts colleges for answers. They come, rather, to learn to ask the right questions; they insist on probing the meaning of meaning.

To maintain church affiliation and the universality of inquiry will probably involve inconsistency. In the [search for truth], it is an imperative that every door be opened, every road explored, no path barred. Sectarian education, by definition, does not meet this need. The church-affiliated college—Catholic, fundamentalist, or any other—however much it may succeed in teaching its students to think, will also be tempted, to a greater or lesser degree, to *instruct* its students in the particular tenets of its religious faith. To teach a student to think about the tenets of several religions is a very different thing from instructing him in the tenets of a religion.

The difference between the two approaches is seen in the answer given by a Manhattanville student, a graduate of a parochial secondary school, to a question put to her by an investigator sent by the State Education Department when the college applied for state aid. . . . He asked her if she could make a distinction between the kinds of teaching in respect to religion that she had received in a parochial school and that she was then receiving at Manhattanville. She replied, "When I was in school, if I hadn't studied for an exam I just wrote down pious answers and always got a good grade for them. Here, though, piety will get you nowhere." I found this a very heartening answer. If you are trying to teach students to think, piety *shouldn't* get them anywhere. Indeed, if it does, then it seems clear to me that the institution involved is teaching such piety and would be ineligible for public funds. Substituting the theology of a single denomination for piety leads, in my opinion, to the same dilemma.

Manhattanville, like so many American institutions of higher learning, was associated in its origins with a particular church. Like others, it has changed. The important point—one that Mr. Buckley distorts—is *why* the college has changed. At the time we were first applying for state funds, many people urged me to forget about it, to avoid the bureaucratic difficulties involved. "Let's go back to where we were," they would say, meaning back to where Manhattanville was ten or fifteen years ago. My answer to that was (and is) "there is no 'back' to go to." The world itself has changed. One may regret the present; some will expend most of their energy upon such regret. But it seems a good deal more fruitful to try to come to terms with the need to see things as they are, not as they were, and thus to construct a realistic base from which to project a better world and seek to bring it into existence. For, if an educational institution's first duty is to teach its students to think, its second duty must be to do all it can to satisfy the needs of the society of which the institution itself is a part. Only by adequately fulfilling these interlocking duties can a college really do its part in serving the present and making the future. Change for the better in our society can be achieved only through the efforts of thinking citizens; and only through education can today's children become the thinking citizens of tomorrow. To achieve that educational and human purpose, Manhattanville has indeed changed.

On *Firing Line,* Mr. Buckley seemed chiefly bent upon getting me to say that I thought the Blaine Amendment should be repealed. It was evident that in his view such an admission would indicate that we were providing, after all, a "palpably Catholic, Catholic higher education," and that we were simply doing our best, by being as impalpable as possible, to get what financial help we could. In such a case, Mr. Buckley would no doubt be willing to forgive us our trespasses.

However, as I have tried to show, the Blaine Amendment is really a false issue. The real issue is education: How can we best teach young people to think, so that they may grow into citizens capable of dealing with the realities of their world? Manhattanville is dedicated to finding the best answer to that question, and in so doing we must ourselves face the realities. Mr. Buckley, unfortunately, does not seem equally willing to do so.

Cordially, Elizabeth McCormack R.S.C.J.

President

Buckley's five-word response appeared below Elizabeth's letter: "Radix omnium malorum cupiditas est." That is, "The love of money is the root of all evil," quoting Saint Paul.

(6)

A New Life

BEFORE THE TAKEOVER of Brownson Hall, Elizabeth and Jerry had worked together for only two months. But spending that week together, night and day under difficult, stressful conditions, allowed them to get to know each another pretty quickly. "By the time that week was over, we really knew one another," Jerry recalled much later. "Without that, it would have taken six months or longer to develop the kind of relationship that we developed in the heat of that thing."

Elizabeth agrees that they developed a special relationship during that intense period. She found his judgment sound and she felt sure she could trust him. And on top of it all, she found that he could discover lightness in almost anything. "One of the things about being with Jerry was that no matter what the circumstances it was fun," she says.

At one point, a bomb threat was phoned into the college. The caller said that he had planted a bomb in one of the buildings and planned to detonate it. Elizabeth immediately ordered the evacuation of the two main buildings—including the one the bomber said he was targeting. Then she called Jerry. "I phoned him, and I said, 'There is nothing to this but you should know that I just emptied the buildings,' and he said that he would come over. I said, 'I don't think it is necessary.' I said, 'It's over.'

A few minutes later Jerry walked into her office "and he said, 'I thought you had said that you had evacuated the building?' I said, 'I did.' He said, 'Then what the hell are you doing here?' I said, 'It's nothing.' I didn't know he was coming, in the main building. Nobody else was in the building because I had evacuated it, and he appeared at the door and he looked in and said, 'What the hell are you doing here?' I said, 'Come in. It's fine.' He said, 'You had told me you evacuated the building. Staying in a building is not evacuating. If it was dangerous enough for you to empty the building, you shouldn't be here.' And I thought, 'He doesn't want me bombed.'"

.   .   .

Bombs, in Vietnam and Cambodia and closer to home, were much on the minds of everyone in those years. A front-page story in the *New York Times* on May 5, 1970, was headlined "34 College Chiefs Urge Nixon Move for Prompt Peace." The headline was next to the now iconic photograph of the girl crying out as she kneels over the body of a dead student at Kent State University. Elizabeth was among the signers of the telegram, which read that "the American invasion of Cambodia and the renewed bombing of North Vietnam have caused extraordinarily severe and widespread apprehensions on our campuses. We share these apprehensions. We implore you to consider the incalculable dangers of an unprecedented alienation of America's youth and to take immediate action to demonstrate unequivocally your determination to end the war quickly."

Three days later, a flyer circulated throughout the Manhattanville campus urging students to participate in a national day of mourning for the four Kent State students who had been killed by the Ohio National Guard. The flyer invited students to an interfaith service on the Manhattanville campus: "Students at Kent State have been killed . . . it could have happened here. What is your Christian commitment?"

The following week Elizabeth joined a group of students traveling to Washington to lobby Congress for an end to the war. She didn't just go, she actually helped organize it. A flyer from Elizabeth went out to the student body announcing that buses would leave campus on May 13 at 4:00 a.m. and return the same day at 6:00 p.m. She noted the cost would be $7.75 per person and that "arrangements can be made for those unable to pay." At the bottom of the flyer, Elizabeth wrote: "I am convinced that this united action will have a positive result."

Elizabeth felt compelled to communicate in writing with parents, many of whom had expressed their concern and anger about the events of the year—a year that had surely been the most turbulent in Manhattanville's history. On May 19, she wrote to parents that

President Nixon's decision about Cambodia had its effect on this campus. I would be disturbed if it had gone unnoticed here. I decided that regular classes would not be held on Tuesday, May 5 so that the day could be devoted to a study of the issues involved in Mr. Nixon's decision. A faculty panel explored the situation from the viewpoints of Political Science, Economics and History. Attendance at the panel proved to be an important educational experience for our students. Regular classes resumed on May 6 and continued until May 15, the last scheduled day of classes.

Some students decided on May 6 that they would "strike" to protest the war. Although these students did not continue to attend classes, the majority of them are completing the work of the year including taking their final examinations this week and next. Already existing academic procedures make it possible to receive "incomplete" in courses under special circumstances.

A few of the most active strikers have, accordingly, made special arrangements with individual professors to complete their tests and other work by September.

Nearly two hundred members of the College—Students, Faculty, administrators—spent Wednesday, May 13 in Washington. Our students went to express their concern about the war to members of Congress. Since I believe that they were acting in the best traditions of our Country, I spent the day with them in the Capitol.

On September 29, 1970, Elizabeth offered some brief thoughts on changes at the college: "educators are responsible for unrest and dissent, President Nixon said at Kansas State recently. He was right and educators should be proud of the fact for only the uneducated are satisfied with the *status quo*. To be educated is to be aware of ideals and of possibilities; therefore, the educated man cannot complacently accept the world as it is."

. . .

The turbulent sixties ushered in a new world. And Elizabeth could see ever more clearly that a Catholic women's college would not compete successfully in that world. There was too much change and turmoil both politically and socially for such an institution to thrive—or perhaps even survive. Change was necessary.

Minutes of a December 17, 1970, meeting indicated that the college had just suffered a half million dollar deficit and anticipated another shortfall in the coming year. At the meeting Jerry Aron said that such a trend could lead to bankruptcy. A decision was made to freeze hiring and attempt to cut expenses by 10 percent.

"I realized that Manhattanville was as successful as it had been because good Roman Catholics like my father believed that their children had to go to Catholic colleges," she says. "That disappeared. That built-in constituency was gone. If the pool of Catholic women was drying up, one had to have a student body from a larger constituency."

She recognized the decline in the popularity of women's colleges, generally, whether Catholic or not. "A few will remain and should remain; like Smith, highly endowed places. It became clear to me that it was change or go out of business and what the change had to be was making the college available to a larger pool of students—Catholic, Protestant, Jewish, male, female." It was change or die. And, in fact, soon Newton College of the Sacred Heart in Massachusetts did not change and fairly quickly closed.

Manhattanville was hardly alone in its internal struggle to decide whether to go coed. Dozens of single-sex colleges across the country faced the same issue. In August 1970, an internal document, produced by Elizabeth and her staff, "Coeducation at Manhattanville College," cited a report done at Connecticut College in New London, formerly Connecticut College for Women. The Manhattanville report noted that Connecticut College was "similar in size and quality to Manhattanville," and they had made the decision to go coed. It noted that the team at Connecticut College "concluded in their decision a year ago to seek full coeducation that 'the historical reasons for single-sex colleges are no longer operative. In fact, there is a national trend toward coeducation, suggesting that sexually segregated colleges are anachronistic.'"

The Manhattanville document referred to single-sex education as "academically inadequate" and noted that "a current survey of 4 year independent colleges in New York state provides more general evidence of the trend. Of 12 colleges which increased their 1970 applications 20% or more over 1969, eight had recently become coeducational. The figures from the eighteen 4-year women's colleges in the state show, on the average, a 7% decline in applications."

Elizabeth was absolutely convinced this was the right path. She believed, in fact, that unless Manhattanville went coed it would almost surely have to close. The Manhattanville board voted on September 19, 1970, to admit male students for the 1971–72 academic year. The shift to coeducation was not easy, but coming as it did after the name change—and to many, identity change—it was relatively manageable. "I think that the public relations, cosmetic change of secularizing Manhattanville was so traumatic to so many people that, in their opinion, the relatively minor change of coeducation went by much more easily," she recalls.

But it did not go easily for some. Telegrams and letters streamed in, some of which objected quite strongly. A correspondent from upstate New York wrote that he and his wife "feel very strongly that coeducation is not appropriate for college years, and does a great deal more harm than good. Regretting very much the steps you are taking. . . ."Another wrote on the impressive letterhead of his law firm expressing his "considerable dismay" about the decision. He noted that his family had been connected with the Sisters of Sacred Heart for four generations: "It is with deep regret that I must advise you of my intention to support no longer financially the religious order or its schools and colleges which have contributed so admirably in the past to the upbringing and education of my grandmother, my mother, my sisters, my wife and my daughters. It is sad, indeed to realize that there no longer exists a similar institution for my granddaughters." While it was eminently clear what his position was, there was no indication of what any of the women in his family, from any generation, thought of the decision.

In addition to the many negative reactions to the decision there were some positive ones. The San Diego College for Women had merged a few years before with San Diego University, a men's college, and Sister Nancy Morris, president of the university's College for Women, wrote to Elizabeth that September: "After three and a half years of the coeducational experience here in San Diego, I can assure you that the activity, both good and ill, is more intense in and outside the classroom." She also noted that her school had achieved a "marked jump" in enrollment.

After male students were admitted, things generally went quite

*Natalie Duffy McCormack with
Elizabeth and George, 1925*

Age four, Larchmont, 1927

*With Grandmother
Elizabeth Ring Duffy, 1927*

High school graduation from Maplehurst, Convent of the Sacred Heart, New York, 1939 (later moved to Greenwich, CT)

Graduation from Manhattanville College, 1944

Inauguration as President of Manhattanville College, December 9, 1966

With Bernard Bailyn,
University Professor of History
at Harvard, 1966,
at the inauguration

With Chief Justice Earl Warren at Manhattanville, where he
received an honorary degree in 1973

With Laurance S. Rockefeller
at Princeton University,
where Elizabeth received an
honorary degree in 1974

*With Richard Lanier
at the Forbidden City
in Beijing, 2002*

*In Hong Kong, 2010, with
Douglas Tong Hsu,
Chairman and CEO
of Far Eastern Group
and an ACC Trustee*

*From left, Linda Goelz, Elizabeth, Valerie Rockefeller Wayne,
Kenneth Fung, Ralph Samuelson, Stephen Heintz, and David
Rockefeller, Jr., meeting during an ACC trip to China, 2002*

The Asian Cultural Council Board at Pocantico, 2010 (standing, left to right): Hope Aldrich, Hans Michael Jebsen, Douglas Tong Hsu, David Rockefeller, Jr., Richard Lanier, Michael Sovern, John Foster, Erh-fei Liu, Ken Miller, Isaac Shapiro, Robert Pirie, Kenneth Fung, Stephen Heintz, and Curtis Greer. (Seated, left to right) Abby O'Neill, Valerie Rockefeller Wayne, Josie Cruz Natori, Elizabeth, Lynne Rutkin, and Wendy O'Neill.

With Katarzyna "Kate" Stich, her friend and assistant, Hong Kong, 2009

The Trust for Mutual Understanding, Budapest, 2010 (from left to right), Barbara Lanciers, Mary Lanier, Sylvia Renner, Blair Ruble, Elizabeth Burke, Jennifer Goodale, Elizabeth, Alina Enggist, Richard Lanier, and Andras Torok

Elizabeth, Jerry Aron, and
Mrs. John Rockefeller, 3rd, at her home,
Fieldwood Farm, Westchester, 1989

From left, Nan Aron, Elena Arons,
Elizabeth, Phoebe Aron, Bernard
Arons, Mark Aron, and Peter Aron
(Emma, Sophie, and Betsy not pictured)

With Nick and Leo,
Jerry's grandchild and great-grandchild

With brother George McCormack and Mary Murray

George McCormack Jr.'s family (from left), Bill Lauck (Jane's husband), Adam McCormack (George 3rd and Corinne's son), Jane McCormack, George 3rd, and George Jr. (Julia and Hugh not pictured)

With Jerry in Antarctica, 1992,
and Russia, 1993

With Jerry and his daughter Betsy, 1969

smoothly at Manhattanville. A year and a half into the coed era, faculty members were asked to evaluate the situation. Most were positive about the change. Male students helped stimulate classroom discussions, and many took their studies seriously. But there were a fair number of negative comments, as well.

One professor wrote: "Manhattanville has not developed its women such that they can deal with the men in class. Dumb men talk while bright women are silent." Another observed that the "boys tend to be more talkative—and less intelligent." In chemistry, a professor wrote that most of the male students consistently ranked at the bottom of the class and did not work as hard as the females.

When the controversies over racial and gender issues began to recede somewhat, Elizabeth was able to effect some important changes to Manhattanville education. In the spring of 1972 the college announced it would set aside its standard grading system in favor of a portfolio system where a body of work—papers, exams, fieldwork, and more—would represent a student's performance. It was not nearly as simple as grades, of course, but it was a deeper, more robust way to try and represent the nature and depth of a student's work.

.   .   .

Around this time, a Manhattanville student Elizabeth knew and respected asked to speak in confidence. She explained she had a younger sister in high school who had gotten pregnant. She said her father was a violent, emotionally unbalanced man. The student told Elizabeth she feared that if the father found out about the pregnancy he might kill his daughter. She looked steadily at Mother McCormack and said she was determined to find someone who would perform an abortion for her sister. Would Mother McCormack help?

Elizabeth had been asked many different questions by many different parents and students at Kenwood, Greenwich, and now Manhattanville.

But never before had anyone asked for help with an abortion—among the most forbidden of all the Catholic mortal sins. But Elizabeth did not hesitate. "Of course," she told the girl. Of course she would help.

"We had never talked about anything like this, but she must have thought I could help her," says Elizabeth. "I always believed that the Christian message is a message of love and understanding and help for people in trouble. That was Jesus' message and certain church teaching is the opposite of that. Well, this was after Vatican II and Vatican II stated—and I knew those documents very well—that the ultimate norm of behavior is the human conscience. Therefore, if you know in your conscience, if you believe that something is right, some rule made not by Jesus but by mortals. . . . And I had no hesitation. I phoned Planned Parenthood and I said how do we do this." They gave her the name of a doctor. She had not consulted her brother as she would have on just about any other medical issue. "George was very anti-abortion."

As she reflected upon that event many decades later, Elizabeth said she had never regretted it. "I believe that there are frivolous reasons for abortions, I believe there are good reasons for abortions," she says. "And I do not believe that abortion is murder. I don't believe that a fetus is a person." In this case, the girl got the abortion and her father never found out about the pregnancy.

"I helped that young woman whom I've never met get an abortion and I never for a moment regretted doing it," she says. "Although if the Cardinal Archbishop of New York knew about it I could have been ex-communicated. But I never worried about it."

.   .   .

For all the difficulties she faced within the college, Elizabeth was perceived outside the campus in a generally positive light. A *New York Times* article on December 6, 1970, was headlined "Manhattanville: Catholic and catholic" and included side-by-side photographs of Elizabeth: one where she was fully covered in her habit and the other where she wore a simple dress and strand of pearls.

The article, by Linda Greenhouse, read in part:

"When I was still wearing the habit I often noticed that everything I said was greatly appreciated. If I said something a little humorous everyone thought it was extremely funny. If I said something a little intelligent, everyone thought it was brilliant. So, too, has it been with this college. As long as people keep the old image, they will always think of us as out of the mainstream, and so we will be."

Miss McCormack, a Roman Catholic nun who has a doctorate in philosophy from Fordham University, made the change to street clothes more than a year ago. Changes at Manhattanville, in their own way, have been equally dramatic during the last few years.

Manhattanville College has dropped "of the Sacred Heart" from its formal name because the president thought it was a misleading name for an independent liberal arts school. The students put out G.D.P., a daily news sheet whose initials stand for General Daily Paper, but which is known to students and administration alike as "goddamned paper." And next September the college will admit its first male undergraduates . . .

But outsiders have remained rather skeptical. Nearly everyone here is actively trying to persuade them, as Franklin Kneedler, vice-president, put it, "that what they think of as a very good, very wealthy, very posh convent is actually a very broke—but very swinging—institution."

It is not an easy task. The image of Manhattanville as an elite place for demure young ladies whose fine minds and proper Catholic upbringing dies hard. And it is scarcely aided by the appearance of the walled convent on the bucolic 260 acre former country estate of Whitelaw Reid—complete with real castle.

The image is also kept alive by the one fact most people know about the school—that it is the alma mater of several Kennedy sisters and wives . . .

"The hardest thing I have to overcome," said Jane Tuohy, a buoyant 1969 alumna who travels throughout the Middle West as an admissions counselor and recruiter, "is that strong Kennedy-girl image, the idea that everyone here is well-bred, well-mannered and well-moneyed. High school students are always surprised when I tell them that only about a third of our students are not receiving financial aid of one kind or another."

The article noted that Manhattanville received no money from the Church and that in February the college was declared eligible for state aid.

A year and a half later, on April 22, 1972, a feature piece, "Where Piety Gets You Nowhere," by Helen Dudar appeared in the *New York Post,* which was at that time a very liberal newspaper:

If you grew up some decades back, a nun was one of the remote and mysterious creatures of the world: a pale face floating out of black drapery, a disturbingly alien figure frozen in the amber of unalterable Catholic tradition, a woman of fervid power who could forbid young girlfriends to wear lipstick to parochial school.

And now one confronts a woman of the church who is serenely demolishing tradition, who is imposing freedom on the young, who couldn't care less how they decorate their faces but is well nigh fanatical about how they embellish their minds. In many ways, she seems as remote and mysterious as ever.

Elizabeth Jane McCormack came to the presidency of Manhattanville College of the Sacred Heart at Purchase, NY not quite six years ago in the usual wimple, medieval robe and large silver cross.

[Now she sits] in her office in a simple, handsome blue day-time dress that stops at her nyloned knees and there is only the wedding band on the usual finger to remind the visitor that she is a sister of the Religious of the Sacred Heart of Jesus, a bride of Christ.

Dudar mentions the increasing secularization of the college and the adverse reactions of many alumnae. Elizabeth explains that the college is "very important to them and therefore it worries them that today's student isn't finding the same thing as they did. Of course, today's student may not be looking for the same thing."

Dudar describes Elizabeth as "a woman who doesn't reach five feet, is round-shouldered and seems to dart rather than walk from place to place. She is brisk, interested and friendly." She quotes a new employee at Manhattanville: "The new treasurer, for example, is a Jew, a garment industry dropout, a former Westchester businessman named Jerome Aron who speaks with fervent awe about his boss. 'There's a wall around this place, a very symbolic one. Until Sister McCormack, the neighborhood never got inside. Symbolically, she has removed the wall.'"

.   .   .

In the spring of 1972, Elizabeth informed the Manhattanville board that she would be stepping down as president in May of 1973. Elizabeth believed that her predecessor, Mother O'Byrne, who had served for twenty years until age seventy, had stayed on the job too long, and Elizabeth did not want to repeat that mistake. During Mother O'Byrne's final few years, Elizabeth was essentially acting president.

"And therefore, my own seven years of presidency, eight by the time I left, had to be thought of in relationship to at least three years when I was doing much of the work. I thought that was long enough. And that it would be good for the college to have somebody else. I had thought initially that I'd stay a maximum of ten years. I also found that so many of the problems kept returning. When faculty and staff came with some new problem, what would flash through my mind, was how many times I've heard this before. And I don't think that's good in a person who's running something, because as the chief executive officer you don't approach the problem the way you should, if you think, 'Well now this came up three years ago and there was nothing to do about it and there's not going to be anything to do about it now,' or whatever. So I just decided I'd had enough of it."

She was fifty years old when she made her decision to leave and informed the board. And she would be just a couple of months past her fifty-first birthday when she actually stepped down.

"I thought that if I was going to do something different, that was the moment to do it. If I waited, I don't know how many years, but if I stayed a certain number of years more, I would stay till I was sixty-five and that would be dreadful both for me and for the College."

.   .   .

Elizabeth had a difficult time in her final years at Manhattanville. When Elizabeth left the college there were many alumni as well as administrators—including one of her successors—who seemed to pretend she had never existed, who seemed to want to wipe her out of the college's collective memory.

Says Jerry: "They started having events celebrating Elizabeth's predecessor, Mother Eleanor O'Byrne. They'd list recent presidents of the college, and her name wasn't listed. She was never invited to a commencement, other than to get the printed form that went out to the world about it." But there was no reaching out to her, no kind notes saying the college leadership would love to see her return for a visit—nothing. It was icy and willfully so.

Much of what Elizabeth accomplished at Manhattanville generated conflict within the institution and among the alumni. The name change was one example, of course, as was the decision to go coed. But many of her accomplishments drew little controversy and set her mark upon the institution for many years to come and affected tens of thousands of students. She started programs for a Master of Arts in Teaching and a Master of Religious Education. She persuaded faculty members from Harvard Divinity School to teach some of the courses. She changed the curriculum in significant ways—to make it more flexible and adaptable for students and their areas of interest. Her adult education program, inaugurated for educational purposes, was a financial lifesaver for the college. And, ultimately, the changes Elizabeth made almost certainly saved the college from closing.

Jerry sums up her tenure at Manhattanville this way: "Her whole life has been the management of trends, which is an extremely difficult thing to do, and one of the key elements you have to have in order to do it is flat-out courage. You have to be able to walk in standing up straight and say it. And you have to think thoughts that your contemporaries are afraid even to mention. You have to think them, say them, and do them. And that's what she did. That's how she salvaged Manhattanville College and got 5,000 women hating her. A single-sex college these days may be fine for Wellesley, but not at Manhattanville. Totally church-oriented can't work. When she became President, the administration of the college was virtually 100% nuns. When she left, there were very few. To hire the first male administrator of Manhattanville College was an act of great courage, and she did that and then followed up with a lot more."

When she became president of Manhattanville she had come to believe that "the idea of a Catholic liberal arts college was a contradiction. When one says 'Catholic' in that sense, one is accepting a whole series of beliefs and dogmas, while the whole idea of a liberal arts institution, where liberal learning takes place, is that there *aren't* answers."

For all the turbulence and difficulty, Elizabeth left Manhattanville with a deep sense of connection to its students. In her final commencement as president, on May 24, 1973, she talked of how in prior years after commencement students had moved on, gone out into the world, while she had remained behind. This year, she said, was different. She, too, would be going out into that world.

．　　　．　　　．

Her work to diversify the college did not go unrecognized in the broader community beyond the campus. A week after her final commencement, the American Jewish Committee in Westchester County gave Elizabeth its First Citizen of Westchester Award. It was given to her at a simple ceremony where the presenter, Raphail Scobey, recalled a meeting he had been invited to at Manhattanville some months earlier. He explained that at the meeting

> a Jesuit priest told us of his plans for the establishment of an accredited college in a penal institution in Bedford Hills in the northern part of our county, and of his hope that out of this college would come poets, artists, teachers.
>
> This was a meeting concerned with bringing education to the most lowly members of our society, and it was no coincidence that it was being held at Manhattanville. The meeting reflected the essence of Elizabeth McCormack's philosophy as an educator; that education has no boundaries; that it must reach out to all segments and elements of our community; and that in a pluralistic society, education must be a civilizing and binding institutional force requiring the cooperative commitment of the administrator, the teacher and the community.
>
> It was to achieve these goals that Elizabeth McCormack opened Manhattanville to students of all faiths, groups, and backgrounds, to young men as well as women . . .

She conceived of Manhattanville as a community institution, one that must not remain apart from the people and problems of the community. Under her direction, Manhattanville instituted a program of continuing education for adults; it set up a special institute for the study of County problems.

These educational achievements of Elizabeth McCormack reflect something very deep in her Catholic heritage and in our Jewish heritage, perhaps best expressed by George Schuster, a former president of Hunter College. "A civilizing education," he said, "cannot aim or wish to produce a nation of saints, philosophers, and artists, but it ought to produce one in which every educated man can to some extent participate in the experience of the saint, the philosopher, and the artist."

During her stewardship of Manhattanville College, Elizabeth McCormack has made the experience of saint, philosopher, and artist available to the citizens of Westchester, and beyond. So it is First Citizen of Westchester Award to Elizabeth McCormack, a warm human being, a gracious lady, a great educator, who has enriched our community with her vision of a civilizing education.

.   .   .

Elizabeth's brother, George, recalls that right after she left Manhattanville she went away on vacation to the island of Antigua. While she was gone, George and his wife, along with friends and co-workers of Elizabeth's from Manhattanville, "rented a truck and brought furniture from her house on the Manhattanville grounds to her new apartment. And she walked into an apartment that had furniture and linens, silver, pictures on the wall, all of it arranged by the Manhattanville faculty plus my wife."

And thus did she start her new life.

(7)

The Love of Her Life

JERRY ARON WAS born in 1917 in Philadelphia. His father was influential in Republican circles as both an attorney and a Pennsylvania state senator. Jerry's paternal grandparents had emigrated from Russia and never learned to speak English. His grandfather had been a tailor in Russia and continued that in the United States, and he was determined to secure the finest possible educations for his children. Of his two sons, one went to medical school, and the other, Jerry's father, to law school, and his law practice proved to be quite lucrative during the 1920s. So lucrative, in fact, that the family employed five domestic servants including a cook, laundress, and chauffeur. But when the market crashed in 1929 the Arons went broke. Jerry's father, ever industrious, went back out and made a good deal of money practicing law all over again.

After graduating from Haverford College in 1939, Jerry moved on to Yale Law School, from which he graduated in 1942. He enlisted in the army and was sent to language school at Stanford to learn Japanese.

He spent several months with the occupation army in Japan, where, as he liked to joke to Elizabeth, his fluency in Japanese amounted to asking "Where is the men's room?"

Jerry married Joan Borgenicht, and, when the war was over, they discussed the possibility of Jerry working in Joan's father's dress business. It was quite a successful company, and though it was not Jerry's preference, he felt a responsibility to the family to get involved—with the idea of eventually taking over from his father-in-law. And that is the unhappy course Jerry followed. They moved to the New York area where Jerry managed a complex company with a design showroom in New York and factories in Pennsylvania, New Jersey, North and South Carolina, and Georgia. They were relatively small factories, but they added up, and the company reached a point where it was making four to five million dresses a year.

But it was never particularly enjoyable or fulfilling for Jerry, and, in 1967, at age forty-eight, he sold the business, created trusts for his five children, and began the process of looking for a new job. In doing so, Jerry wrote several dozen letters to universities and companies, but received only a few replies. When he was mailing the letters he noticed that he had written the incorrect address for Manhattanville College and put the envelope aside. After weeks passed and he had received few responses, he remembered the Manhattanville letter, dug it out, corrected the address, and mailed it. Soon after, he received a job offer from Teachers College, Columbia University for the CFO position. As he was considering whether to accept the job, he received a call inviting him to Manhattanville for an interview.

A few years into Elizabeth's tenure as president of Manhattanville, there was no longer a nun available to fill the position of CFO. In 1969, she went to her friend Peter McColough, then chairman of Xerox and of the Manhattanville board, who offered his company's search firm to help find someone. But the firm sent her "a whole group of losers," as Elizabeth put it, and she phoned McColough and said, "Peter, I don't know how good the search firm is for Xerox, but it's no good for me." McColough got involved, and the firm stepped it up. And the first résumé they plucked from the pile of applicants was Jerry's. He came in for a round of interviews starting with Elizabeth.

"I met him and I thought you know this man is smart and of course by then I didn't wear a habit and we talked," Elizabeth recalls. They talked for some time, quite easily and amiably. He did not have accounting skill but she didn't need that—she had a good accountant. What he did have was extensive business and financial experience, having run a company. After their conversation, Elizabeth sent Jerry around to talk with the dean of the faculty and several others. The feedback from each of the interviews was very positive.

By the end of the day, Jerry returned to Elizabeth's office, and she said she and everybody else was impressed. "If your references check out, would you like the job?"

"I think I would," he said.

And that was it—at least, that was the professional side of the story that day. But something else had happened in that office. For it was that day, the very first time Jerry and Elizabeth met, that Jerry Aron decided that one day he and Elizabeth would marry.

Elizabeth had no knowledge of what he was thinking until he revealed it to her years later. He said he vividly recalled every detail of their first meeting including the fact that it was late morning and she wore "a beautiful blue dress," which she says she never owned. She thought Jerry was a nice-looking man. At five feet eight, he towered over her. With deep brown eyes and thinning hair, he had something of the rumpled appearance of a Beat poet.

Jerry was quickly welcomed into the administrative ranks at Manhattanville. People found him bright, likeable, and easy to work with. He dove into his role as chief financial officer, working collaboratively and well with colleagues. When there was a need for a teacher to fill in leading a philosophy class he was delighted to oblige. When a theater group needed him for a bit part in a college theatrical production, he jumped in with both feet.

From the start of their professional relationship, Elizabeth found she could rely on Jerry. She trusted his judgment, liked the way he thought and analyzed issues, and appreciated his candor. Very quickly she was relying upon him more and more, and the two were spending a great deal of time together at the office. She could trust Jerry on matters reaching far beyond the financial. "He was my partner," Elizabeth says. "I began by consulting him on things. Until he came, I had been doing this job alone from 1966. There was nobody to talk to about anything."

It did not take long for Jerry to become deeply impressed with Elizabeth. He would see that she was far more worldly than other nuns at Manhattanville. She had frequently gone off campus to travel—for educational meetings, fund-raisers, alumni events, and more. "She did a lot of networking," Jerry recalled. "She got out, got to know people, they got to know her. She had a kind of sophistication most of [the other nuns] didn't have."

Dealing with her on a wide variety of college challenges, Jerry saw that she was exceptionally intelligent and quite tough. "She has determination of steel," he said. "A mind like a metal trap. Boom, doesn't have to sit and think about it. And she also doesn't cry over spilt milk. She's an amazing person. Amazing."

Jerry marveled at how excellent Elizabeth was at her job, particularly during what was one of the most difficult times ever to be a college president. When he told her this, she replied: "I am as effective as I am because everybody knows I have no agenda."

Jerry refined the point. "The interesting thing is, she does have an agenda, but it's not a personal agenda," he says. "Her agenda is what's going to be good for this institution."

.   .   .

For Elizabeth, there was no *aha!* moment when she fell in love with Jerry. But surely it happened very quickly—only a matter of months after Jerry arrived at Manhattanville. Others at the college were keenly aware that they had a special bond, and Elizabeth's secretary expressed concern about the closeness of the relationship.

"I don't remember when it changed from just being a wonderful co-worker, a friend to the man I was happy to marry but it happened," says Elizabeth. "My secretary, Elizabeth Porter, asked me, 'Why are you always going to consult with Mr. Aron? Why do you need to talk to him about everything?' And I thought, 'Boy, I do need to talk to him about everything.' So it kind of came on me, this realization."

Cynthia Hettinger (later Bennett), one of the young nuns who had removed the crucifixes at Manhattanville, said years later that she believed that Jerry "fell in love with her long before she fell in love with him." For a time, Cynthia lived in the same house as Elizabeth on the Manhattanville campus, and one day in 1972 or 1973, when no one else was nearby, Elizabeth stopped her.

"Elizabeth said, 'I want to ask you something,'" recalls Cynthia. "And she said to me, 'Do you think Jerry Aron looks at me?' And I said, 'Yes, absolutely.' She said, 'How do you know?' I said, 'It's very clear.' And she sat me down on the staircase and she sort of asked me basically to explain."

.   .   .

Elizabeth was forty-seven when she met Jerry, who was then fifty-two. It had been twenty-six years since she had dated a man. Since that time she had devoted herself to her religious vocation and never had any inkling that she might one day again become involved with a man. When she fell in love with Jerry, was there ever a time when she thought, *I don't know how to do this. I don't know how to ride this bicycle?* She says emphatically, "No, never, because it is not a hard bicycle to ride. I mean you don't have to take lessons."

She says they never discussed deciding to have a romantic relationship. "Never," she emphasizes. "He wasn't good at talking about things."

It was obvious that Elizabeth trusted Jerry and respected his judgment, obvious that she relied upon him. And as time passed, it also became clear to those who worked with them that there was a certain level of affection between them. This was so clear, in fact, that many staff and faculty at Manhattanville believed that Elizabeth and Jerry were having an affair. People perceived a warmth and closeness there that they thought went well beyond a strong working relationship or friendship. "Everyone thought we were having an affair," says Elizabeth, who says it never happened.

There was a slight scent of scandal in the air. Here was a nun, the president of the college, with a close relationship—perhaps an affair, many thought—with a Jewish married man, a father of five.

.   .   .

At the end of each year senior employees at Manhattanville signed a letter of reappointment for their personnel files. The letters outlined their duties, stated their salaries and other details. The employee would then sign the letter, thus agreeing to the terms, and the letter would go to the human resources department. The second year Jerry was at Manhattanville he signed his letter, then appended a note to the bottom of the page, writing: "My role here has changed living to life."

Years later, Jerry's daughter Nan said she had no doubt what the implicit message was. "He was saying that he was in love with her," says Nan. Though he had not previously expressed feelings for Elizabeth, that is how Elizabeth read it as well.

It seemed clear Elizabeth had developed feelings for Jerry when she received a phone call from Jerry's wife, Joan. Jerry was prone to difficult and sometimes acute nosebleeds. Elizabeth recalls that Joan called to say he would not be coming to work because he was hospitalized with a particularly bad nosebleed. It was serious enough to require surgery.

"I was terrified that he might be dying and Joan was as matter of fact as if she were saying, 'He has a headache. He won't be in today.'"

The surgery left scars on Jerry's face, so he grew a beard to mask them.

People at Manhattanville really liked Jerry. He got on well with students and faculty as well as his fellow administrators. And he was always available to pitch in and do whatever was needed. Jerry liked working with the nuns and found them smart and creative.

In the summer of 1969, Jerry got a call from one of the nuns— Mother Ann Conroy, the dean of students, who said she urgently needed Jerry's help. Mother Conroy explained that a Manhattanville student had just been arrested in White Plains for shoplifting. Mother Conroy wanted to go and get the girl out of custody right away. Everybody knew Jerry was a lawyer, and Mother Conroy thought it would be useful to have Jerry's expertise at hand if needed.

By this point most of the nuns were wearing civilian clothes. But before they left to go to White Plains, Mother Conroy quickly changed back into her habit. "She swooshes into my office in full regalia, full black habit, white hat, right out of the Vatican," says Jerry. "First time I had ever seen her dressed up. We go to White Plains; it took her two minutes with the judge to get him to release this girl into her custody. It was a performance. Back in the habit."

Jerry's daughter Nan says he loved Manhattanville right from the start. "He was a wonderful storyteller and he would regale us with stories about the college," says Nan. "When you talked with him he was filled with a sense of adventure."

Jerry had never been happy in his marriage. His relationship with Joan was contentious and always difficult. The tension was palpable throughout the years, and it seemed there was hardly ever a moment of real peace, let alone deep affection and intimacy. "We hadn't seen our father happy in many, many years—ever really," recalls Nan. "He and my mother had a very tough marriage."

Nan was married in 1969, and Jerry brought Elizabeth to the wedding, "which was a little bit of a signal to me that this was serious," says Nan. "It wasn't just bringing a friend to a wedding." Unsurprisingly, Joan was quite unhappy that Jerry had brought Elizabeth. "She was not happy about this because Jerry was still married and still living in the house with my mother and Elizabeth walks in," recalls Nan. "Everyone knew they were very close, and my mother would in fact make reference to it. Not romantically. I know my mother knew Jerry was close to Elizabeth. I knew she knew there was a special relationship."

Even in a house filled with tension and animosity, there were moments of warmth and tenderness. Jerry and the kids, in fact, had a nighttime ritual after Joan had gone to bed. Nan recalls, "We used to have this tradition at home where we'd congregate in the kitchen at eleven o'clock every night. He would cook or open cheese and salami, drink his favorite beer, and we would review our day."

And after he started working at Manhattanville, his whole outlook changed. "Clearly he loved what he was doing," says Nan. "He loved Manhattanville. He would describe in great detail his interactions with people on the faculty and students and what came through those discussions was his work with Elizabeth and how important that was to him. . . . It was just a moment in the house where you could kind of have just a little bit of fun. We took sips of my father's beer. I'm not sure he ever drank a full glass.

Nan says she saw her father was transformed after he met Elizabeth. From her point of view there was no doubt that her father and Elizabeth "carried on a several-year flirtation. And Jerry was clearly smitten. . . . He was gone. You could tell. . . . He wouldn't say because that wasn't his manner." But Nan knew her father well, and she could see, with absolute clarity, that although he still lived at home, he "was very much in love with Elizabeth."

Jerry did not talk with Elizabeth much those days about how unhappy he was in his marriage. Later, after he divorced Joan, he revealed
more, but even then, it was not something he went into very often. "Jerry
was extremely loyal," says Elizabeth. "We did not talk, in fact, ever, even
after we were married, about how really hard it was to be married to
Joan. He didn't talk about that." But, one day when Elizabeth and Jerry
were driving into New York City they passed a movie theater in Yonkers.
As they did so Jerry pointed it out and told Elizabeth that when things
at home got too tough, he would drive over to the movies, sit back in
the theater and fall asleep, spending the entire night there.

.   .   .

Jerry needed to get out of the marriage. He had decided that he
wasn't going anywhere until his youngest child had completed high
school, which came in 1960. During the late 1950s, Joan worked hard
in a PhD program in public administration at New York University,
eventually earning her doctorate and going on to teach there. That
achievement for a busy suburban mother was "very impressive, incredibly impressive," says Nan. "She really wanted a career."

As part of Elizabeth's final Manhattanville commencement, in 1973,
Jerry and Joan hosted a dinner at Joan's home for the recipients of honorary degrees. Elizabeth's brother, George, attended the dinner and, at
a certain point, had a conversation with Joan. After dinner, George and
Elizabeth were driving back to Elizabeth's residence on campus. Elizabeth respected her brother's views and, given his extensive experience
in a series of marriages, she knew he knew something about relationships—particularly bad ones. "As we were driving back in the car," Elizabeth recalls, "he said to me: 'Joan has no regard for Jerry.'" He said it
definitively, without elaboration or discussion, and Elizabeth knew he
was right.

While Elizabeth was president of Manhattanville, she would drive to Larchmont to visit her mother, who was slowly failing during the final year of her life. Jerry would often accompany Elizabeth on these visits, and he came to know her mother. Later, after Elizabeth had ended her years as a nun, Mrs. McCormack told Jerry she was worried about Elizabeth since she was no longer a nun. Elizabeth's mother told Jerry that she did not mind that her daughter was no longer a nun, but she did worry about her being alone—going through life on her own.

"So she said to him," Elizabeth recalls, "'Jerry, will you promise me that you will see to it that Betty marries someone just like you?' And Jerry said, 'I promise!'"

Manhattanville reenergized Jerry. "It was a new world for him," says Elizabeth. "The job, me, and he began to be appreciated. The people he met through me, the people we met together, he became very popular. People loved him and the thing was with Joan, he was always compared with people and she would say you should be like so and so and you're not, so he had a hard life."

When her father fell in love with Elizabeth, Nan says, "I had never seen my father so happy before. And it struck me that this was the first time he had a relationship that was so satisfying. And it was so unexpected. She was a nun and committed to higher education. He was a businessman and father of five children. And yet they found each others' company so comfortable and satisfying."

And he expressed his feelings in 1973 in a letter he wrote to all of his children:

Dear kids—

Having pulled away from 260 Mamaroneck Road on June 25th, I am now in the tenth day of solitary liberation. I expected it to hurt—and it does. I walk around with a vague feeling that something is missing—I have a tendency to look over my shoulder in search of something. I guess thirty-two years of being half a pair is a long experience suddenly to terminate.

I must add, however, that I have great conviction that I did the right thing—and I am fortified by the rapidity with which I turn away fleeting thoughts of running home. Such an act would be a disaster, of course, and it will not happen. If Mom and I ever do get together again, it will only be after a long period of brushing the cobwebs away . . . and I have strong doubts about it.

Mom asked me to clarify a point and I think I should. I'm sure I gave you the impression that I at long last made up my mind to split—and took off. It didn't quite happen that way. I did make a decision at Christmas to leave—but I couldn't leave. I had been agonizing continuously over it, and discussed it with Mom any number of times. Perhaps it would be more honest to describe some of those "discussions" as rather having been threats. Finally, a couple weeks ago, Mom said that she couldn't go on in such an ambiguous and ambivalent condition. It was clear that she was right, and that neither of us could live that way. She asked that I make a commitment to reach for a total and happy relationship—and that short of that we could not continue. I told her that I couldn't do it—that I was simply unable to make such a commitment. I then left.

I guess this is the moment to try to explain the whole goddam ball of wax (and if I pull it off I will photocopy this letter and send it to all of you guys, since I cannot do it five times). Little explanation is necessary concerning thirty-two years of conflict, of a mutually destructive relationship, of two people satisfying unknown inner needs by scratching at the other—all the while leaning on the other, supporting the other—and sharing both moments of happiness, and long-lasting great events—such as the five of you. But it was sick. Sick. And it never stopped.

The past several years were somewhat easier, I must say, mainly because of a slackening of pressures—a smaller household, fewer people around, less cooking. Her involvement in her own career became more absorbing and siphoned off a good measure of her tensions. But certainly not all of them—and when pressures mounted, such as a visit by several of you at a time like Christmas, it was the old ball-game all over again. What that said was that we had to live a crisis-free life in order to live a friction-free life. I am afraid that it is given to no one to forever avoid crises. They are inevitable and are the very moments when two people are supposed to be able to rely on the support of the other rather than the reverse.

Enter my memory. I suppose part of my own fucked up head is an inability to forget fierce and bitter conflicts—and in this case that includes the horrible, horrible inability to forgive. This is even more dreadful since what Mom was doing was interacting with me—I am convinced that I was asking for it. Hence my guilt. Hence, my hostility.

Enter Manhattanville College. A new and beautiful life—an environment in which I sense a mission, fulfillment, where I am respected and looked to for leadership and the formulations of important decisions, void of bitter memories. There are some lovely people—there are some bastards. The challenge is engaging and the stakes are high. I feel good. Very good.

Enter Elizabeth McCormack. Delightful, charming, witty, a razor-sharp mind, with a value system and set of objectives which parallel mine. We think alike. We can communicate in silence. (I can be driving with her in a car, and after a period of long silence she will say: "Isn't it interesting how happy I can be with you even when we say nothing.") She trusts me. I trust her. At some point I find I love her—and when she leaves the order she tells me she loves me. She does.

Query: did I leave Mom for Elizabeth? Answer: No. Query: did I leave Mom because of Elizabeth? Answer: undoubtedly yes. She was the catalytic agent—the embodiment of the possibility of

peace—of freedom—of gentleness—of kindness—of commitment—of love. Of course, nothing will really ever be any good
for me, or for Mom for that matter, until we sort out the crud in
our heads—and that I intend to make a strenuous effort to do.
Never will there have been so well worked-over a shrunk as mine.

And so in the midst of such relief and optimism there is pain
and hurt. Maybe you guys can place all of the above into a coher-
ent pattern. I'm sure you are aware of much that I have failed to
say—that has escaped me—wherein I am wrong—perhaps unfair
or unjust. It is a pillar of strength to me—critically important—
to know that the five of you love Mom very, very much, and that
you will stay close to her, and help her, and support her. Because
oddly enough I still love her. I always have. I always will. I just
can't live with her. But she, like I, is suffering—and needs you.

I have been living in a motel—but I sign a lease tomorrow for
an apartment. I know how to get there, but I don't know the address. It is in Port Chester—five minutes from the college. I will
send you the information when I have it. Incidentally, in addition
to a kitchen and a bathroom, the apartment has a living room and
a bedroom. That means there will be room for visitors to sleep
over—and one and all are welcome.

I love all of you,

Dad

(8)

Light of Reason

THERE HAD LONG BEEN a sense of innocence about Elizabeth Mc-Cormack. Perhaps innocence is the wrong word. Perhaps it was her simple acceptance of faith, her conviction that she was doing what God wanted her to do. During her early years in the convent she received a call from her brother delivering the news that he was separating from his wife.

As George later remembered: "I called my sister and I told her and I remember what she said word for word. She said, 'That is fine, George, but don't remarry because if you remarry you cannot go to heaven and if you don't go there I don't want to go there either.'"

"Do you see what my faith was like then?" she asks. "That I believed that you died and you went somewhere and that we would be together. I wish it were true." She shrugs. "Might be."

She pauses, reflecting, then says: "500 billion people all milling around somewhere?"

.　　　.　　　.

One evening in 1973, while still president of Manhattanville, Elizabeth was scheduled to speak before a Westchester Jewish group. As she sat in the hall waiting to be introduced she noticed a small brochure and began skimming it. "It stated, 'a doubt is a belief that is still alive,'" she recalls. She immediately saw it differently. She saw a doubt as "a belief that is dying."

Elizabeth had believed everything she was asked to believe because her life was based on that simple foundation—that she was doing God's will.

"I think that in order to live the life of a nun you have to believe that whatever you are told to do is the will of God and once you begin to question that it all unravels quickly. Faith is a very mysterious thing, and very intelligent people can be, and many are, strong believers, but they are able to separate their belief from the rational light of reason." Many others, however, struggle mightily to reconcile faith and reason. "Once you begin to bring them together for some people—for *me*—it begins to disintegrate."

The doubts and questions she had back in 1967 in Rome were about the Society itself—not about faith. But in Elizabeth's case, there seemed to be a progression. In 1967 she had questioned the competence, vision, and leadership of the Society.

"I never questioned *anything* until then," she says. "These people there were the instrument of the will of God for seven thousand people. Should they be the instruments of the will of God? I realized that this group of eighty-five women representing seven thousand didn't know what they were doing and that was very alarming. I questioned the wisdom of the people governing the Society. Their naïveté. Did I want to be a part of this?"

This was new to Elizabeth. She had lived so much of her life as a member of a semi-cloistered order of nuns. She was not out in the world where people engaged in vigorous debate over matters of faith and religion. Her formidable habit, in fact, was a massive and visible barrier that helped prevent any such discussions. A tiny woman wearing such a medieval costume was not likely to be the target of a proselytizing atheist. She lived in a Catholic world where even the non-Catholic faculty members—some of whom were certainly non-believers—would never have dared attack the central belief of her life, to assail the very foundation of her Society.

As time passed, she found herself privately questioning some of the rules of the Church. She questioned whether papal encyclicals contained the wisdom they were supposed to.

Her faith had been a given. She had a beating heart that enabled her to live. And she had faith. Faith and reason had coexisted within her quite comfortably for decades, and then there was conflict—a classic clash that has existed within mankind for centuries.

"I never saw any contradiction—for years." And when she saw a contradiction, she saw not just a small piece of a new picture—she saw the whole picture at once. She was questioning everything—Church teachings on divorce, remarriage, homosexuality, and abortion. "I don't think those rules have anything to do with the Christian teaching and Jesus. . . . There is no relationship. The Church is not unchanging—it has changed very much. Things have evolved. That is a historical fact."

Being a nun, she says, is a "total commitment, the total life, almost unexamined. And the reason that it's unexamined is because even though this thing or that thing may not make much sense, the whole thing is what God wants from you, and therefore to look at one part of it is not called for, it shouldn't even be done. And if you begin to question, your belief goes to dust in your hands. The reason that many nuns have left religious life is that they begin to question."

She wondered about the beatific vision that would come with death. "Just think of that," she says. "That is what you are going to get when you die. The beatific vision. What does that mean?"

She began to question fundamental beliefs she had never before questioned: "You take the light of reason and you shine it on what you did not question."

She no longer believed in transubstantiation, in Hell. She reflected upon certain prayers. Church teachings were that these prayers were literally true, but as Elizabeth reflected upon the Creed, she had difficulty with this notion. "I know the Creed by heart—'He descended into hell and on the third day he rose again from the dead. He ascended into heaven and sits at the right hand of the father.' Thinking this cannot be literal. This is not so. This is not what Jesus told us to believe. It's the Nicene Creed and therefore it was drafted by a Church council. This is what you have to believe to be a Catholic. I do not believe in this literally. I began thinking about the words 'born of the Virgin Mary, suffered under Pontius Pilate, and on the third day rose again from the dead.' No he didn't. That didn't happen—it was written in gospels years later."

"What has birth control got to do with the Christian message?" she asks. "Nothing. And yet it's the Catholic rule. What is infallibility—when the pope speaks *ex cathedra*—in matters of faith and morals? Who believes that anymore? Nobody. Not educated Catholics in the first world.

"I was in Poland a few years ago being shown around by a very attractive young guide. Poland is ninety-five percent Catholic and I asked if she was Catholic and she said, 'Of course.' And I said, 'How do you feel about the teachings of the Church on birth control, marriage, homosexuality, etc.' and she said, 'I think they are all wonderful ideals.' And I said, 'Do you live by them?' And she said, 'Of course not. Nobody does.'"

Elizabeth loved the Mass when she was a nun. She relished the ceremony of it and she believed in it—believed in the idea of transubstantiation, the literal interpretation of the words of Jesus—*This is my body, this is my blood.*

"I used to believe the literal meaning of those words without reflecting upon what they meant, on what I was believing. It's *the real presence*. Until you begin to think, 'What am I believing? That the actual body and blood of Jesus Christ are there in that wafer and that wine?'"

Shouldn't it mean, she asks, that the bread and wine *signify* Jesus' body and blood, rather than that the bread and wine are Jesus' *actual* body and blood? "Does it take away from the value of the Eucharist to think it *symbolizes*, it memorializes, that it brings into our lives the life of Jesus, but that it doesn't mean he is actually bodily present there?

"In 1944 when I entered the convent I believed a great many things," she says. "I bought the whole 'ball of wax.' I believed that everything I was told to do was the will of God—*very specifically*. When the bell rings to go to meals, answering that bell is answering the voice of God."

From when she entered at Kenwood in September 1944 to the Rome session twenty-three years later, Elizabeth "never had a question about the Society, the Church, the whole thing." But from the meeting in Rome in 1967 through 1973—for six solid years—she examined everything; she studied everything; she *questioned* everything. She asked herself what it was, exactly, that she believed? "During the next six years I questioned not just the Society, but the Church and everything else." She reflected upon the most fundamental question: "What do I believe?"

"I believe that the human mind cannot know all of reality," she says. "I do believe there is a realm that is real—call it spiritual—that's beyond the power of human reasoning. I think it exists. I cannot believe that the human mind can grasp the whole of reality. I just have problems when that realm is defined.

"I believe that there is reality beyond what the human mind can understand. I believe that. Whatever it is. Call it God. Call it supernatural. Call it spiritual. Call it whatever you want. And it is about that reality that you have faith. You believe in it, and faith is a kind of light that gives you hints into that reality."

None of this is to suggest that intelligent people cannot embrace both science and rationality as well as faith. She mentions her friend Frank Rhodes, president of Cornell University from 1977 to 1995, whom

Elizabeth regards as a brilliant man and a strong Christian believer. "His faith, I think, guides his life," she says, "and he's a strong intellectual. I am not as intelligent as he is. I find that when you take your reason, your critical judgment, and you look at the things you believe—I found it difficult. And for me my faith wavered. For many people it does not—it has no effect."

What impact, if any, did Jerry's views on faith have on Elizabeth?

"Jerry was very respectful of my beliefs," says Elizabeth. "Wherever we were traveling, Jerry took me to Mass every Sunday—until I decided I didn't need to go every Sunday."

Jerry had no religious affiliation, no faith. "I don't think he was a believer at all," says Elizabeth. "His story was that when he was a young boy at camp, eight years old, he wandered off from the group into the woods near the camp where it was very quiet. And he could hear birds and insects and the sounds of the forest and he thought, these creatures that I hear live by destroying one another. They eat each other. It is such an awful thing there can't be a god."

Richard and Mary Lanier were close friends of Elizabeth and Jerry and spent a good deal of time with them, and they both agree that "Jerry was a dedicated atheist who was pretty cynical about blind faith and religion. He was a real rationalist." Says Richard Lanier: "Jerry would often say, 'Vas you dere, Richard?'" Meaning that if you did not see something—witness it firsthand with your own eyes—then it was not something that could be proven or believed in. Perhaps Jerry was echoing a popular radio and movie comedian of the 1930s, Jack Pearl, playing Baron Munchausen, spinner of yarns of his incredible adventures. When someone doubted him, he would reply, "Vas you dere, Charley?"

. . .

Elizabeth is very much a liberal thinker, but she also believes that the very rapid change in Catholic institutions was destructive. "I've always been of the opinion that Vatican II was a response to change that had already taken place, and was the cause for further change. It wasn't as though everything was status quo and then there was Vatican II and everything changed. A great many things were changed before and the change was made legitimate by Vatican II. Having made legitimate the change that had taken place, the Church made more change follow inevitably."

At Manhattanville the nuns' habits were worn throughout the 1968–69 academic year. But by the fall of 1969, there was the option to wear civilian clothes. The overwhelming majority of the nuns chose that option. Elizabeth says, "Some never took off the habit—the very old and the very conservative didn't. Eventually, except for a very small group of very conservative people, everyone else did. I was very, very hesitant to do it. I felt that it was a very big step and I didn't know, even though some of the nuns were doing it, whether I would do it, at the college, or not. I thought a lot about it and decided that, if most were making the change, the president of the college should.

"Why? Because those who really believed in this felt that the habit was a barrier to doing one's educational job. I didn't really believe that. I do know that on a given day, after having worn a habit from 1944 to 1969, and I then decided to put on a normal dress, I thought it would be very traumatic. It really wasn't, however, because one doesn't look at oneself in the mirror all the time—you quickly forget what you have on.

"What was amazing and what I believe was part of the reason that many people during those years left religious orders is the dramatic change in the way people treated you when you weren't wearing religious dress. *Absolutely amazing*. I remember very soon after, I began wearing a very simple black dress. I was coming down the stairs in the Castle at Manhattanville and at the bottom of the stairs was Robert O'Clair, a member of the faculty whom I knew quite well. As I walked down the stairs he looked up and he said, 'Mother McCormack, welcome to the human race.' People treated me very differently. Before that

I had gone to many, many educational meetings and knew many people. When I was wearing a habit, never did anyone at the mid-morning
coffee break say, 'Come on, I'll buy you a cup of coffee.' No one ever
said that. If you wanted a cup of coffee you went yourself and got yourself a cup of coffee.

"The minute you didn't have the habit on people treated you the
way they treated everybody else. You were a member of the human race
again. Barriers were down—that's really what it was. Not that you felt
differently, but people felt differently *about* you and if you have a long
enough experience with that, you *became* different, in my opinion. Not
because you didn't have a habit on, but because you had more normal
relationships."

From a practical standpoint, Elizabeth found the change to civilian
clothes annoying. She did not like having to shop for clothes, nor did
she like worrying about or having to decide what to wear.

But in America's fashion-conscious culture, things changed fairly
quickly for the nuns in mufti. Gradually, nuns began to assemble more
diverse wardrobes. Some wore only the plainest outfits while others
opted for something more stylish and some even had their hair styled
and used some make-up.

What she really objected to were the fundamental changes in the
life she had led as a nun—a life that seemed to be evaporating before
her eyes. "By this time in the Society's evolution, in the late 1960s,
Sacred Heart nuns were no longer required to pursue academic careers
as they had been in the past," writes author V. V. Harrison in *Changing Habits*. "Now there was a practice of 'discernment,' which translated into a dialogue between individuals and their provincial to
determine what ministry would best suit their temperament, specific
area of interest, and sometimes their politics. There was now an acceptance of diversity and a freedom to choose, where there had been
none before."

The rules, to Elizabeth's chagrin, seemed to erode all too rapidly.

Postulants lived in the outside world rather than in a strict convent setting. They had the freedom to come and go as they pleased. The sense of community—that intense connection the women felt in a cloistered setting where prayer and reflection defined their lives—was gone. "The very fact that those years were rigorous and different and demanded a lot of you I found made it worth doing," she says.

The liberalization within the order troubled her. She watched it not as a change but as a kind of disintegration of what the order had been all about, of what she had devoted her life to. "So your life disintegrates at two levels—both what you do and what you believe."

Elizabeth believed that Pope John XXIII, while a simple and deeply holy man, was also naïve and had no real vision for what was to come. She read his autobiography, *Journal of a Soul,* later and felt that "had he been able to know what would happen, I think he would have been appalled. I don't think he could have stopped certain things that had already happened. I think things would have continued to happen, but he made them legitimate and therefore the people who wouldn't have changed at all changed because of him."

The Sacred Heart nuns took three vows: poverty, chastity, and obedience. "I believe today the only one of those that remains is chastity and how much of that remains I have no idea," she says. "But poverty doesn't. They don't live like poor people. Obedience—each religious is told to do what she feels called upon by God to do. She doesn't obey. She can choose.

"We lived a common life: when you rose, when you went to bed, went to chapel and when you went to meals—only talked on feast days—common life and common mission—which was the education of children in the schools; if you were less educated you cooked the meal for the children—that was the mission. Now there is no common life and each religious does what she believes she was called by God to do. So what's left? I believe that once you make the life more ordinary—*easier*—it's the beginning of the end."

When Elizabeth entered the Society in 1944 there were 100 young women entering the noviceship in the United States. By 2010 that had shrunk to perhaps one to three.

.   .   .

Elizabeth had earned an influential role within the Society of the Sacred Heart. She had been asked to take on some of the more challenging, high-profile roles—Headmistress of The Sacred Heart Academy in Greenwich, delegate to the General Chapter in Rome, and the presidency of Manhattanville. Thus, when she told the Manhattanville board she would be staying just one more year, she expected her superior, the Provincial, to suggest other assignments.

"I fully expected her to say to me, 'O.K. when the year is up *this* is what I want you to do. I would like you to do this, this, this or this. You know, we are starting a school in Uganda and after you have been at Manhattanville when this is over next year go run that school.' And she never did. I was an old-fashioned nun. I was shocked when I was not offered another job."

Not only was Elizabeth surprised that she was not offered another position within the Society fairly promptly, she was hurt as well. She had, after all, devoted nearly thirty years of her life to the order. She had sacrificed in ways that are, today, unimaginable in our society— she had given up personal freedom, offered absolute obedience, promised not to have sex or marry or make money. Jerry saw all of this up close and could see that Elizabeth was profoundly distressed. "I think it would have been a source of great comfort to her," he says, "had they asked her to do something."

But now that she would be stepping down as president—with no new assignment on the horizon—what would she do? The more she reflected upon it the more deeply disillusioned she became.

That summer of 1973, she made her decision. She would leave the

Society. In October, she visited the Society's Provincial, Mother Margaret Coakley, and told her. Mother Coakley suggested that she make a retreat and reflect and pray about this decision.

"I said, 'No, I've been thinking about it a few years and I no longer believe—my faith is gone.' She said, 'Then there's no point in making a retreat.'"

The Church required that Elizabeth write two letters—one to the Pope and the other to the Society's Mother General in Rome—asking to leave the Society. She did, and Jerry could see that it was "damn traumatic" for Elizabeth.

Many people believed Elizabeth was leaving the Society because of Jerry. "I said to Jerry, 'I find that disturbing.' And he said, 'We know it's not true.' We never had an affair, ever, and nobody would ever believe that, and so Jerry said, 'What difference does it make what people believe?'" In 2010, she says emphatically: "I was considering it, questioning it. I did not stop being a nun because of Jerry."

Perhaps the passage of time—nearly four decades—has somehow shrouded the reality of that period in her life. But there is powerful evidence that Elizabeth did, in fact, leave the Society for Jerry. On October 2, 1973—before visiting the provincial to say she intended to leave the Society—Elizabeth wrote Jerry an intensely personal letter from London. The purpose of her trip is unclear, but she wrote on the stationery of the Great Western Royal Hotel in Paddington on October 2 at 11:00 p.m.

> Dearest Jerry,
>
> Last night at JFK my feelings, heart, mind—all can be described as one word—EMPTY—new and strange sensation for me, but very real. . . . Between arrival and dinner I slept in this old, rather nice hotel. Now it is time to go to bed and I want to get off the Mayflower.
>
> Already I long for JFK on the 10th. I don't know myself in these reactions. More tomorrow. I love you, Elizabeth

A letter from the same trip—she had travelled from London to Ditchley Park, Enstone, Oxfordshire, for a meeting of the Ditchley Park Foundation, for which she was a member of the U.S. Board, begins: "Dear Jerry, I MISS you." And ends: "You know all the right things to say. I only know and say that I LOVE YOU. Elizabeth."

A much earlier and briefer note written by Elizabeth—nearly two years earlier, in fact (December 1, 1971), read:

Jerry—
    Rest, read, relax, forget. Ask me for any help I may be able to give now and forever. Elizabeth M.

According to her close friend Linda Goelz, "Elizabeth says that Jerry was not the reason that she left but Jerry played a very big role in why she gave it up."

.   .   .

What made deciding to leave the order so difficult was not that Elizabeth would have to face an entirely different kind of life outside the convent. "It was the people, two or three people who had counted on me. They were my security, wonderful women."

She reflected upon this at length, troubled by how disappointed they would be. Elizabeth's main concern was for the Reverend Mother Helen Fitzgerald, who had assigned her to Manhattanville. "She was a wonderful woman and she counted on me. I don't think she had any of the doubts that I had and, therefore, I had to say to myself if she believes all this and she is intelligent, why do I have a problem with it? Who do I think I am? Do I know that she didn't have a lot of questions? Of course not. She would not have told me."

The other woman she did not want to disappoint was Mother Elizabeth Cavanagh, who had taught Elizabeth in high school. "I found telling her that I was going to leave the Society the hardest thing, because it was so disappointing to her, so unintelligible to her. I knew both women well and loved them and admired them both, and they were always very supportive of what I wanted to do once I began thinking of what I wanted to do."

Years later, when Mother Cavanagh was dying, Elizabeth went to visit her "and she said to me, 'Don't you regret what you did, to leave?' And I said, 'Not for a minute.'"

Ultimately, Elizabeth McCormack left the Society of the Sacred Heart because her doubts had grown so strong. On January 14, 1974, she wrote a letter to friends and colleagues at Manhattanville: "I have asked and have been authorized to leave the Society of the Sacred Heart. I came to this decision with sadness and after several years of reflection. . . . The world in which we live is dynamic. It is inevitable that both institutions and individuals evolve as they are moved by the forces of life. The commitment I made in 1944 can no longer be fulfilled by me within the Society."

The decision to leave was an exceptionally difficult one. She called it "the most painful period of my life. I agonized about the decision." It was also hard on Elizabeth's mother, who was in her eighties and still living in Larchmont. "This decision of mine to leave the Society was very hard on her. Not from a religious point of view, she took that in stride, but she was terribly worried about me. 'What will you do at this age? What will you live on? How will you cope?' She was very concerned."

The *New York Times* reported Elizabeth's decision in an article on January 16, 1974.

In an interview, the 51-year-old educator said that an underlying factor in her decision was a fundamental disagreement with the order over the nature of the religious life.

"The major focus of the institution that I joined was education," she said. "Now it is education but also community living, identification with the poor and solidarity with the Third World. At a time when the order faces diminishing resources, especially people, I think that it is unwise to diversify."

She also noted that in the last few years the Sacred Heart Society, like other communities of nuns, had shifted its style of living from large groups of nuns working in the same school to smaller groups in which the emphasis is on mutual support.

"This represents a major shift," she said. "The question is whether the community is organized to meet the needs of the world or whether the central thing is the religious life of the members."

Elizabeth worried for a while about being alone. After all, she had lived with her family or at a school or in a community of nuns her entire life. "And then suddenly I was going to be in a flat on 82nd Street, all by myself." But it wasn't difficult at all, she says, because she was so active and busy and because so many friends reached out to her to make sure she was never lonely. Also, she had Jerry. That first year, in particular, she was constantly being invited to dinners and other events by a wide variety of people including Bob Bernstein, then head of Random House, and his wife Helen. "They would phone and say, 'We're alone in this big house. Count on this place any weekend. Just arrive. The children are away and we have lots of space.'" Elizabeth never did it, but she very much appreciated their thinking of her. And as she reflected back upon it she says that "among those supportive people there wasn't a single Roman Catholic."

．　　．　　．

In December 1974, Elizabeth received a response to her letters asking to be released from her vows. The response, which arrived by mail, was a form letter on a mimeographed sheet. And she was shocked by the coldness of it.

Thirty-five years later, Elizabeth McCormack is nearly speechless when asked about this. "Thirty years. Mimeographed form." She shakes her head. *"Horrified."*

She was sure that the Mother General would contact her. "I was absolutely convinced, that she would write or cable or telephone and say, 'I want to talk to you. You know I'm not going to try and change your mind but I want to know your reasons, I want to see you.' I was convinced that was going to happen. When it didn't happen, and when a mimeographed form came, it confirmed the wisdom of the decision."

While many women were leaving various orders at the time, Elizabeth was different. "Because of my role at the college, and because of the role I had played in the Society, my leaving was particularly threatening. I believe, therefore, that they may well have dealt with it far less kindly because they just didn't want to think about it. Had I left with a serious financial problem, they would have helped me."

. . .

In 1973, soon after the announcement was made public that Elizabeth would be stepping down as president, but before her decision to leave the order, she received a call from William Dietel, vice president of the Rockefeller Brothers Fund. Dietel and Dana Creel, then president of the Brothers Fund, had watched Elizabeth's performance at Manhattanville over the years and were impressed. They would like to talk about her working with them.

Elizabeth had met William Dietel many years earlier when she and others within the Sacred Heart Society were rethinking some of their educational approaches. Dietel was then headmaster at the Emma Willard School in Troy, New York, a private school for girls. Elizabeth wanted to get a better understanding of some of the educational approaches used at Emma Willard, and she contacted Dietel to see if she could have a conversation with him. She drove up to Troy and they had an extensive and valuable discussion. Dietel was taken aback when Elizabeth arrived at his office. He did not know she was a nun when she called for an appointment, and he was struck by her habit, "which was darned so much it looked like it would fall apart."

Now, Elizabeth, Dietel, and Creel agreed to sit down for a discussion. For this meeting, she was of course wearing civilian clothes, not a habit. After it, the men said they would like to hire her, to have her come and work for the Rockefellers. She was genuinely surprised. "I found it amazing that they would hire a nun," she says.

"They were looking for someone who could do two things: one was relating to the fourth generation after John D. Rockefeller's," she says. "We are talking back in 1974 about the cousins' generation; the members were just out of college or out of law school and to introduce them to the world of philanthropy about which I knew very little. That was one thing I was supposed to do and the second thing I was supposed to do was to create an office. The idea was to establish a philanthropic office for the Rockefeller family members to use if they wished for individual philanthropic advice and for distribution from charitable trusts. First they had to be sure that I could relate to a younger generation before I began to establish the office."

She accepted the job. During her final year as president of Manhattanville, she spent some time getting to know the Rockefeller office and learning some basics about the world of philanthropy.

Creel and Dietel were concerned that she was lacking funds on which to live. "They said, 'You must have no money,' and, of course, they were correct. When I had entered the Society in 1944, my father gave them $10,000 and when I left I was given back the $10,000, plus an additional $4,000."

Creel and Dietel thought she should put that aside, and they paid Elizabeth as a consultant during her final year at Manhattanville. "So they gave me, for doing virtually nothing, $1,500 a month. So that by the time I left I had $14,000 plus $1,500 a month for a year. So I had a little money."

They also thought perhaps she would need help with tax issues and put her together with one of the lawyers at the Rockefeller offices. He visited her at her Manhattanville residence, and she pulled out past checks that she had received as salary for being the college president— seven years' worth of checks and every one—one after the other—was signed over to the Society of the Sacred Heart. She had never cashed her paychecks.

The lawyer was astonished. He had seen all manner of financial situations through the years, but he had never before seen anything like this.

"We talk about generous philanthropy," he said to Elizabeth. "You gave over every penny. This is *total* philanthropy!"

. . .

Elizabeth would soon sense an undercurrent from others that she had somehow squandered nearly three decades in religious life. Even her brother, George, said to her, "Isn't it a shame that you wasted thirty years? When you look at your career and what has become of it and how much greater it might have been." And Elizabeth said to him, "I didn't waste thirty years. If I hadn't entered the convent I would have spent my life driving children around Westchester County. I have loved my life and, I believe, I have done some good."

She believed, in fact, that she had had a productive and thoroughly enjoyable life as a nun. She had, for most of those years, loved being a nun, loved being an educator. She would not put it this way, but it seems clear enough that she loved being a woman with authority, a woman with power. She also knew, in those years, that the alternative to being a nun was not for her.

"I think now in retrospect I didn't want the life that I would have had had I not become a nun. I actually, from many points of view, had a much fuller life. I had a career. I was educated. I learned leadership. It really gave me an awfully good life. Not many women my age now have had as full a life as I have."

The only real sacrifice was giving up the opportunity to have children. "That's the only thing I gave up," she says. "What I would have had is a husband—God knows what he would have been like. We would have been in suburbia. Had children.

"I look at the lives of my friends after college—no careers, married, lots of children. I would have loved to have had children," she says, but in a matter-of-fact way, not wistfully, not in any way suggesting that she would go back and alter her course if she could rewind history. "Oh, no," she says. "You don't regret. It was a good life and it wasn't as though during those years I was just doing nothing but believing and praying. I mean, I was involved in education that whole time. I still see people to whom I was a big help, whom I taught."

(9)

Rebirth

IN DECEMBER 1973, Elizabeth received the infamous mimeographed letter from Rome freeing her from her vows. She was required to sign a document included in the package and mail it back. When she received the mailing, she phoned Jerry, and he came over to her house on campus.

In the letter she had sent to the Society's Mother General in Rome, she was supposed to say that she was "no longer able" to live by her vows, but she had written instead that she "no longer wished" to do so. Now, she was required to sign an additional form with some bureaucratic language to satisfy an administrator in Rome.

When Jerry arrived at her house, she showed him the documents, then asked him: "Should I sign this?"

"It's not up to me to decide whether you should," Jerry said.

Elizabeth thought a moment and said: "Well, I'll sign it if you'll mail it."

Deal. Elizabeth signed and sealed it and handed the envelope to Jerry. As he was walking out the door he turned back to her and said, "By the way, I'm getting a divorce. Will you marry me?"

And Elizabeth replied, "Of course!"

.   .   .

Jerry needed to break free of the unhappy life he had had with Joan for so many years. He needed to get away and start a new life with Elizabeth. Joan, however, did not want a divorce. "She was afraid of being alone, mostly," says their daughter Nan. "She had spent so much time working that her social network had shrunk. She had less time for friends. Her kids had moved on. She knew she'd be alone in a big house and that was very scary. Jerry would fix things. He was a huge help and source of support in many ways." Joan did not want to let him go.

But Jerry was not to be denied. Elizabeth recalls that, in the face of Joan's opposition, "he said, 'I want this divorce. The only way I'm going to get it is to give her everything.' Which is what he did." Elizabeth completely agreed with this approach. "Give her everything. Who cares? Who needs *things?* That's what happened."

With Joan agreeing to the terms, the most expeditious way to formalize the divorce was in Haiti, and Jerry quickly flew to Port-au-Prince. Elizabeth's understanding of the process was that Jerry arrived in Port-au-Prince and met with a lawyer who took him to a court "and the judge said, 'Is there any possibility of reconciliation?' 'No.' And that second you're divorced. On the plane coming back, he wrote this out, exactly what was said, and always had it in his wallet, that little paper."

.   .   .

After Elizabeth stopped being a nun, her relationship with Jerry remained essentially the same as it had been while she was a nun. "It

should have changed radically, but it didn't," she says. "I should have gone and lived with him, but I didn't." Elizabeth rented an apartment at 82nd Street and Lexington Avenue, while Jerry had a very modest basement apartment elsewhere on the East Side.

Jerry had been married for so long that the divorce could not immediately sever all entanglements with Joan. Jerry would spend most evenings with Elizabeth at her place. But when he was there, he had to set call-forwarding of his apartment phone to Elizabeth's phone. When Joan called him, as she did every night, she would think he was at home, not at Elizabeth's. Why so many calls after the divorce? Nan explains that it was very rough on her mother. The divorce had taken a toll on Jerry, as well. There were emotional scars—some difficulty with one of his children and a sense of having failed in a marriage that had lasted for so many years.

But finally, Elizabeth and Jerry began living together. In the early part of 1976, Jerry had to undergo back surgery. The doctor said he would need post-surgical care. He could not live alone in his apartment. One option was a rehabilitation facility, but both Jerry and Elizabeth opposed that. And so Jerry came to live with Elizabeth at East 82nd Street.

Because of the terms of the divorce, Jerry was basically broke. He had given everything to Joan and was left with nothing. When Elizabeth and Jerry eventually did get married, they went to a lawyer friend to set up a will. When the attorney was done going through it with them he joked: "Well, this will is the short and simple annals of the poor."

Says Elizabeth: "When we were married we had nothing—nothing."

.   .   .

The plan was simple: They would marry in the Catholic Church and then again in a Jewish ceremony. "We were going to be married by Father Vincent O'Connor, a wonderful priest, on a given Saturday, and then we were going to go the next week and be married by Jerry's mother's rabbi

because that would mean something to her," says Elizabeth. "Jerry asked if I minded being married by a rabbi, and I said, 'Of course not!'"

Even though she had left the Society of the Sacred Heart, Elizabeth very much wanted to be married in the Church. She had, after all, grown up in a Catholic household where she and her brother held their breath passing a Presbyterian church en route to Sunday Mass; where there was not even a possibility she would go to anything but a Catholic grammar and high school; where the thought that she might go to other than a Catholic college was dismissed out of hand by her father. She had spent twenty-nine years of her life as a nun and been president of a Catholic college. Of course she would be married in the Church, and given the enormous contribution she had made to the Church, there couldn't possibly be any problem.

But there was a glitch. A week before the scheduled ceremony, Father O'Connor telephoned Elizabeth and said there a problem with the bishop, and he said it was going to take time to resolve. He asked if she still wanted to get married in the Church, and Elizabeth said absolutely. The priest replied he would not be able to perform the ceremony the following weekend as planned. He said there might be a couple months' wait.

As she talked on the phone with the priest, Jerry could see that Elizabeth was upset. "So Jerry said to me, 'Give me the phone,' and he spoke with Father O'Connor and he said the delay was fine and that the priest could just let them know when the path was cleared." Jerry was about to finish the call when Elizabeth wanted the phone back. She told Father O'Connor that she planned to be married by the rabbi the following week, that they were simply reversing the original order.

Meanwhile, Jerry's mother phoned him and said that Rabbi David Weiss would like to meet him and Elizabeth before the ceremony. Jerry was frustrated, but his mother reassured him. "It is going to be fine, Jerome, it is going to be fine, but Rabbi Weiss wants to meet you and Elizabeth," his mother said.

"And I am sitting right there," recalls Elizabeth, "and Jerry says, 'Jesus Christ, Mother, haven't I had enough to deal with the Church? Do I have to now deal with your rabbi?'"

But Jerry and Elizabeth went to see the rabbi, and Elizabeth was impressed by him. He asked them only one question, and it was put to Elizabeth. Rabbi Weiss asked whether her being married by a rabbi "would cause suffering to my family." And the answer was certainly not. The only family Elizabeth had left was her brother, George, and, as Elizabeth put it, given his serial divorce history, "George gets married every few minutes."

And so, Elizabeth and Jerry were married on December 23, 1976, at the synagogue Jerry's mother attended in Philadelphia with Rabbi Weiss presiding. Elizabeth's friend, and former nun, Cynthia Bennett attended, as did George McCormack and his wife, Joy. Two of Jerry's children, Nan and Betsy, were there as well. It was the simplest possible ceremony lasting only five or six minutes, and then it was back to Jerry's mother's home on Rittenhouse Square for a party.

Elizabeth and Jerry were now married, and they turned their attention to working toward a Catholic wedding as well. The Jewish marriage was not an obstacle in any serious way because the Roman Catholic Church simply did not recognize it as a legitimate marriage. Church officials referred to it, says Elizabeth, as "the attempted marriage."

Because the wedding was planned for Connecticut, Jerry and his mother had to travel to Bridgeport to answer questions from an Ecclesiastical Court. Priests wanted to understand what had gone wrong with Jerry's marriage, why he had gotten divorced. A priest questioned both Jerry and his mother. "It was all about what had been the matter with his marriage. What kind of scandal this marriage was."

The review process would prove to be arduous and lengthy. At one point priests questioned Jerry, Jerry's mother, and Elizabeth's friend Cynthia, who as a young nun had been involved in the nocturnal crucifix gathering at Manhattanville. All three interviews were conducted in separate rooms, and all three were recorded by a stenographer.

Jerry recalls, "Elizabeth wasn't invited to appear at all. The complaint which the Bishop of Bridgeport entertained was that if we were married, it would cause 'wonderment' in the community. That was the charge. So all of us appear in an office someplace in Bridgeport—a kind of large room with small rooms off the side. And in each room there was a priest at a desk with a tape recorder." Cynthia, Jerry, and Jerry's mother were asked many questions, including whether the marriage would cause "wonderment." Elizabeth had never heard this term before—not during nearly thirty years as a nun, not as the president of a college, not during her PhD process—never. "Wonderment," she says. "A nice word for scandal, I guess. Would people be shocked?"

Cynthia, Jerry, and his mother were questioned intensively. He was asked what had happened to his marriage and whether Elizabeth was the cause of its breakup. Jerry's mother was asked why Jerry had had five children, and she said to the priest: "Have you ever heard of sex?"

When it was over, says Jerry, "I was kind of numb. None of them made any sense to me, but there we were, and finally we were dismissed. The tapes were transcribed and sent to Rome for Papal determination."

Decades later, Elizabeth becomes visibly angry about the process—the fact that her good friend Cynthia along with Jerry and his elderly mother had to be put through it. "I should not have put us through all that but I did it because I wanted to be married in the Church," she says. "I could have left the Society without getting a release. I could have married Jerry without getting the release. But I was a Catholic and I wanted to be married in the Church."

She shakes her head: "It was outrageous."

In January 1977, Jerry wrote a letter to Pope Paul VI:

> Your Holiness:
> I request to enter into a Marriage with Elizabeth J. McCor-

mack within the Roman Catholic Church. I was formerly married to Joan Borgenicht Aron by Rabbi Louis Wolsey on May 2, 1943 in New York City. Both Joan and I are Jewish by birth and religion and we have never been part of the Christian Church; consequently, neither of us has ever been baptized. Our marriage was a dismal failure for decades and has been legally dissolved. I have lived entirely apart from Joan for the past two and a half years, and there is no possibility of a reconciliation. Because of the above facts, I request that the Privilege of Faith be granted to me.

It was accompanied by two other brief letters, one each by Jerry and Elizabeth promising to raise their children as Catholics "were it physiologically possible" to have children, "which it is not." Elizabeth also pledged that after marrying Jerry she will "continue to practice my Catholic faith."

Had she been a low-profile nun she suspects the process would have been far simpler, but given her prominence, she believes the Church turned up the heat. A year went by. Questions were asked and answered, and weeks, then months stretched on without anything happening.

"Well, a year goes by," says Jerry, "and we don't hear a word. So we're having dinner one night with our friends, the Klines. Ed Kline inherited a chain of thirteen middle-size Midwest department stores from his father and he couldn't have been less interested, so he sold them. He got a tutor and learned to speak Russian and became very interested in the dissident movement out of Russia and became a critical part of bringing these dissidents here. When Andrei Sakharov was awarded the Nobel Prize and was not permitted to leave Russia to accept it, he asked Ed Kline to go in his stead.

"We're having dinner, and I was telling him about this process and that it's been a year, and I'm just on the verge of getting myself a canon lawyer to look into it. And Ed says, 'Don't get a canon lawyer. That's not the way you deal with these people. I have become an expert on the Soviet government, and I know exactly how these bureaucrats work, and the Soviet bureaucrats and the Vatican bureaucrats are the same thing. Don't do it.'

"About a month later," says Jerry, "a monsignor from Notre Dame came to see Elizabeth about fundraising for the university. They got very friendly, and somehow or other she told him the story of our problem and he was horrified. He said, 'What a terrible thing to do to you. I'll deal with this, Elizabeth. Tomorrow I will phone my friend, Cardinal Somebody in the Vatican, and we'll get this thing moving.' Well, he did. Two weeks later, I get a letter from Bridgeport: 'His Eminence, the Holy Father, has determined blah, blah, blah, that you and Elizabeth can be married in the Church.'"

In the letter, Reverend Jerald A. Doyle of the Tribunal within the Diocese of Bridgeport wrote that the pope had "granted the dissolution of your marriage to Joan Borgenicht in favor of your entering marriage with Elizabeth McCormack according to the laws of the Catholic Church." The Pope's action came on December 16, 1977, and Jerry was notified by Reverend Doyle's letter dated December 28, 1977.

"During the course of this year from time to time, I'd say to Elizabeth, let's make a contribution to the poor box at the Church because that will get things going," says Jerry. "We had a trustee at Manhattanville—eleven children and he got an annulment to marry another woman. God knows what that cost. Elizabeth said, 'We will not pay a penny. I will not pay for this.' So the final paragraph of the letter: The cost of the transcripts was $175.00. 'I would appreciate your remitting that amount at your earliest convenience. Yours in Christ, Father So and So.' So it cost us 175 bucks, and then Father O'Connor married us."

.　　.　　.

Along the way, Elizabeth's thinking on the matter took an interesting turn. She wanted very much to marry in the Church, and she was so deeply grateful that Jerry was so persistent in his efforts to move it forward. It was such a tangible demonstration of his love for her, and she deeply appreciated it. But the more bureaucratic and absurd the process grew, the less important it became to Elizabeth. There had been something ugly, something medieval about the process.

She had devoted thirty years of her life to service of the Roman Catholic Church, and this was how she, and many other Catholics, for that matter, were treated. She found it intolerable. A process that was originally supposed to take a week took more than a year.

"This was very important to me, but the worse the procedure got, the less important it seemed," she says. "I began to think that this has no relationship to Jesus, to the Christian message. This is just awful stuff. Awful. It absolutely destroyed my faith in the Church. It did. After that for some time I went to Mass every Sunday. No matter where we were Jerry would drive me to Mass and then I finally said, 'You know, I am not doing this anymore.'"

Just when you think the Roman Catholic Church is a hopeless, un-Christian institution, however, along comes a person who represents the best of the Church. Elizabeth and Jerry were married on January 14, 1978, in the garden of Saint Catherine's Church in Riverside, Connecticut, with Father Vincent O'Connor officiating. There were only a few friends and Jerry's mother, as Elizabeth and Jerry wanted it. And Father O'Connor did something important, something truly special. He made a point of recognizing the legitimacy of the Jewish ceremony, a point he did not need to make, a point in conflict with the Church's official teachings, but a point that recognized what Rabbi Weiss had done. In fact, Elizabeth and Jerry were already married. So Father O'Connor said, "If I had had the privilege of marrying you, I would have said, 'Do you, Jerry, take Elizabeth for your lawful wife? . . . '" Father O'Connor's beautiful act of generosity so touched Jerry's mother that she began weeping with joy.

.   .   .

Elizabeth and Jerry drove out to Montauk for their honeymoon. Before they left, Elizabeth spoke to George's wife, Joy, who predicted that she and Jerry would have their first marital fight while driving to Montauk. When Elizabeth recounted this to Jerry, he said, "See what people's relationships are like!"

In fact, they did *not* fight during the drive—or ever. "We didn't know how to fight," Elizabeth says. "We never had a fight, never. I think we were both old enough to know that the things you fight about don't make any difference. You can have a human reaction, that's human, but expressing it is a whole other story. I believe what has stayed with me from twenty-nine years as a nun is discipline."

Elizabeth learned as a nun never to complain. "You just don't," she says. She recalls sweltering Albany summers where she was dressed in a heavy habit, yet the thought of complaining never even crossed her mind. The discipline she learned as a nun, Elizabeth believes, was actually excellent preparation for marriage. She had never been a complainer and part of her training was to avoid complaining. And a spouse who does not complain, Elizabeth believes, is sending a powerfully healthy signal within a marriage. As Jerry told an interviewer years after the wedding: "I met Elizabeth in October of '69. Not once since that moment has either of us raised his voice to the other."

.   .   .

Elizabeth McCormack was fifty-five years old and a married woman. And she had never been so happy in her life. It was not that she had ever been unhappy. Remarkably enough, Elizabeth had lived her entire life without ever experiencing any real unhappiness. Trying to decide whether to leave the order had made for a difficult and trying time, but not an unhappy one. Even much later when Jerry grew ill, she was deeply concerned, but she was not unhappy with her life or her marriage.

There was something deeply loving about her relationship with Jerry. She loved him for his kindness and his intelligence, for the joy he took in music, conversation, the study of American history, and much more. And his love for her was so palpable, so real—and it seemed to surround her. And he was never boring. They loved listening to music together, classical, jazz, musicals, everything. They traveled to Paris and stayed at a small hotel on the Left Bank. "And Jerry said the greatest tomb in the world was Napoleon's tomb so every time we went to Paris we had to visit Napoleon's tomb. We just loved Paris."

Linda Goelz knew Elizabeth and Jerry well. She worked with Elizabeth for more than twenty years at the Rockefellers, and she would eventually move into the building where Elizabeth lives. "Elizabeth and Jerry found each other at crucial times in their lives," says Linda. "People at Manhattanville saw sparks from the very beginning. Both gave up very established lives. They came together completely in sync with each other. It was so new to Elizabeth. All of a sudden she is in this relationship.

"I have never heard them quarrel. I don't even know if they disagreed. They never did it publicly. He showed her a completely different world from the world she had and he took her away—far away from where she had been. It was almost a rebirth into this life—freedom to leave the Catholic Church behind and to be free to do anything you want with someone you love."

At one point when they were discussing possible trips, Elizabeth said she wanted to visit Antarctica, but Jerry didn't like that idea at all. But two years later he surprised her. "You know, I have been thinking about it," he said to her. "You said you would like to go to Antarctica." And she replied, "Oh, Jerry that was nothing." And he said, "Well, I have made the arrangements, and we are going." And they went. Elizabeth remembers, "You have to be with a group and you go to Buenos

Aires for a couple of days and then you go to Tierra del Fuego and you get on a ship and go through the roughest sea in the world and then Antarctica, which was fabulous. And my doctor brother gave us pills for seasickness and going through the Strait [of Magellan] we were the only people in the dining room. Everyone was sick. It was so rough—just that part of it. Out the window were nothing but waves. You couldn't see anything. It was great. We loved that trip."

Another time they took a cruise on a large liner through the Caribbean. They disliked just about everything about it—the crowded ship, poor food, stopping on every other island—but because they were together, they had a ball. They took another cruise, this time on a small Swedish ship with just 100 passengers through the Panama Canal. "It was wonderful," she recalls. "Jerry was fun to travel with."

Richard Lanier and his wife, Mary, were close friends of Elizabeth and Jerry, and the two couples would often travel together. "They had about as close a relationship as I have ever seen in a married couple of any age," says Richard.

Not long after they married, Elizabeth and Jerry traveled to California for an Aron family event. Joan, Jerry's former wife, was there, and she and Elizabeth chatted. Joan said, "Since Jerry married you, he is more eccentric than ever." And Elizabeth replied, 'Is he? I like him that way.'"

Dorothy Samuels, former head of the New York Civil Liberties Union and now a member of the Editorial Board of the *New York Times*, knew Elizabeth first and, through her, got to know Jerry. She described him as "one of the most down-to-earth, funniest, unique people in the world. There's no bull factor with Jerry. Jerry just sees through everything and has this wonderful sense of humor about the world in which he's operating, and he's a man of passion, which is wonderful. And the two—Elizabeth has quiet passion, and she has a wonderful way of modulating herself so you know when she feels very strongly about something or whatever, but she uses it to get things done. And it just always seems to me that they're such a loving couple that complement each other, and once you enter the world of Elizabeth and Jerry, the world seems so much safer. And the times in my life when I've had problems, including some political problems when I left the ACLU . . . any time there's been any kind of struggle in my life . . . they're always there."

.   .   .

Jerry and Elizabeth had spent some time upstate, and they both loved being out in the country—a peaceful respite from the city. They had rented a small home in the town of Copake, in Dutchess County, but it was quite a distance from the city, 113 miles, and they were looking for something that might be closer but still bucolic.

A couple of years after they were married, they saw an ad in the newspaper for a small house on a large piece of land in Pawling, which is 40 miles closer than Copake. The price was $130,000. Elizabeth pointed it out to Jerry, who said there was no way they could afford that kind of money. But, by this point, Elizabeth had been working for the Rockefellers for nine years, and she had inherited $50,000 after her mother's death. Elizabeth suggested they at least drive up and look at it, and they did so.

"Jerry said, 'Why don't we just buy it? Let's offer them $80,000.'" They made that offer to the real estate agent, who balked at suggesting it to the owner. "I remember distinctly, Jerry said, 'You represent the buyer and the seller. I'm the buyer. I'll give you $80,000. You've got to tell her that.'" And in a day or so the deal was struck—for $85,000.

"That was the first house I'd ever had other than the convent and a rental apartment," says Elizabeth, who was sixty-one years old at the time. "We got a couch at Altman's. Then over the next six months we gradually furnished it. We bought new, not too expensive Scandinavian furniture. We bought a couch and he had an Army cot, and it was great fun. We were behaving as though we were twenty-one. *Oh, we had a great time.*"

They drove up to Pawling almost every weekend, usually leaving the city around 5:30 p.m. Friday and returning after dinner on Sunday. "Jerry really didn't love New York City but he loved the country. *Loved it*. And I used to say to him, 'Look, I can quit everything. Let's sell the apartment and just move to Pawling.' And he would say, 'That would be very short-sighted.' We didn't make friends up there. He didn't *want* friends there. We have loads of friends here but up there we didn't. I remember we went to a fancy dinner party in the city one night, and I was at a different table from his, and after dinner a woman came over to me and said, 'I understand you have a house in Pawling. I do, too. I sat next to your husband and he let me know that you don't want to make friends in Pawling.' He used to say, 'If we get to know everyone, it will be just like the city and we will have to move somewhere else.'"

Jerry reveled in the peace and quiet of the place. He would often sit in his favorite chair in the living room sifting through record albums in a collection that seemed to grow organically. He would puff on his pipe and examine album covers, silently making judgments about what music best suited the mood that given day. After a time he would make his selection, put the record on the turntable, sit back, and enjoy it.

Jerry and Elizabeth spent countless hours in Pawling talking . . . and talking . . . and talking some more. Says Nan: "I never heard two people talk so much in my life."

They discovered little shops and second-hand places where they bought inexpensive furniture. They would take walks through the meadows on their property.

There was a little restaurant nearby called McKinney and Doyle, which made prepared foods that patrons bought and then heated up at home. It was convenient, and the food was delicious. Jerry loved their soup, especially one that mixed sautéed shrimp and scallops in a sauterne leek cream. He frequently bought that, and he and Elizabeth would enjoy it for lunch or dinner. Jerry so loved the soup and bought it so often that when the owners of the store opened a restaurant on the premises, they put the special soup on the menu and named it *Jerry Aron's Favorite*. Jerry was so fanatical about the soup, in fact, that for a dinner party in the city he once dispatched a hired car up to Pawling to pick up a sufficient supply for the guests.

.   .   .

During these years, Elizabeth was deeply engaged with her work in the rarified air of the Rockefeller family, playing increasingly major roles in the philanthropic world. Jerry was active in Open Space Institute and Literacy Volunteers, where he furthered his interests in the environment and education.

Whenever Elizabeth traveled, which was not infrequently, she either tried to do so with him or, if without him, she phoned him every day. And she would often discover that he had been up most of the night watching old movies. He was unsettled when she was away, unable to rest. When she would return, he was far more comfortable and he would sleep at night.

Another problem in their lives was Jerry's health. He had long been a heavy smoker. The first butt was lit with coffee in the morning and the habit continued until bedtime. He was well aware of the danger, of course, and knew he should quit. Elizabeth never complained about his smoking or nagged him about quitting. She figured that if he wanted to quit badly enough, he would.

One New Year's Eve, when Jerry was in his mid-sixties, he and Elizabeth dined at the apartment of friends. Throughout the evening he never stopped smoking. "The next morning, New Year's Day, I said to Jerry, 'I'll get your cigs.' 'Oh,' he said, 'didn't I tell you? I'm not smoking anymore?' And he never had another cigarette."

Elizabeth was a woman of immense strength, but not about any illness or malady affecting Jerry. When Jerry had his back surgery, they agreed that she would not go to visit him until the third or fourth post-operative day," recalls George, "because the idea of seeing him in pain was intolerable to her. And so on the third or fourth day, I took her to the hospital, and I went with her to Jerry's room, and he was still obviously in considerable discomfort, and she walked in and she saw his face and bang, like that, she passed out. Just like that. I mean instantaneous. She ended up on the floor. And I knelt down alongside her and felt her pulse and felt her forehead and you know she is going to come to, and she did come to in a few minutes. And when she did, I was laughing. And she said, 'What's so goddamn funny?'" George laughs heartily. "She is not good with illness."

Nan believes her father was determined not to go near the subject of his own mortality for Elizabeth's sake. When a tumor was discovered in Jerry's colon, George McCormack knew about it because Jerry consulted him on medical issues, but they kept the news from Elizabeth. "He was going to have it removed ten days hence and he didn't tell Elizabeth about it until the night before he was going in the hospital, because he said it would have been ten days of anguish," says George. "So the night before, he told her, and he said, we sat on our couch and she had her head on his shoulder and she cried for three hours."

When someone else died—a friend of Nan's mother's—Nan recalls Jerry saying, "'Dying is excruciating. It's terrorizing.' He hated the idea of dying. He always had this thing growing up, where he said, 'I don't believe there's a God. I don't believe in an afterlife.' It's a little like Woody Allen, who says, 'I don't believe in an afterlife, but I'm taking my underwear with me just in case.' Jerry was very realistic in his view of death, that there was nothing afterwards, but then he'd make a joke like, 'Who knows? Maybe I'll be surprised.'

Elizabeth, though, could not help but raise the issue sometimes. "I used to say to Jerry, 'What worries me is I am becoming totally dependent on you.' When we were going to be married I used to say that to him all the time. He was five years older, had been a big smoker. I knew I would outlive him, and I said, 'You know I am able to function by myself but I may not be able to,' and he said, 'Don't be crazy, of course you will be able to.'" But Elizabeth wasn't at all sure how Jerry would do if she were to die first. "He was no good without me," she says. "It would have been harder for him for me to die first and he always said that and he was right."

.   .   .

Jerry's health steadily deteriorated. In 2004, he was diagnosed with liver cancer and required surgery. The prognosis was grim. Jerry was anxious and depressed and Nan's husband, Bernard Arons, who is a psychiatrist, suggested medication to help calm Jerry a bit, to ease his anxiety. "I said to Jerry, 'Bernie's ready to get that. It would be good for depression.' And Jerry said to me, 'That's for depression when everything is fine and you get depressed. I've got a goddamn good reason to be depressed. No pill is going to do anything.'"

They heard about another treatment, experimental in nature, that sounded as though it might hold some promise. Elizabeth researched it on the Internet and the information she found indicated that the treatment was accompanied by horrific side effects. She printed the information out and gave it to Jerry.

"I said you must read this and make a decision because no one has told us that this is a cure. He read it and he said, 'No, you are right. I am not going to do it.'"

"There is nothing else to be done."

"That was an awful moment because it was over," she says.

Though Jerry was gravely ill, Elizabeth cared for him herself. But she could now see that she very much needed help.

Their friend Ed Kline recommended a nurse who was a wonderful cook. The plan was for Aset Chadayeva to come over on Saturday night and cook a meal, but on Friday evening Jerry suddenly got very weak. Elizabeth phoned Aset and asked if she could come over right away. She was at the movies but left at once and was soon at the apartment. She cared for Jerry that night and the next day, and Jerry learned that she was friends with the Klines and assumed, because of their Russian connections, that she was Russian.

"And she said, 'No, I'm Chechen,' and he said, 'Then you must be a Muslim.' He was very smart, and she said, 'Yes I am a Muslim.' And of course he was Jewish, and she said, 'Is that okay with you?' And he said, 'It is fine. I like you.'

"And I called a hospice on Sunday, the Fourth of July, and they said they would come Monday morning. So this hospice nurse came and said, 'Has he a living will?' and I said 'Of course' and she went in to talk to him.

"On Monday morning she said to me, 'I think he will die today.' I said, *'What?'* She said, 'I am not sure but I think he will.'"

Elizabeth called family members and relayed what the nurse had said. "Nan was in Washington and said, 'Dad bounces back.' I said, 'Nan, I am not telling you what I think. This is his nurse and they know what they are talking about.' She said, 'We will come.'" Nan and her husband traveled from Washington, as did Nan's brother Peter, while Mark boarded a plane in Oregon. The youngest, Betsy, was already there.

"I went in to him when the hospice nurse left," remembers Elizabeth, "and I leaned over and I said, 'Jerry, you know I love you.' And he said, 'And of course I love you.' He never said another word. He was dead three hours later."

.　　.　　.

Jerry was buried two days later in the family plot in Philadelphia. It was the worst of times for Elizabeth, of course, but she was thankful that the end had not dragged on for months with Jerry suffering. She was grateful for the swiftness of it. For his comfort and peace. "I'm not for these long deaths," says Elizabeth. "I mean, he had dinner on Sunday and he was dead by Monday."

When they returned to New York from Philadelphia, Jerry's children stayed with her for a few nights. The day Jerry died his family was with him. His granddaughter, Emma, sat with him for several hours as he gradually lost consciousness, and Elizabeth says, "I will always have a special bond with her for that." By Friday, Peter, Nan, Mark, and Betsy had to return to their homes. Kate Stich, Jerry's assistant, and her friend Martin Bieniek stayed over with Elizabeth the Friday and Saturday nights after his death. Elizabeth barely knew Kate and Martin (they later married), and recalls an anecdote when "one day after Kate arrived and I happened to be home, she said in surprise: 'Oh, are you going to be with us today?' Jerry enjoyed that question. From that day to the present, Kate and Martin have become a second family for me."

By Sunday Elizabeth knew she had to face the new reality of her life alone. "Of course I couldn't stop crying, which was awful but I decided right then that I will stay here for a week but then I am going back to the office because I cannot give up and so I must keep going."

But, of course, in the process of keeping going, there are moments, reminders that are a kind of energy field that strike with unseen power—particularly music. "Music is amazingly difficult," says Elizabeth. "The New Year's Eve after he died I went to a friend's house and there was a guy who began playing the piano just before midnight with love songs and I went out of the living room and this man followed me and he said, 'The woman I have lived with for ten years just died. We cannot stay in that room.' And I said, 'No we can't.'"

She still misses him terribly. "Jerry was not only wonderful and supportive but he was fun," she says. "I was so lucky to have him and for 27 years." The love they found with one another was precious, and as Elizabeth says: "We never took it for granted."

Jerry's death was the worst loss Elizabeth ever suffered. But after his death, there was another loss: the failure of faith to provide any solace.

"No help at all," she says, regretfully. "None. Zero. Because by that time—and I don't know how much you should write of this because it would shock people. I don't believe in an afterlife and that is the only way faith could help me . . . if I thought this was temporary. I mean I think the hardest thing about the death of someone you love is the finality of it.

"How would faith have been helpful?" she asks. "It would have been very helpful if I could have believed that I would eventually see Jerry again."

So, she is asked, you believe that when the lights go out, the lights go out? Yes, she replies.

she says. "I believe that they are going to be known in the history of this country as probably the greatest philanthropic family. Why? They used money for institution building. Institutions will change; they will evolve but they will continue to have impact. They are not ephemeral. The Rockefellers, more than other families, have not been distracted by money. As children, they gave dimes away. They were taught philanthropy." While they were very rich, Elizabeth learned quite quickly that the Rockefellers' "values were always human values, not materialistic ones."

. . .

The Rockefeller Brothers Fund is a foundation established for the five sons of John D. Rockefeller, Jr. The brothers—John D. 3rd, Nelson, Laurance, Winthrop, and David—along with their sister Abby Rockefeller Mauzé—constituted the third generation of the Rockefeller family.

"They each did something pretty outstanding with their lives," says Elizabeth. "Nelson was governor and vice president. Laurance was one of the first venture capitalists. David was CEO of the Chase Bank and an investor. Winthrop was the governor of Arkansas. *They did things.* John, the oldest of them, never was a businessman of any kind, but he was a great philanthropist and his philanthropy was his business. He was in his office, which was near my office, nine to five every day."

There was a distinctive character to their sense of philanthropy. William Dietel, who served as president of the Rockefeller Brothers Fund (and who hired Elizabeth), says an important inheritance to the brothers was their father's idea that simply giving away money was insufficient. "They gave away their time, they gave away their experience, their network of contacts," says Dietel. They became active participants in the organizations to which they contributed—serving on boards, attending the meetings, actively engaging in the issues and challenges. "*They worked at it,*" says Dietel.

Rockefellers

ELIZABETH KNEW ENOUGH about the Rockefellers and their history to admire what they had accomplished individually and collectively. The family's contributions to American life were everywhere: Acadia and Grand Teton National Parks; Spelman College; the University of Chicago; Rockefeller University; Lincoln Center for the Performing Arts; Rockefeller Center; the Museum of Modern Art; Colonial Williamsburg; the United Nations (they donated the land for the headquarters), and so much more.

"You have the first Mr. Rockefeller, Standard Oil, then you have his son Junior, who wasn't apparently that kind of a person at all," she says. "He created Rockefeller Center. Then you have the brothers and large money for philanthropy. Someone told me that John D. Rockefeller, the first, the founder, had a larger percentage of GNP than Bill Gates has now."

From the start, she was deeply impressed with the Rockefellers and their impact on the world of philanthropy. "They created *institutions*,"

The 56th floor of 30 Rockefeller Plaza was the family floor, the brothers' floor. This was a world unto itself. Suite 5600 at 30 Rock, known simply as 5600 among the family and staff, was the nerve center of the Rockefeller philanthropic empire. It contained dozens of offices, many with breathtaking views of the Manhattan skyline and the New York and New Jersey countryside. And the walls of the long hallways were lined with some of the finest art in the world—from Matisse to de Kooning.

"Since they were all Rockefellers, the brothers were called Mr. John, Mr. David, Mr. Nelson, Mr. Laurance, and the story is that Bayard Rustin, the African-American civil rights leader, arrived one day and the receptionist said, 'Do you want to see Mr. John, Mr. David, Mr. Nelson, or Mr. Laurance?' And Bayard Rustin said, 'I thought this was a *foundation,* not a *plantation.'"* After recounting the anecdote, Elizabeth laughs and wonders aloud, "I wonder if that ever really happened."

The fourth Rockefeller generation—the twenty-two children of the brothers and Abby—is known as "the cousins." And it was the coming of age of the cousins' generation that created challenges that Elizabeth was hired to advise. The world was changing and, perhaps more to the point, the culture in America and beyond was changing in a fundamental way. Many of the cousins chafed at their parents' culture and traditions. Most of the female Rockefeller cousins changed their names to try to distance themselves from the Rockefeller name.

"There was a period in the 1970s when to be the child of a Rockefeller was a burden," says Richard Lanier, an advisor in the Rockefeller Family office. "There were questions of identity: Who am I? What is expected of me? What should I do?"

The Rockefellers believed Elizabeth was the right person to relate to the cousins' generation. This was a time of extraordinary cultural turmoil in the United States, and Elizabeth had demonstrated—as an educator and college president—an impressive ability to relate to younger people in a thoughtful way. That was a skill the brothers and the administrators of the Brothers' Fund needed.

Elizabeth proved to be a comfortable fit with the generation of cousins who came of age in the 1960s and 1970s. Many were very bright, accomplished academically, and active in the central political causes of the time, including the movements on behalf of civil rights, the environment, women's rights, and against the war in Vietnam. Elizabeth was a liberal thinker, an educator who had been on the front lines dealing with the seismic cultural changes of the time.

In 1974, the members of the cousins' generation ranged in age from the early twenties to the early forties. Many were at key points in their careers, striving to establish professional identities and to determine the precise course of their philanthropic endeavors. When Elizabeth arrived at 30 Rock, Steven Rockefeller, son of Nelson and among the oldest of the cousins' generation, was thirty-eight. He had earned degrees from Princeton (BA), the Union Theological Seminary (MDiv), and a PhD in the philosophy of religion from Columbia. He went on to become a professor of religion at Middlebury College. David Rockefeller Jr. was thirty-three at the time and had graduated from Harvard and Harvard Law School. After law school he worked for the Boston Symphony Orchestra and served on the board of the National Endowment for the Arts. Jay Rockefeller was thirty-seven and had an undergraduate degree from Harvard in Far Eastern Languages. After college he joined the Peace Corps and Vista Volunteers. At the other end of the cousins' generation was Eileen Rockefeller Growald, who was twenty-two when Elizabeth McCormack arrived at 30 Rock. Eileen received a BA from Middlebury College and an MA in Early Childhood Education at Lesley College in Cambridge, Massachusetts. Her older sister Peggy Dulany, twenty-seven, graduated from Harvard and earned an EdD from the Harvard graduate school of Education.

Elizabeth's job was to help to guide the cousins' generation into and through the world of philanthropy. She was also charged with setting up an office especially for them. "The idea was to establish a philanthropic office for the Rockefeller family members to use if they wished for philanthropic advice and for charitable trusts, but they wanted to be sure that I could relate to a younger generation before I began that job," she says. "So the first two years I was a staff member at the Rockefeller Brothers Fund getting to know the family, learning more about philanthropy.

"For people of inherited wealth who came out of the Vietnam War era, to be part of the establishment was a curse," says Elizabeth. "They were ashamed of being Rockefellers. It was the anti-establishment era during and after Vietnam. As I learned to know them they began talking to me negatively about their parents and I said to them, to each one of them, 'You know, that is so boring. Everyone your age is doing that—everyone. Let's talk about something else. Sure you are angry at them, sure they don't understand you, sure, sure, sure. Okay, now what should we talk about?'"

She liked the cousins right away. She recognized them instantly, for she had just been in the presence of people like them at Manhattanville. "It was the Vietnam War era and they had the same sentiment, same approaches, most of them, as Manhattanville students," she says. The cousins were sometimes portrayed as radicals, but she says that was not at all the case. "They were children of their times," she says.

.　　.　　.

Steven Rockefeller recalled the initial meeting between Elizabeth and the cousins. It took place during the cousins' semi-annual gathering at Pocantico, the family's vast estate in North Tarrytown, New York, in June 1974. "She met with all of us in the living room where the cousins gathered every June—semi-annual meeting," Steven recalled. "And Elizabeth conducted a wonderful conversation with all of us, and I think she demonstrated, number one, that she understood the social, political, and economic situation of the nation and was someone who readily understood the way many of us felt about the war, about human and civil rights, about the feminist movement and other major currents of social affairs in this country. And she won the confidence of everybody. I think she also demonstrated that she was a very smart, highly competent person with the administrative and organizational skills to manage the department superbly. So I think that she impressed everybody in terms of her interpersonal skills. She's quiet. She's direct. She is not threatening in any way, which is very important. In other words, she didn't come in like a very imposing, grand figure who was going to be intimidating."

This was important, says Steven, because "there was a reaction in the sixties and seventies on the part of many cousins to being managed by a group of professionals at 5600 who were basically the appointees of their parents, and so there was a . . . concern. The cousins did not want a person that anyone in the group was going to feel was intimidating. Elizabeth is remarkable because on the one hand, she has all the ability and confidence of any other member in the Rockefeller world of associates and advisors, but she is low key. She is quiet and thoughtful and does not come across in any way, shape or form as an intimidating kind of personality."

"They were just a little older, most of them, than the students that I had been dealing with at Manhattanville," Elizabeth says. People said to her before the meeting that she might find them difficult, that they were very liberal, even radical. "People thought they were because they were a younger generation. So at that meeting I found that I liked them. They asked me a lot of questions. They weren't antagonistic. They were not threatening. It was a lovely meeting."

After the meeting, one of the cousins said to her: "In this family no one confronts anyone about anything. They disagree, they pass it over. You are going to find that difficult." But, Elizabeth says, "I didn't find it difficult but it was absolutely true. They can disagree but it is all very civilized and they don't confront one another. You know I have come to know quite a few wealthy families of all kinds and they are very different. There are no family fights among the Rockefellers. That is a very good thing."

Elizabeth's first assignment, in collaboration with Bill Dietel, was to evaluate West Virginia Wesleyan University, which had offered Jay Rockefeller, JDR 3rd's son, the position of president. Jay was living in West Virginia, where he had just lost a race for public office, and he was looking for a new position that would enable him to remain in West Virginia and build a platform for a future run for office. Elizabeth and two others visited the college, and she returned with an evaluation of the situation.

She was direct. She told Jay that he and the college were not a good fit. It had many needs, but he didn't know anything about running a college. A week later Jay phoned Elizabeth and said he wanted to stay in West Virginia and that he was going to take the job.

"I think we were very naïve about the politics," says Bill Dietel. "We really didn't understand that this was a leg-up. He had lost the election, he needed a base of operations and he needed to show he was going to stay in West Virginia. They all started accusing him of being a carpetbagger."

But it worked out well. Jay soon was elected governor and, subsequently, United States Senator.

Annually, each member of the cousins' generation was given what was known within the family as the Blue Book, which detailed several years of their personal giving—money the individual cousin donated to a variety of causes—money other than that given by the Foundation or any other Rockefeller-related entity. Elizabeth began a series of individual meetings with the cousins to discuss their personal philanthropic priorities and goals.

"I studied the Blue Book before I met with each one of them," she recalls, "and I would say, 'I have studied your last few years of philanthropy and I think I understand what you have given. These are your primary interests and you think you can achieve these goals in this way.' Nine times out of ten they would say, 'That is not my primary interest.' Then I would say, 'Well, then you are not giving correctly.' 'Well, I give because people ask me to.' 'Okay, so let's put some kind of order in this. You should decide how much you are able to give every year. Whatever it is, decide that a certain amount of that will be reaction to your friends who say, 'I have gotten very interested in this. Will you contribute to it?' An amount every year that you will give in this way and when you have given that amount you say, 'My budget is finished. I give that much to my friends, to their interests but most of what I do has to do with my interests.'"

Fairly often, cousins changed their approach to giving as a result of conversations with Elizabeth. But she knew, going into the job, that she would never bat a thousand. "When your work is advising, it is very important, I believe, that you give the advice that you think is right, is sound, but you know that it won't always be taken and that doesn't matter. If your aim is to get your advice taken, then you don't give good advice." If that is your aim, she says, you will then tell someone what he or she wants to hear.

She spent two years on the staff of the Rockefeller Brothers Fund, from 1974 to 1976. Then she established and headed the Rockefeller Family Philanthropic Office, whose mission was to provide thoughtful advice to family members on their personal philanthropy. Forming the Family Philanthropic Office was a relatively simple matter: Elizabeth identified some talented people, hired them, and set them up as advisors to the cousins. The office described Elizabeth's duties as including "management of the philanthropic office; oversight of program areas and recommendations; special responsibilities for the following program areas: education, arts and culture, world religions, international issues; representation of the family at various philanthropic meetings; and meetings with persons and organizations seeking family support."

. . .

The Rockefeller brothers had long been interested in conservation, which is an essential element within the environmental movement. But that movement was rapidly evolving, and newer, much more aggressive environmental organizations were forming. Founded in 1967, the Natural Resources Defense Council's (NRDC) mission was to litigate when environmental laws were broken. This newer, more aggressive approach to the environment was greeted with enthusiasm by a number of the cousins. And some of the cousins got involved at the front lines. Laurance Rockefeller's son Larry became an attorney and went to work at NRDC.

"It became very clear to me early on that there are many ways one could support the environment depending on temperament," says Elizabeth. "One is conservation and the donor might then give to the Audubon Society. Education is another. One might then find projects in schools which teach particularly very young children about protecting the environment, and then an NRDC type which litigates to protect the environment. I found in those years that that fourth generation of Rockefellers was interested in the environment, so my work was to find appropriate institutions in the different areas, conservation, education, and litigation, to which they could contribute. These were the early years of NRDC and the cousins played a role in making it the strong institution it is today."

The cousins had had far less wealth than the brothers' generation, yet they still had access collectively to hundreds of millions of dollars. And they also—at least many of them—had the Rockefeller name, and Elizabeth clearly saw this as an important asset in leveraging additional donations.

"Their giving was more influential than the amounts of money they gave," she says.

The cousins were "profoundly impressed with Elizabeth as a person and a human being," says Steven. "Many of the cousins were involved in a religious or spiritual search in their own way, and it took many, many different forms. And with the 1960s and moving into the 1970s, there was a new interest in Eastern religions and meditation and mysticism which had regenerated interest in Jewish Christian monasticism and contemplative prayer and so forth, and the cousins were all in touch with that. The other thing is that the cousins were actively trying to eliminate in their dealings with each other any elements of gender inequality and were certainly very aware of the international and national women's movement and for the most part, very supportive of it. So the idea of having a woman coming in to take over a major office of the family was something that appealed to all of us."

At the same time, says Steven, Elizabeth is a rock-solid personality whose ego does not intrude.

"Elizabeth is steel," says Steven. "She's just made of steel. She has the quickest intellect in terms of forming judgments of any person I know. Elizabeth is not a person who likes to mull decisions or issues for a long time, and she combines both the capacity for rigorous analysis with a marvelous intuitive ability, and she makes judgments and decisions very quickly."

Different family members relied upon Elizabeth for different things. "I certainly relied heavily on Elizabeth for advice in philanthropy," says Steven, "and I'm sure I talked with her about personal decisions and boards and all that kind of thing. However, I know that some members of the family turned to Elizabeth for guidance in a lot of areas. . . . She'll tell you the truth—what she thinks."

Bill Dietel believes a key reason Elizabeth was successful with the cousins was because "she is a very, very good listener. And she heard these kids. She also came in with the reputation of having been a rebel. I mean, she took Manhattanville and absolutely turned it around. Well, that generation loved that."

Peggy Dulany, a daughter of David, recalled that Elizabeth "really valued what we wanted to do and what we believed in . . . and in those somewhat fragile years of the seventies . . . to have an adult in a responsible position really affirming the values with regard to philanthropy that we were making and encouraging us to do it better and more and use our leverage, not just our dollars, was a pretty big thing."

Elizabeth played a role in a particularly sensitive area within the family—solicitation of one family member by another to donate to a particular cause.

"The general policy is you don't solicit another family member unless they've given you permission to do it," says Steven. "They turned to the Philanthropy Department to kind of mediate that, and procedures were set up so that if some member of the family was deeply engaged in some board and institution and thought other members of the family would be interested, Elizabeth would go to them and say, 'Your cousin is doing this, and they need a little extra money, and this is a good cause. If you're not interested, just tell me, and that's the end of it.' And the cousins, then, don't have to talk to each other about it . . . so that I don't have to write a letter to my sister and have to go through the whole thing about this is a wonderful project, but. . . . You just say to Elizabeth, 'I'm not interested,' and that's the end of it.

"If you don't do this, what happens is that at every social occasion, all family members are pulling each other aside and asking for money, and the whole event is ruined, basically. It becomes a big solicitation. And then, you see, the brothers didn't do this, and the cousins learned from the brothers because in the RBF, when it was first set up as the Rockefeller Brothers Fund, there was sort of an unwritten rule that everybody got a piece of the pie. Part of what caused the tension between Father [Nelson] and John was the fighting over this pot and who got what. So it became very important for our generation not to let philanthropy and fundraising become an issue among us."

.   .   .

Elizabeth developed a particular fondness for JDR 3rd. He was shy, she says, "reflective, serious, and quite intelligent. His whole life had been philanthropy and he did what major philanthropists have to do if they are to do a good job and learned about, in depth, the areas in which he was going to give money." He had a broad portfolio of interests including Asia, cultural exchange, agricultural exchange, women's issues, and much more. He believed deeply in the power of bringing people together and enabling them to learn from one another, and he was passionate about working to have the United States and Asia understand one another.

"He was very active in revitalizing the Japan Society after the war," says Elizabeth. "He went to Japan after the war and said he wanted to meet Japanese people and was staying at the Imperial Hotel, and he said, 'I want a suite because I want to visit with Japanese friends,' and Japanese were not allowed in a hotel to go above a certain floor. This was right after the war. So he said, 'well, make it a suite on whatever floor they can visit, and so he became a friend of the Japanese."

Elizabeth arrived at the Rockefellers in 1974 and JDR 3rd died four years later. During that time she came to know him well. She worked with him on two of the organizations most important to him—the Population Council, which he created, and the Asian Cultural Exchange Program. "JDR chose what area he was going to discuss with each advisor, and he talked to me about his family—[about] his children because they were ones I had gotten to know, the fourth generation, the cousins, Sandra, Jay, Hope, and Alida."

One time he sat down with her and sought her counsel on a particular donation that Nelson wanted the Rockefeller Brothers Fund to make. "JDR had a very clear idea of what the Rockefeller Brothers' Fund was," she says. "It was a foundation with programs and a staff, *not* a pot of money to be given away at the whim of the brothers, and Nelson wanted to give money to a Dr. Ryland who was an osteopath. JDR 3rd was totally opposed to it, not because of what it was, but it was not a program of the Brothers Fund. It was of interest to one brother, Nelson. So John talked to me about this and I said, 'JDR, Nelson wants this. He is going to get it. Don't fight him. He is a better fighter. He is a politician. Don't fight him. It isn't that important.'"

Some time passed and late one night she received a phone call. "I was all alone in my little rented apartment, 11:30 at night I get a call. I think something has happened to somebody. I say, 'Hello.'

"'This is John Rockefeller. I lost.'

"I said, 'Oh.'

"He said, 'You told me not to fight him.'

"I said, 'Now that you've done it, it was a good fight, and it's only money.'

"He said, 'What?'

"I said, 'That's all it is. It's only money. Go to bed. Go to sleep. Forget it and it was a good fight.'

"He said, 'But you knew I'd lose.'

"I said, 'Yeah. Nelson wasn't the governor and vice president for nothing.'"

.   .   .

A decision reached by the brothers—in which Elizabeth would become involved—was to donate half of the assets of the Rockefeller Brothers Fund to philanthropic organizations the family had long supported. This grants program was known as the Creel Committee after Dana Creel, who was president of RBF at the time. Hundreds of millions of dollars were at stake, and the funds would be distributed on the recommendation of the three brothers most directly involved—JDR 3rd, David, and Laurance (Winthrop had died in 1973).

"They were all getting older and the younger generation was becoming prominent on the board of the Brothers Fund and they had different interests from their parents," says Elizabeth. "Thus, the brothers decided on the strategy of giving half the money away. In doing so, they would target major institutions and organizations that had enjoyed longstanding Rockefeller support. The gifts would be major—extremely large in some cases—and in some cases the gifts would come with the message that this was the end of major Rockefeller funding."

While JDR, David, and Laurance worked to try to figure out where the money should go, Nelson was "the odd man out," as Dietel puts it. As governor and then vice president, Nelson had his hands full. Nelson had been appointed vice president by Gerald Ford, who had been vice president under Richard Nixon and became president after Nixon's resignation. But for his 1976 presidential campaign, Ford instead chose Sen. Robert Dole of Kansas to run with him.

"The minute Jerry Ford dumps him, Nelson comes back to New York and he's really the proverbial bull in the china shop," says Dietel. "He can't wait to get his hands on all the levers of power in every area of the family. Which brings him into conflict with John and David."

Laurance was supportive of Nelson. "Laurance was his best friend," says Dietel. "They were very, very close. Laurance got Nelson out of scrapes again and again and again.

"Nelson returns, tries to take over and run the family show and all of a sudden here is this pot of money he sees as belonging to the brothers and he believes it should be divided equally into four shares among them."

But JDR 3rd had very different ideas. He did not think of the funds as being assigned to individual brothers to allocate as they wished, but rather as a pool of funds for the family to think about allocating in a thoughtful and strategic way. And because Elizabeth was close to JDR—in fact she served as his senior advisor on philanthropy—she was drawn into the conflict with Nelson.

"So Elizabeth did cross swords with Nelson but it was on behalf of trying to defend John's views," says Dietel. "Elizabeth admired John and Blanchette, she liked the children and she began to think that Nelson was really hustling Johnny. And so she begins to resist this." Nelson recognized Elizabeth's skills. He once said that "there are three politicians in this office: me, Dietel and Elizabeth."

Steven Rockefeller believes that when his father returned to New York "he was interested in re-establishing himself in the position of major leadership of the family. And for whatever reason he saw Elizabeth as somebody with an independent mind who was deeply engaged with the cousins and understood them and supported them in many ways. I think he didn't think that Elizabeth was going to be one of his soldiers. And Nelson's approach in many ways was: 'You're either with me or against me, and I want people who are absolutely loyal.' And I think that he saw in Elizabeth someone who was very smart, tough, and clear in her mind about matters and that she was not going to be someone to whom he could say, 'Elizabeth, I want you to get control of X,' and she was going to just do what he said. So . . . there was tension between them, and I don't know what exchanges they had, but there was a meeting between the brothers and the cousins, and it was the only one that ever occurred. It was formally a meeting of the brothers and the cousins . . . and one of the [agenda items] was the cousins communicating to my father that he could not let Elizabeth McCormack go—that we wanted her to continue as the director of the Philanthropy Department, and he didn't push that . . . that if there was any thought being given to letting Elizabeth go, this was not acceptable to us, and we wanted her to stay and that settled the matter."

Elizabeth was asked to persuade Nelson Rockefeller to speak at a dinner meeting of the NAACP, and she told him that his presence would be positive not only for the organization but for him as well. He had recently returned to New York from Washington and his appearance before the NAACP would serve as a kind of re-entry into the not-for-profit world.

"I made my request and added, 'Personally I do not care whether you accept my recommendation.' He replied: 'Really?' And I answered, 'Really.' He then said, 'You are the only person at 5600 who does not mind if a recommendation is not taken.' I asked him why he thought that this was true and he said: 'Because you did harder things before you came to work for the Rockefeller Family.' And he was right."

.   .   .

A tragic moment came in 1978 when John D. Rockefeller 3rd died in an automobile accident. He was seventy-three. After his death, the question was what to do about the projects he had funded through a personal funding mechanism called the JDR 3rd Fund, which did not have an endowment. JDR would fund it from his own wealth, usually to the tune of $10 million annually.

The task of sorting out what to do in the wake of his death would prove immensely challenging. Many people helped out over time, but the work was led, right from the start, by Elizabeth and Richard Lanier. Lanier had worked for JDR 3rd on many issues since 1972 and had a deep knowledge of JDR's interests and vision.

"When he died the question became what to do with some of the philanthropies he contributed to annually," says Lanier. "His m.o. was to get a program started or help to do so and fund it annually with un-restricted money. Every year he would write a check for the program— for the JDR 3rd Fund. It supported agricultural development internationally, the Asia Society, the Pop Council." But after his death, says Lanier, "there was no provision for ongoing support" for any of these organizations—"other than a $2 million reserve fund we used as the beginning of a little endowment."

Before JDR's death, Elizabeth and Lanier knew one another, though not well. JDR's death brought them into a close working relationship that lasted for years. They had to face a number of questions. "Since the JDR 3rd Fund had been funded annually, should we put it to bed

and let it go out of business?" says Lanier. "Should we find another organization to place it under? Or should we set it up and go it alone? A
lot of people said it's done, let it die and we began looking around to
see what institutions we might affiliate with."

There were three major programs JDR had been funding. "One
was Arts and Education, and the woman who ran that was retiring so
that was discontinued," says Elizabeth. "The second was a program of
awards for very bright young people going into public service rather
than making money; public service awards administered by Princeton.
I looked into it, and the JDR 3rd Fund was paying Princeton more to
administer this than the grants. So I went to see the president at Princeton and I said, 'We're closing it down. The foundation is finished.' He
said, 'It's a great program.' I said, 'It is, but it's finished.'"

The third program JDR had been funding was the Asian Cultural
Exchange Program, later known as the Asian Cultural Council. This
was something that had been particularly important to JDR, and everyone close to him knew that. It had to be maintained. It was remarkably
simple in its conception. The program identified young people from
Asia with a particular talent in music, dance, or theater, and brought
them to the United States, usually New York—and U.S. citizens were
sent to Asia—to connect with others in their field, to learn and grow.
Grants were from six months to a year, and the program made sure that
grantees had whatever they needed.

Elizabeth worked closely with Lanier as well as with JDR's family,
and they raised enough money to keep the JDR 3rd Fund going. They
raised some from Rockefeller family members and from foundations
including Starr and AIG foundations, and from a very wealthy and generous anonymous donor in Tokyo.

Like JDR 3rd, Elizabeth believed passionately in the Asian Cultural
Council's mission. "I think it is very important," she says. "First of
all, what it isn't: It's not about big groups. It brings individuals and we
have a special IRS ruling that we can give grants to individuals and so

American individuals go to Asia, Asians come here. We have offices in Taiwan, Hong Kong, Tokyo, and the Philippines, little offices and we do not simply give away money, we program the people, get them to meet the right people, for example, director of a symphony from Taiwan spends time with conductors in this country. It is my belief that the way to bring the world together is not diplomacy. God knows it is not war. It's to bring individuals together whose common interests go beyond their differences, so people in the arts are at home with one another no matter what country they come from." Through the years, there have been more than 6,000 such exchanges. The positive contribution to world understanding and peace is perhaps small and certainly not measurable, but JDR believed deeply in its efficacy and Elizabeth shares that belief.

Traveling in Asia Elizabeth frequently hears from people who proudly proclaim that they were JDR 3rd fellows. "When we travel in Asia and we say we are from the Asian Cultural Council, people say, 'Oh, I was an ACC grantee' or 'I was JDR 3rd fund grantee.' This recognition includes museum directors, actors, dancers and when you talk with them they say, 'it changed my life. I knew nothing except what it was like to be Taiwanese and I learned what it was like to be an American.'"

.   .   .

Elizabeth believes that JDR 3rd changed the field of population studies. He had delved deeply into the population issue through the Population Council, which he had founded and funded. He had been invited to address the 1974 UN conference on population in Bucharest well in advance and he and his staff, especially Joan Dunlop, put a good deal of thought and effort into his remarks. He took full advantage of the opportunity of having a large international audience. In his speech, he stressed the need to shift the focus from birth control and family planning to the education of women. "JDR argued that it was often not in the self-interest of women to have many children—for emotional and practical reasons," says Elizabeth. "And because of who he was he was listened to."

Not long after JDR's death, the president of the Population Council called Elizabeth and asked her to serve on the board, as he put it, "to hold a place for a Rockefeller." Elizabeth readily agreed. Her expectation was that a Rockefeller family member would be recruited to serve and she would then quietly exit. And while there were family members who served on the Population Council board at various times through the years, Elizabeth's tenure stretched out over nearly three decades.

Many years later, after Elizabeth had left the board, she was asked to return. McGeorge Bundy, national security advisor under Presidents Kennedy and Johnson, was chairman and not well. "You know, Mac really has to step down," a fellow board member told Elizabeth. "He shouldn't continue as chairman and he knows that but every name we suggest to replace him does not satisfy him, so would you come back on the board as vice chairman to help him to find someone to replace him?"

Elizabeth agreed, but she wanted to make sure Mac was comfortable with the idea. She said she would return if Mac himself asked her. She arrived at her office one day soon after and found a phone message from him, but when she returned his call he did not remember why he had phoned her. "I said, 'Mac, I think it had something to do with my coming back on the board,' and he said, 'Elizabeth, now you know how much I need you.'"

McGeorge Bundy died soon after, and Elizabeth took over as chair of the board. She believed that the Population Council was doing truly important work. "The Population Council is a research organization comprised primarily of social scientists and then a small group of natural scientists, basic scientists, who develop various birth control devices," she says. "When we give them to a pharmaceutical company we do so with the agreement that they will be sold at low cost in the third world. So that is one side of it and the people who do that have their offices at Rockefeller University and they are scientists. When the social scientists do various social science studies in the third world, they have offices in many countries. What I think is important about it is that it is not studies simply for reports which then are read by other social scientists. They are social science reports *to influence policy* in countries."

And the model often works very well. Elizabeth and other board members frequently traveled to poorer nations where the Pop Council's work was focused. During a trip to Mexico she and Rodney Wagner, the Council board chairman, met with the Mexican minister of health, who mentioned the council's research and observed: "In this Catholic country that research helped get through the legislature birth control legislation."

.   .   .

As the years passed, Elizabeth served in a variety of roles for the Rockefeller family, including as a general advisor on an array of topics. An April 25, 1988, list of "Items for discussion with Laurance S. Rockefeller" is typical of her work:

Institute of Noetic Sciences
Historic Hudson Valley
Michael Murphy concerning Princeton's Philosophy Department
Pastoral institute of Grace cathedral
Institute for the Advancement of Health
Earlham College
Wainwright House
Jung Institute of SF
Tibet House
Herbert Benson

Elizabeth de Cuevas sculpture

Scott Jones

New School for Social Research

Gordon Conwell

Walter Burke

Asia Society

Elizabeth talked each item through with Laurance, and he did, in fact, provide some sort of funding for many of them. Historic Hudson Valley was an example of an organization that had enjoyed strong Rockefeller family support in large measure because family property bordered the Hudson. The Princeton Philosophy Department listing was a particular interest of Laurance's. "He graduated from Princeton and wanted to give them money and he did," she says. "He was the original funder of the Center for Human Values, which he envisioned having an important spiritual component."

Laurance was drawn to spiritual causes, and he liked the California Institute of Integral Studies because "it was dealing with east-west psychology, philosophy and religion—bringing them together, teaching them. He gave them several million dollars and asked me to be chairman of the board." The Institute for the Advancement of Health was founded by Laurance's niece, Eileen Growald, and he naturally contributed to that. "Many things Laurance contributed to were a little fringy," says Elizabeth. "And he knew they were but he was a venture capitalist and if he thought there was a little validity in these things he'd put money into them."

The Gordon Conwell Seminary, says Elizabeth, "was much too middle-of-the-road Protestant for him but his wife Mary loved it and she was on the board." Laurance was suspicious of organized religion, says Elizabeth. "We were at Union Theological School once and Laurance walked up to a group of faculty members and asked: 'In your opinion does religion divide or unite?' The faculty members were taken aback, but Elizabeth says Laurance strongly believed that organized religion was a divisive force in the world—organized religion as distinct from spirituality.

Laurance felt a spiritual kinship with Elizabeth, and during an interview he reflected on that. "Elizabeth and I have been spiritual partners on many things. . . . You might say that a spiritual influence and talent are desperately needed in a very secular world. . . . I have a concept of funds to enhance the human spirit and I couldn't have found a better ally than Elizabeth." He characterized her as "a major force" in his family as well as that of his brother John.

Laurance said that when Thornton Bradshaw was asked to become chair of the MacArthur he said he would do so, according to Laurance, "'provided Elizabeth McCormack goes with me because she knows about philanthropy.' So she goes out there . . . several years later he dies of a heart attack—so guess who becomes chairman?"

.   .   .

Sandra Ferry, a daughter of JDR 3rd, may not have wanted her name to be Rockefeller, but she possessed the classic Rockefeller sense for philanthropy. She contributed funds to many different causes and organizations, but she did more than that. She created a new organization called the Trust for Mutual Understanding, which is devoted to cultural exchange and environmental issues. Instead of giving money to individuals, the funds go to organizations, which in turn do the work of identifying grant recipients.

How anonymous was Sandra Ferry? She never attended a single board meeting of the organization she envisioned, founded, and sustained with her personal funds. She never went on a single trip with the organization. Elizabeth, however, knew Sandra took great pride in the work of the organization. Some years ago, during a gathering of grantees in the Czech Republic, individual recipients spoke extemporaneously about how much the experience had meant in their lives. In the midst of this, Elizabeth was so moved that she stood up and addressed them.

"You all know that the person who created this trust, that you are all so thankful for, wants to be anonymous," she said. "But let's pretend that her name is Sandra. And let's thank her—let's thank Sandra.' And they all stood up and applauded and when I phoned Sandra I said, 'I broke the rule. I used your first name.' She loved it." And for years after that, grant recipients would say to Elizabeth—having no idea who Sandra was—"Would you please thank Sandra for me?"

.   .   .

One oddity about the Rockefellers, which may apply to some other old-line wealthy families as well, is their inability to handle money in certain circumstances. For example, when Elizabeth first joined the Rockefellers, she had dinner with a member of the fourth generation of the family. "She called and said, 'We want to get to know you. Let's have dinner in New York. Get a restaurant and the three of us will have dinner. A good restaurant.'"

Elizabeth did so, and the appointed evening arrived. "We had a wonderful dinner, good conversation. The end of dinner the cousin gets the bill. He says, 'This is extremely expensive.' I said, 'Mr. Rockefeller, your wife said a good restaurant. This is a good restaurant.' He said, 'I don't have this kind of cash.' I said, 'It's okay, they will take a credit card.' 'I never carry a credit card.' I said, 'Have you got a check?' 'No.' I said, 'Mr. Rockefeller, I'll pay for dinner.' Which I did.

"The general principle is that people born to money don't understand money. They either are overly generous or they think just a little money is too much. They don't get it. When I get a bill in a restaurant, I look at the bottom line and I think that's about right. I never add it up, never. Most Rockefellers do. They add it up and they say, 'Did we really have . . . ?' Yeah, we did."

One theory, of course, is that people born to such wealth are taught early on that some people will try to take advantage of them. "I think one of the things that makes them suffer," says Elizabeth, "is that it is very hard for them to know who their friends are."

.　　.　　.

Blanchette Rockefeller, the wife of JDR 3rd, remained largely in the background while her husband was alive—"in John's shadow philanthropically," as Richard Lanier puts it. She was keenly interested in the Museum of Modern Art, but not much beyond that. But after her husband's death, says Lanier, "she began to come out into her own"—and Elizabeth played a pivotal role in helping her do so. "Elizabeth helped her with everything—dealing with the aftermath of John's death, invitations to events. She would ask Elizabeth, 'Should I do this or that?' and Elizabeth is quick on the draw and she would be able to make quick decisions. She wouldn't equivocate—'This is what you should do or what you shouldn't do.'"

Elizabeth got to know Blanchette particularly well during a trip to Japan after JDR's death. Their mission was personally to thank many people in Japan for all they had given to the Asia Society in his memory.

During the trip to Japan they were invited to tea by the nuns at Sacred Heart College in Tokyo. During the conversation Blanchette told the nuns: "You may think Elizabeth is doing very different things now, but, actually, she is doing what she has always done: teaching and instructing young people. The only difference is that now her students are all named Rockefeller."

They were two genuine, caring women operating in a man's world, says Lanier, and they got along beautifully. In time, says Lanier, Blanchette "blossomed. She became the center of attention when she would go to a museum opening or a cultural event. She was no longer on the arm of JDR 3rd and she was amused by some would-be suitors.

She was kind of girlish—full of life and energetic. And Elizabeth," says Lanier, "was her number one confidante, advisor, and friend. They traveled together. Blanchette and Elizabeth and Jerry took vacations together and Jerry was very good with Blanchette. She had led a life of such great privilege and she would ask, 'How much do you tip the bellboy?'"

Blanchette suffered from dementia in later years and declined rapidly. She died on November 29, 1992. Elizabeth remained close to her to the end. Three months after her death, Elizabeth received a letter from Senator Jay Rockefeller. He wrote that Blanchette had set aside a trust for the benefit of "individuals who had been closely associated with her during her life." Jay noted that a gift to Elizabeth from the trust—the check was enclosed—amounted to $300,000. The letter concluded with "Sincerely yours," but Jay crossed that out and wrote "Love." He added a handwritten P.S. "You *are* a saint. Jay."

.　　　.　　　.

In 1988, at age sixty-six, Elizabeth officially retired from her position with the Rockefellers. An article in the *New York Times* noted that she had "advised three generations of Rockefellers about their charitable interests."

Many Rockefellers wrote her notes of gratitude. David and Laurence wrote. Members of the cousins' generation wrote, including John D. Rockefeller IV, Jay. In a handwritten note, he wrote:

> Dear Elizabeth, I care for you so much, and I am grateful to you for so many acts of help and wisdom that I am feeling very prideful that I had a small part in encouraging you to work at the office. . . . Elizabeth, you are one of a relatively few people I trust totally. Xeroxed Latin "dismissed" from the Vatican notwithstanding, you are glorious. Love, Jay

Writing from Middlebury College, Steven Rockefeller wrote:

> You have followed a path that has led you into the cloister and back out into the world. In the process you have succeeded in combining in a wonderfully creative fashion the religious spirit of self-discipline, clarity of mind and compassion with an active concern for the quality of everyday existence and the social institutions that so profoundly shape our lives. Our world hungers for your kind of integration of the spiritual and the secular.
>
> All of us in the family are deeply grateful to you for joining us as an associate at a critical time in our family history and nation's history. You built up our confidence as individuals and as a group and strengthened our sense of purpose.

Elizabeth had officially retired, but she continued working out of a Rockefeller Center office and counseling a number of the cousins. And she continued serving on more than a dozen boards. Approaching her ninetieth year, she still practices the art of philanthropy.

(11)

The Fine Art of Philanthropy

E LIZABETH MCCORMACK LEARNED the art of philanthropy from many sources, including the Rockefellers, of course, and particularly John D. Rockefeller 3rd. Her participation in the Filer Commission on Private Philanthropy and Public Needs also taught her a lot. The commission was formed in 1973 by JDR 3rd and the Treasury Secretary at that time, George P. Shultz, and a former Treasury Secretary, William E. Simon. Simon knew Elizabeth—his sisters had gone to Manhattanville—and he suggested that she be appointed a member.

"Before I accepted, I went to see JDR 3rd, who was funding the commission, and I said, 'I am ready to do this, but I want it understood by you that I am not going to have a Rockefeller position. I am going to have my own opinion. Is that okay?' He said, 'Of course.'" This did not prevent C. Douglas Dillon, yet another former Treasury Secretary and commission member, from accusing Elizabeth of being a mouthpiece for the Rockefellers. The Filer Commission provided Elizabeth with a strong, foundational understanding of American philanthropy before she started working for the Rockefellers. Thus, by the time she began her new job in 1974 she spoke the language.

She would also come to learn a great deal about philanthropy from Bill Dietel at the Rockefeller Brothers Fund and from William Bowen, president of Princeton and later head of the Mellon Foundation. And, of course, she learned by applying her own intelligence, common sense, and curiosity. "I talked with many people. I learned about philanthropy through talking to people who knew about it, who *did* it. I was changed into a philanthropist."

Elizabeth has always possessed the academic's thirst for knowledge, which has spurred her to dig into aspects of philanthropy and learn continuously. She has never been static in her thinking.

"I learned in those early years that foundations often gave to bring about policy change while individuals often make gifts that are humanitarian," she says. "Foundations will give to stop homelessness and individuals will give support to organizations which help homeless people. Foundations work for policy change, and as individuals become more educated in their giving, they tend to move toward policy change as well.

"On the other hand, policy change takes years and a new administration can change a progressive policy. Therefore, I suggest that an individual philanthropist give some support to 'charity' and some to policy change because people will die in the streets waiting for that policy change. I think those who give away money should give some for housing or food for health care for the poor while at the same time trying to influence policy to help in a bigger way."

There are many much smaller examples of humanitarian philanthropy. She mentions a New York City organization, Sanctuary for Families, which provides shelter for battered women and their children. "That is a humanitarian project to which I personally give a little money. Some people may be negative about that kind of giving. They say that's old-fashioned charity. Whereas changing policy is real philanthropy. I don't buy that. I think both are needed.

"Humanitarian giving is often called charity. To give food to the hungry in a city is a humanitarian initiative. While to advocate for a city or state food program involves policy change. Most major foundations attempt to bring about policy change through demonstration projects, advocacy, education, etc. In advising younger members of the Rockefeller family, my suggestion about their individual giving was to do both. A government program helps many more people, but it can take years to become law and in the meantime many will die of hunger. Why not help some now work for later change?"

She recognizes the constraints on policy change, as well, since it is often at the mercy—or whim—of political change. "Many foundations, including Atlantic Philanthropies and George Soros, have worked for years on the elimination of the death penalty. In many states it has been eliminated. But as politicians change so does policy!"

That argues for foundations helping to strengthen organizations that will sustain the effort—to fight the death penalty or whatever other issue might be in play. Organizations working to change policies are relying heavily on advocacy, working from the grassroots upward. Advocacy, she says, "is a tool to try to bring about change," and she sees advocacy efforts increasing within the philanthropic world.

"No matter how big a private organization may be, its resources are limited compared to public money," she says. "If you look at a problem, whatever it is—the environment, death penalty, torture, population— if you are to be effective you have to look at the big problem and say, 'This is what we are interested in and this is a little piece of it that we are going to try to do something about. Because if it is scatter-shot, it's going to get nowhere.'

"To give away money very well is not easy," she says. "The wise way to give is to look for synergy so that one's own donations—in collaboration with support from other individuals or organizations—may have a powerful impact. If I give wisely to some good purpose the impact is made not only by my gift but by everyone's giving. I have to be sure that the combination of my own funds and other funds from individuals and foundations have the greatest chance of something good resulting."

.　　　.　　　.

As far back as 1980, six years after she started working for the Rocke-fellers, Bill Dietel saw that Elizabeth had become "a very real substantial person in New York City and increasingly outside the city in her own right." Part of her appeal was her close association with the Rockefellers, of course. As her friend Thornton Bradshaw, former CEO of both RCA and Atlantic Richfield, put it, she was "an ambassador for the Rocke-feller family to the philanthropic world."

But it was more than just her association with the Rockefellers, says Dietel: "It was her talent. She begins to crop up on important boards and she plays important roles on those boards. She's not just a board member, she ends up running the governance committee, she ends up running the board.

"By the time you get to 1985, people are coming from all across the United States to see Elizabeth. . . . People would talk to me and they would say, 'We've got this terrible problem, we've got this organization, we don't know who the hell to put on it. Where do you go to get good names?' You go to Elizabeth. . . . And before you know it, everybody and his cousin claims some kind of connection to her."

Part of her appeal was her intelligence and judgment, says Dietel, but another important component was her openness to new ideas. "Elizabeth isn't afraid of failure," he says. "Elizabeth is interested in cre-ating new things. She's interested in the new and the different . . . and she's got a strong enough ego that she could afford to take a risk with her reputation. And that really won her legions of friends."

Why was she so sought after by a handful of the most elite organizations in the country? Steven Rockefeller says it is "her ability to take big complex issues, cut right down to the nub of the matter and then get something done. And she's got an extraordinary network of people whom she can contact."

Elizabeth's ability to cut to the chase is a key element of her appeal, says Dorothy Samuels. She says Elizabeth constantly pushes to find common ground where a solution might exist. Elizabeth, she says, will often stop a conversation "and ask the key question. 'OK, so what has to be done to make it work? What do you need to do to make it right? Maybe you can't do *all* of it, but if you were going to do one thing, what would you do?'" Samuels says that Elizabeth "never gets mired in the problems. It's: How do you do it? What would you need to do if you wanted to do it? If you wanted to fix it? She is into fixing. She's into making better. She understands the other guy's side."

Dorothy Samuels was appointed executive director of the New York Civil Liberties Union in 1979 at the tender age of 27, and as she set about the difficult task of raising money she was introduced to Elizabeth by Aryeh Neier, leader of the American Civil Liberties Union. "I had never been in any office that grand," she says of her first visit to Room 5600 at 30 Rockefeller Plaza. "Even my law office at a Wall Street firm was nothing like that, and I remember Elizabeth taking us to her club high atop Rockefeller Center and being very dazzled by that. I'm there to ask for money for what was this fairly struggling group I was leading and we were in this very grand surrounding, and yet, I was sitting with this very tiny woman with this wonderful smile and this very warm manner that was anything but formal. She was just so down to earth that it was in very sharp contrast to the whole surroundings. . . . And I found that within just a few minutes she had basically found out everything about my life. I don't know how she did it because she never asks intrusive questions. She just gets people to talk."

During that lunch, Dorothy talked about her idea for a new initiative on privacy rights "that would be based with the New York affiliate of the Civil Liberties Union," she says, "but would be a model project that looked at some of the emerging issues of privacy rights, the sharing of Social Security numbers, and the new ability given the emerging technology of governments or even health organizations or schools or large institutions of any kind to assemble dossiers in a way that was going to be different than the old way of assembling documents in Hoover's FBI, say, which was sort of primitive files."

In 1979 this was a visionary notion and Elizabeth McCormack understood right away and followed up with a series of practical questions. How could you make it happen? How do you frame it? At the conclusion of the lunch, Elizabeth asked Dorothy to write a letter explaining her idea. A couple of months passed without a word. Dorothy had half forgotten about it when the mail arrived at her office one day with a note from an anonymous donor and a check for $50,000.

"For us in those days it was enormous!" says Samuels. "And it was done not like foundation executives usually operated, which is it's not their money, but they're dying to take credit and to make sure they get the thanks and the aggrandizement and compliments. Instead, it just modestly arrives in the mail with a note that it's anonymous and 'Keep me posted.'"

That same year, 1979, a Manhattanville graduate named Beth Pettit found her way to Elizabeth's office—like Dorothy Samuels in search of help. Beth had been a teacher in Harlem, but she was not allowed to set up the special reading program she wanted in a public school. She then found her way to a parochial school—St. Aloysius—and established the St. Aloysius Education Clinic to teach children how to read and write well. Beth was seeking to adopt a new program called Reading Is Fundamental, but she did not have the books her young pupils needed. She told Elizabeth she needed $5,000 to get the program off the ground. She said she thought it would have a real impact on the lives of thousands of kids who needed academic support.

Before Beth had left her office, Elizabeth had written to two major corporations and, very soon thereafter, Beth got the $5,000 she needed from IBM. Some time passed and Elizabeth told others about the great work Beth was doing at St. Aloysius and some of them volunteered donations. "A little while later I called Beth," says Elizabeth, "and I said, 'I have some more money.' And Beth said, 'Thank you very much but I don't need any more money.'"

That was perhaps the first and only time Elizabeth had ever heard those words. Elizabeth continued to be helpful through the years in times when Beth did, in fact, need money. Thirty-one years after Elizabeth and Beth first met, Beth hosted a ceremony honoring three people, including Elizabeth. Beth emphasized that she wanted to honor people who had stuck with her since the very beginning.

.   .   .

For all of Elizabeth's empathy and ability to target potentially productive causes, her record is, of course, imperfect. As a member of the General Foods board when it was acquired by Philip Morris in 1985, Elizabeth was asked to join the new board. She hesitated. This was one of the world's largest purveyors of a legal product known to kill millions. But she was persuaded to do so by David Rockefeller and joined the board in January of 1986.

"I said to David Rockefeller, 'should I do this, should I go on the board of a cigarette company?' He said, 'well by saying no you won't keep a single person from smoking.'"

David Rockefeller was a very smart man, but was he right? Would a refusal by Elizabeth to join the board have been seen as further demonization of the tobacco industry and its practices? Or had the industry been so thoroughly demonized by then—so thoroughly in disrepute—that nothing she did would have an impact? But if the latter is true then why would she want to join the board at all? Why would she be affiliated with a company peddling such a demonstrably lethal product? An industry where company leaders stubbornly refused to acknowledge the scientific truth—that their products were dangerous.

Could it be that Elizabeth was blinded at that moment by the bright lights of the corporate world? That she was—for that moment—seduced by it? Often in her life she stood on principle. Elizabeth's deepening friendship with Thornton Bradshaw was opening more opportunities in the corporate world. They served together on the boards of the Aspen Institute and the John D. and Catherine T. MacArthur Foundation, and Bradshaw was instrumental in bringing Elizabeth onto the board of the Institute for Advanced Studies at Princeton.

When Bradshaw was asked to take over as chair of the MacArthur Foundation, he told Elizabeth that he had agreed to do it provided that she join him on the board. This was an interesting opportunity. Elizabeth was aware that MacArthur was having difficult governance issues with board members pushing themselves into program areas that happened to be directly in line with their professional interests. This hindered the Foundation's ability to establish and sustain a clear, well-focused mission.

She was swamped with obligations when Bradshaw asked her to join the MacArthur Board, but she could not resist. Bradshaw and Elizabeth would travel to MacArthur Board meetings together, taking the RCA helicopter from Manhattan to Westchester and then boarding the RCA jet to Chicago. They spent countless hours in the air through the years and got to know one another very well.

"He was a real intellectual, which was very unusual in the business world," says Elizabeth. "He was unlike most CEOs I know—he was a much more humane person." She admired his ability to examine and understand complex issues from various perspectives. "So often people in the corporate world have a completely erroneous idea of what the nonprofit world is all about and vice versa. For instance, to be very involved in the Earth Justice through board membership and to be on the Champion International board, a paper company, and to hear absolutely rational but opposite positions on cutting down trees is a real education."

At the end of 1995, then MacArthur Foundation board chair John Corbally sought opinions from board members concerning the overall direction of the foundation. In her letter to Corbally dated January 10, 1996, Elizabeth included the following list.

1. We make far too many small grants—too many to be researched or evaluated.
2. Our staff is too large. The current size is the result of the large number of small grants in far flung places.
3. We make too few general operating grants. Our project-program grants often cost our grantees more than we give them. Were we to concentrate far more on general operating grants we would be unique among foundations.
4. We operate in too many countries. Because we do not have on-site staff (except in Moscow) our Chicago staff must be continually on the road and in the air. I cannot believe that it is possible for them to know in depth so many very different cultures.
5. I believe in grassroots giving, but it should be balanced by grants to major organizations. In other words, more of our grants should be "wholesale." Too many are "retail."
6. It should be the task of the officers of the Foundation to identify "big bet" opportunities. Only for these will we be remembered as having made a significant identifiable difference. This does not mean always creating new institutions. We should be proud of WRI and the Energy Foundation, but also our grants to Bill Moyers. I recently heard of a six-million dollar grant from the Wallace Funds to the College Board for "Equity 2000." This might prove to be a good bet.

7. The world—economically, politically, and socially—is experiencing an era of sea change comparable to the Industrial Revolution or even the Renaissance. (Note the communications revolution and the global economy—AT&T downsizing by 40,000 jobs, most of them in the U.S.) These movements cannot be reversed, certainly not by foundations or even by individual nations. But this new reality must be factored into everything the Foundation does. To divide programs into national and international is consequently obsolete. No challenge is simply a U.S. challenge or an international one. Everything we do should have both dimensions.

8. The Foundation should use its voice to spread awareness of the fact that this is a new world. It should make grants to those who will analyze the new problems created by these changes. It is time for thinking and analysis.

9. Much work has already been done on the idea of "Healthy Communities." I do not like it, as it says everything and nothing. Also, it is supposed to be our "national program," which I do not believe we should have.

10. Whatever programs we eventually settle on should be focused. I suggest a few programs, each with a clear focus.

11. I believe there should always be a large general grants budget without any program focus. This would enable us to seize opportunities, initiatives, and make "big bets."

.　　.　　.

Jonathan Fanton was president of the New School in New York when he joined the board of the Rockefeller Brothers Fund and got to know Elizabeth. He came to know her better and better through the years, and, by the late 1990s, when Elizabeth was chair of the MacArthur Foundation board looking for a new president, she nominated Fanton.

There were three search committee members, but Fanton says "she was clearly the dominant force on the committee and she was very supportive of my candidacy.

"The board was famously difficult," says Fanton. Board members often behaved as though they were staff—pushing for grants in their pet areas and then, staff-like, micromanaging those grants.

Elizabeth saw that the foundation was a mess at the governance level. Certain board members, including some truly distinguished people, had used their clout to promote philanthropy in their own areas of interest. "They were on the board but they were acting like super program staff," she says. "Each staff person had to report to the president but also to the board member who had created the program and who was still running it. It is an inappropriate role for the board."

A big part of the problem at MacArthur was a lack of focus. It seemed to lurch from one issue to another, all too often taking on mega-problems. In general, Elizabeth believes that philanthropic organizations have a tendency to overreach. In their desire and often passion to take on large problems, they too often don't target their gifts effectively enough. "You have to take on big things, but you have to do it saying we're not going to accomplish it. We're taking this one little piece. When foundations take up huge things like climate change, they have to pick some small aspect that is meaningful—teaching schoolchildren the implications of climate change, for example. You are not going to end climate change quickly. I believe foundations attempt to do things much too big which they can't possibly do."

She once said to her fellow board members at MacArthur that "if a man from Mars came to a MacArthur board meeting and spent two days with us listening to our plans and grants and then went back to Mars he would announce to his fellow Martians: 'We have nothing to worry about as far as planet Earth goes—the MacArthur Foundation is taking care of it.'"

Fanton says MacArthur trustees tended to remain on the board too long, preventing the injection of new blood and fresh ideas. Elizabeth and Bradshaw worked diligently to change that throughout the 1990s and, in fact, managed to establish ten-year term limits for members.

Elizabeth played an important role in shifting the organizational culture, says Fanton. "With reforms such as board term limits also comes a general disposition to respect staff and back the board out of some of the micromanaging they were doing," says Fanton. "Elizabeth understood how a professional foundation ought to work and that it should not be a collection of strong personalities pushing the staff around and pushing their hobby horses."

Once board term limits were established, a number of trustees sought exemptions, but Fanton says Elizabeth held fast. The result was a considerable amount of much-needed board turnover, and Fanton asked Elizabeth to chair the nominating committee to select new trustees.

She also played an important role in working with Fanton and board members to steer the foundation away from smaller grants to many organizations and toward making considerably larger grants to many fewer organizations.

"She thought you should pick good people running good organizations and you should trust them without a lot of jerking around," says Fanton. "Give them freedom to do their work. She had the right balance between wanting some evidence of impact but not believing everything can be measured—taking some risks in organizations we believed in."

Occasionally, foundations identify a problem but cannot find an organization to deal with it. And so they create a new organization, which is what MacArthur did at one point. MacArthur wanted to play a role in protecting the environment and noted what was obvious—countless organizations, large and small, already occupy that space. As officials at MacArthur studied the situation they found what they thought was an unfilled need in the environmental movement. They found that, perhaps not surprisingly, most existing environmental groups were hostile to business and corporate interests.

MacArthur saw the need for something different—a collaborative approach with the corporate world. Since no organization existed to facilitate that, MacArthur used its considerable clout to create a new organization from scratch. Thus was born the World Resources Institute, which works with business to find opportunities to improve the environment. Since its founding in 1982, the World Resources Institute has grown into a respected environmental think tank that seeks to provide solutions "grounded in sound science and objective analysis."

.   .   .

While Elizabeth has served on many boards of very large, prominent organizations, one of her most rewarding boards is Hamilton College, a small, liberal arts school in Clinton, New York, where the board consists largely of graduates of the college. She was one of the first three women to join. "It's a wonderful board, and there aren't many really good boards," she says. "Boards fail in one of two ways. The members go to meetings. They like the people they meet. They like the parties. They do nothing. That is one problem. The other is that the board tries to manage, and that is worse because no board can manage anything."

During the 1960s, Hamilton's leaders established a women's college, Kirkland College, as a companion school. Originally, Elizabeth served on the Kirkland board at the invitation of her friend Walter Beinecke, who had been a trustee at Hamilton since 1960 and played a central role in the creation of Kirkland. But Kirkland was in trouble. Hamilton was paying a variety of costs to keep it going, and pressure was mounting for something to happen. At a meeting in the late 1970s, Elizabeth said to her Kirkland board colleagues: "Could we, for the moment, pretend we are Hamilton's board—not Kirkland-Hamilton's. Could we as

Hamilton's board continue paying a large percent of Kirkland's annual costs, when we of Kirkland are not able to tell Hamilton how long this has to go on? We see no end to it, and if we think of ourselves as Hamilton's board, could we, with our fiduciary responsibility, go along with this?"

The answer was obvious. The chairman then called for a coffee break from the meeting, and during the interval several board members told Elizabeth she was right. She told them there was no value in saying that during a break—that they should repeat it when the meeting reconvened. In 1978, Hamilton and Kirkland merged.

Elizabeth joined the Hamilton board in 1978 as its first female member and was elected a Life Trustee in 1991. She served on the board as Charter Trustee with many distinguished people, including Sol M. Linowitz, a Hamilton graduate and a businessman, diplomat, and advisor to presidents.

"He was a wonderful man and I remember one of my first board meetings when the president had trouble after the merger. Martin Carovano was the president and a group of faculty asked to meet with the board and Martin said at a board meeting that a group of faculty wanted to meet with the board. He said, 'Maybe it should be the executive committee and I am ready to arrange it.'" Sol Linowitz put his hand up: 'We don't want you to arrange that. We don't meet with faculty. We meet with you. Now *you* tell us what the faculty are upset about and we will make a judgment about it, but we will not let the faculty go around you to get to us.'"

"It is a board," she says, "that knows how to be a board."

.   .   .

As one of a rapidly growing number of prominent women in philanthropy, Elizabeth is a role model for other women. "Women in philanthropy are so few and far between," says Nan Aron, Elizabeth's step-daughter and president of the Washington-based Alliance for Justice. "I think women, particularly in philanthropy, don't get their just due, and while many work in the field, most foundations are run by men. I think that Elizabeth's role as a board member on so many foundations and corporations has had an important impact."

"Being a woman, a real minority on boards (two women on Champion board, three on Philip Morris board, the only one on American Savings Bank board), gave me a great, great advantage. I know how to use it; I don't talk a lot. When I do speak, I have impact. The men listen," says Elizabeth.

Asked in 1991 what she would tell a young person seeking work in the foundation world, Elizabeth replied: "I would tell any young person who came to me not to do it as a first job, or even as an early job, because I think that there are many pitfalls connected with giving away money, and one of them is that you become very arrogant. No one ever tells you the truth, ever, and that the only way to remain honest is if one has some other experiences . . . the philanthropic world is not the real world. It's once removed from the real world. . . . Giving money facilitates other people doing important things. These other people are much more important than the philanthropists. And I think it's easy to forget that."

One lesson Elizabeth learned from being around so many wealthy people was that more real-world experience would benefit them greatly. She believes that when a wealthy young person graduates from college he or she should have to work for ten years and cover all of their own living expenses—with no help from parents. Working to "have a roof over your head and food on the table makes you a different person. It is a discipline."

.　　.　　.

When she was chair of the MacArthur Foundation, Elizabeth

helped one of her favorite causes, Cambridge College. Based in Cambridge, Massachusetts, the college serves a lower-income, highly diverse population of adult students. Elizabeth worked closely with Peggy Rockefeller Dulany, David Rockefeller's daughter, to help the college survive and eventually thrive. In May 1994, Elizabeth was presented with an honorary degree at the college. At the ceremony, Peggy Dulany spoke of having tried through the years to figure out what the "secret qualities" were that made Elizabeth so effective. "Here is the tip of the iceberg that I have been able to discern:

- A quick wit that diffuses often sticky situations;
- A nearly mock naiveté that expresses surprise and interest at what her interlocutor is saying, and draws him out further;
- An infinite generosity of spirit that makes room for everyone in her impossible calendar; and
- A secret weapon of secret weapons—a mental database that far exceeds the largest capacity computer, and that is capable of popping out just the right name at the very moment that everyone was despairing in the knowledge that we just couldn't make it."

Fundamentally, Elizabeth says, philanthropy is about common sense. "It is an art, not a science. You have to believe in what you are giving to, and the only way you can give money is to people. No other way. A great idea is a great idea and you can be captivated by it, but unless you can find gifted people who believe in that idea and, in fact, whose idea it *is*, no donor, no foundation really can be the creator of the ideas. If they are, they have to sell the idea and someone who is going to implement it has to take that idea and make it his own. My theory is that the gifted person in the area in which the donor is interested has better strategies than any ivy tower donor. So I quickly concluded that donees know more than donors."

She is concerned about some of the current trends in philanthropy, particularly the push toward excessive measurement. The question asked throughout the philanthropic world is how do we *know* we are effective? How do we know our programs are working as we intend?

"It is good to evaluate what you do," she says. "If a grantee says he is going to do X then you look—is he really trying to do that? Does it have any impact? Some things can be measured in that way and some can't. But we've gone crazy with evaluations—really crazy. Foundations are thinking and spending a lot of money trying to see what they're doing." Elizabeth is fond of citing Einstein on this matter. On his office wall in Princeton, Einstein had a sign which read: "Not everything that counts can be counted and not everything that can be counted counts."

Elizabeth understands that it is important to get away from board meetings and see for yourself the effects of your decisions. She and some colleagues from the Population Council visited India and met with officials working on population issues. From New Delhi, they traveled by bus to small villages where Population Council staff members were conducting research.

"At the Pop Council we always say that women should have a choice of contraceptives," she says. "They should make a decision about whether they would use a permanent method or one which involves visiting a doctor on a regular basis." And the theory of giving the women a choice of birth control methods was perfectly rational, until, that is, one saw the reality of these women's lives.

"How could these poor women have a choice?" she asks. "How would they get it? If they were using a certain kind of contraceptive method, they would have to go every few months to a doctor. We were hours on a bus to get to their village. So this business of choice for many poor women in the third world is probably just a myth of first world people."

Elizabeth's toughness and willingness to do the dirty work—especially involving personnel decisions—are legendary. Through the years, she has proven to be fearless in making and executing difficult personnel decisions.

John Mroz, president of the Institute for East West Policy Studies, recalls a particular Ford Foundation meeting where "I was with two academics whom she did not respect, if I could put it mildly. They had written an op-ed together and she apparently had really let them know what she thought of it and it was so funny because she's tiny and these are two big guys. . . . When she walked into the room one of them says, 'Oh, shit,' and I said, 'What's the matter?' And he said, 'Here she comes . . . she's going to blast us.' . . . If she thought you were wrong she would come up and tell you."

When Elizabeth first joined the board at Memorial Sloan-Kettering, she met the new CEO, a medical school classmate of her brother, George, from Columbia. "He wanted to have the right of making tenured appointments on the faculty there," says George. "That was his request. And he didn't come to the board meeting [when] his request came up. Some people didn't want to do it. And she said, 'Look, he has just started here, we cannot turn down his first request. It's not right.'" But when next she saw the CEO, says George, "She said to him, 'I voted for you to be allowed to give tenure. But the next time you have a request like that and you don't show up at the board meeting, I am going to make sure that it doesn't go through.'"

.   .   .

While Elizabeth has played major roles at major institutions, she has also devoted considerable time and energy to much smaller endeavors. Two of the most notable are Cambridge College and Marlboro College. Neither is at all a particularly elite institution, but both, she says, do crucial work. Cambridge educates adults, many of whom come from diverse backgrounds and who are well into their thirties, forties, and older. Marlboro College in Marlboro, Vermont, describes itself as offering "a student-centered approach to education that is structurally and culturally different from other colleges. Unfettered by generic course requirements, each student works with their faculty advisor to choose an individualized course of study. For graduation, seniors complete a self-designed 'Plan of Concentration' that is reviewed by an outside evaluator who is an expert in the student's field."

Joel L. Fleishman, professor of law and public policy sciences at Duke, knows Elizabeth very well and admires her devotion to these two colleges. "Think about the special nature of Marlboro, the special nature of Cambridge College," he says. "They are two institutions that are serving people who especially need education in new ways, and she cares deeply about that."

Over time, she would come to serve on several dozen boards of directors of a variety of not-for-profit organizations—mostly universities and foundations. But she had just as deep and profound a commitment to helping Marlboro and Cambridge colleges as to helping Dorothy Samuels and Beth Pettit.

In December 2006, the Elizabeth J. McCormack Seminar Room was dedicated at the MacArthur Foundation with remarks from the board chair, Sara Lawrence-Lightfoot:

> You can see the fire in her eyes. That is the first thing I felt when I met Elizabeth McCormack more than twenty-five years ago when we were both on the Board of my alma mater Swarthmore College. Here was this diminutive woman, looking exactly as she looks today, with a simplicity and alacrity that masked a fierce energy, with a spare truth-telling that is grounded in an amazing self-confidence. But it was her eyes I noticed that revealed the passion. At Swarthmore, we were part of a small cabal of trustees urging the college to divest its investments in South Africa.

Ultimately successful in our quest, it was Elizabeth who listened astutely, spoke rarely, and made sense. It was Elizabeth who helped to move—through a steady, quiet insistence and a moral assurity— this Quaker board to a fragile consensus. This was the first place where I witnessed Elizabeth, the consummate trustee at work. Choosing my mentor very carefully, I watched her moves, her style, her timing. I listened for her voice; and noticed her strategic silences. With Elizabeth, the quiet is always more than half the story.

(12)

Today

Elizabeth McCormack's life has taken her from the convent, where she had no personal possessions other than a couple of habits, where she had no assets of any kind, to working with one of the wealthiest families in history.

Making money never motivated Elizabeth, but she did not mind having it, for it enabled her to travel with Jerry, spend time in Pawling—to enjoy life. She was also quite generous with it, both philanthropically and personally. She was compensated well by the Rockefellers and she also earned substantial fees—and in some cases generous stock options—for her work on various corporate boards such as Philip Morris, Champion, and United Health Care.

At one point, her brother, George, and his wife were living in a lovely apartment on East 72nd Street. When they divorced and sold the unit, George moved into a second-story walk-up studio. "And Elizabeth came up one day," says George, "and said, 'This is an awful place where you live. Buy yourself an apartment and let me know what it costs.' She sold I don't know how many shares of United Health Care and gave me the money to buy an apartment."

When she was chair of the MacArthur Foundation board, she became close to its president, John Corbally. "After she had been in the chair five years and I was asked to replace her, I said I would do it only if Elizabeth would be vice chair. . . . We had some fun with this. We had met at the Drake Hotel in Chicago for years when Elizabeth was chair and she always had a room at the end of the tenth floor, a two-room suite with a little dining room overlooking the lake where we would often have breakfast meetings. When she became vice chair she laughingly said, 'Well, I'll be vice chair if I can keep the suite.' She has the suite."

Jerome Kohlberg and his wife Nancy have been generous and caring friends of Elizabeth. She spends time with them at their Martha's Vineyard home and recently joined them there for Thanksgiving. When Elizabeth turned eighty, Jerry Kohlberg said he did not want her wandering around hailing cabs and arranged an account for her so a car would always be available—and she would never see a bill. She refers to it as her K-Car.

"It seems to me," says Dorothy Samuels of the *New York Times*, that "she emerged from the Manhattanville experience—the student takeover, the publicity and controversy, the reshaping of the school, and then leaving the order to marry Jerry, which got very big publicity as a semi-celebrity, was something that somehow never left her. Celebrity may be too strong a word, but certainly, she's a very well-known figure. . . . Hers is a name that people know . . . a grand name and it did change her life."

In 2011, it had been sixty-seven years since she made the decision to enter the convent; sixty-seven years since that summer in Lake Placid when she planned to spend the rest of her life as a member of the Society of the Sacred Heart unquestioningly obeying the will of God. Her plan was to spend her life as a single woman—never to marry, have children, own possessions or wear anything other than her habit.

She regrets some of the changes in the Sacred Heart Society. She valued the strictness and severity of the life, the rigor. It mattered. It contained a richness and depth of commitment and meaning for her.

More than a decade after the 1967 Sacred Heart Society gathering in Rome—known within the Society as the Chapter—Elizabeth and Jerry were traveling in England. They visited the convent in Oxford where she had stayed while she was working on her PhD thesis. They knocked on the convent door and a nun appeared. Elizabeth said she wondered whether she could look around—she explained that she had lived there years ago as a student.

"My name is Elizabeth McCormack," she said, and the nun acted with a sense of wonder.

"Elizabeth McCormack!" she replied. "Come in and tell us what really happened at the Chapter."

It is quite a journey from being a twenty-two-year-old nun who believed unquestioningly that any sort of birth control was sinful and wrong to being a particularly influential member of the board of directors of the Population Council, where you travel to Mexico, India, and other nations to support research concerning women's health, AIDS, and family planning. "It is a long journey," says Elizabeth, "and in the old days you could be excommunicated for being involved in the Population Council."

.   .   .

Perhaps the most important questions about Elizabeth concern her spiritual life. Questions she finds difficult to answer. She often reflects upon the differences between the Old and New Testaments, particularly the focus in the Old on retribution—"an eye for an eye. . . ." She spoke of a luncheon she attends annually run by an organization called

Survivor Corps "created by a man named Jerry White who had a leg blown off in Israel. Its message is that to survive when you are injured, when you have had an awful experience, you cannot think of yourself as a victim, you have to make things better for other people; you cannot survive alone.

"At the luncheon the Niarchos Foundation presents an award to survivors and one was to a Palestinian doctor, a Muslim, I guess. In an Israeli bombing he lost his three daughters and he is now promoting peace between those two countries and not condemning the Israelis . . . that's the Christian message, turn the other cheek. Could I do that?"

Elizabeth has always asked questions. "The most fundamental one is: what is the meaning of life? Who is God?" The search for meaning defines her life. It is a question that is never answered, but it controls her behavior. "Do unto others as you would have them do to you." The Christian code is, she says, "a simple guiding principle of life."

Years ago she read *The Secular City* by Harvey Cox, and today she is reading *The Future of Faith*. Each book articulates what she finds difficult to say herself. Cox defines the nature of faith. He distinguishes between faith and beliefs. Beliefs differ but faith is universal. Christian, Jew, Muslim differ in belief. They believe according to the culture of each. The myths differ but faith is universal.

She quotes Harvey Cox: "Rabbi Herbert S. Goldstein fired off a telegram to Albert Einstein. 'Do you believe in God? Stop. Answer paid. 50 words.' Einstein's response follows. 'The most beautiful emotion we can experience is the mysterious. It is the fundamental emotion that stands at the cradle of all true art and science. He to whom this emotion is a stranger, who can no longer wonder and stand rapt in awe, is as good as dead, a snuffed-out candle. To sense that behind anything that can be experienced there is something that our minds cannot grasp, whose beauty and sublimity reaches us only indirectly: this is religiousness. In this case, and in this sense, and in this sense only, I am a devoutly religious man.'"

Einstein's words speak to Elizabeth. She says that to experience a sense of awe and wonder in the presence of great beauty is to experience the unknown God.

Linda Goelz, who has worked for the Rockefeller family for thirty years, is Elizabeth's friend and neighbor. They live in the same building near the UN and talk nearly every day. Linda says that "there are two wonderful churches over by where we live and she hasn't been to either one."

Her views of the Church are one thing—she has little respect for the institutional Roman Catholic Church. "My brother had to have a priest when he was dying," she says. "He was scared." Many decades earlier George had gotten a girl pregnant and she had had an abortion and "he spent his life worried about that. I don't think I'll need a priest when I'm dying. I hope there's an afterlife. I don't think there is but I hope there is. And if there is I will be part of it and I won't need a priest to get me there.

"I remember one of the nuns—a good friend of mine, Cora Brady, who died a nun—saying to me years ago, 'Whichever one of us dies first, if there is an afterlife when the other one comes and looks at the coffin, the dead one should knock.'"

Elizabeth went to Cora's wake, but there was no knock from the coffin.

.   .   .

She has a sense of humor even where the loss of Jerry is concerned. When Gara LaMarche became CEO of Atlantic Philanthropies, he visited Elizabeth at her apartment. When she offered him a drink, he noticed a bottle of Laphroaig, single-malt Islay Scotch whiskey. He reached toward it, and she looked at him and said, "That was Jerry's." Gara felt as though he had "treaded on hallowed ground," yet a moment later Elizabeth reflected upon it and said, "He's dead. He's not going to have any."

But the truth was that she missed Jerry terribly and had a difficult time being alone after he died: "My life changed after Jerry's death," she says. "The hardest part was and is the realization that death is final. I will never see him again. But the years since 2004 have not been empty. I have done many things with many people, but the greatest help and, in fact, happiness has come from Jerry's family and from Katarzyna Stich [Jerry's assistant] and from Martin Bieniek [Kate Stich's husband].

"Jerry's four children are my children. I speak on the telephone to Peter at least three times each week. Nan often stays with me in New York City, we speak frequently about the Alliance for Justice, political events, and family matters. Mark, who lives in Oregon, comes east approximately once a year and keeps in touch in between visits. Betsy is Jerry's youngest daughter and is my daughter in a very special way.

"Of course the grandchildren are my teachers. They help me to understand and to live in the modern world. Nan and Bernie's children live in New York City and visit frequently. Nick is a storyteller like his grandfather and regales me with tales of his experiences in international law. His wife, Vivien, shares an interest in philanthropy. Their son Leo is my first great grandchild and gives me a new kind of joy.

"Emma, a psychologist, has wonderful memories of time spent with Jerry and me and will remind me of them when I see her and her fiancé Eric, and Leni, our family politico, keeps me current on the activities happening in my neighborhood.

"Shortly before my ninetieth birthday, Phoebe, Peter, and Helen's daughter, and I hosted twenty-one of Phoebe's Whipporwill campers. I am anxious to see how Sophie, their other daughter, will integrate her travels and humanitarian work in Haiti and Africa into her life. As for Mark's sons, I helped arrange an interview for Gabe to meet with Philip Glass, a modern composer, and am so relieved that Sam returned from his military stint in Iraq safe and sound. I also enjoyed watching him on Skype.

"Of course, I am in touch with my brother's children, Jane, Hugh,

George, and Julia. My brother's oldest daughter, Jane, is a very successful clinical sociologist with a PhD from the University of Chicago. We discuss advances in her field. Her brother Hugh has varied interests, among them sailing, which he learned from his father. George is an administrator and a teacher at LaGuardia Community College. Math is second nature to him! George's youngest daughter Julia is an expert fundraiser. When I was on the Board of Memorial Sloan Kettering, I was proud to know that my niece was so successful in bringing major support to the hospital. I spent Christmas in 2011 with them and learned to know Adam, George, and Corinne's son. He is smart and fun to be with.

"For the last five years of Jerry's life Kate Stich was his assistant. She managed our two homes and fulfilled numerous tasks that he requested. He taught Kate the value of education so that after his death she completed her BA at Marymount Manhattan College. From his death to this day Kate and Martin have been a major part of my life. She now works for the Rockefeller Family and Associates as my assistant. Kate and her family have joined my family in giving me a full life."

"After Jerry died she was very emotionally fragile," says Linda Goelz. And she dealt with that not by slowing down, as some people do. Rather, she has chosen to accelerate. "People underestimate how strong she is," says Linda. "She looks frail but she's not frail at all." She travels frequently—both domestically and internationally—and she is out for luncheon and dinner engagements virtually every day of the week.

Elizabeth is most content, says Linda, when she is busy and around other people—especially when she is being asked for help or advice. "Feeling useful is important to her," says Linda. "Feeling she is making a difference in someone's life and can be useful. Being asked for advice is important to her still."

Bill Dietel says she stays active because "she knows in her bones that that's how you stay alive. That if you don't stay engaged you are going to die." She remains on a number of boards. "The Juilliard board is very special to me. I enjoy being a member and I hope to contribute to this great institution." Elizabeth serves as a connector of scores of people and institutions throughout the not-for-profit—and sometimes the corporate—worlds.

And she has even added a new interest to her portfolio—palliative care: that is, the area of medicine focusing on the prevention and relief of patients' suffering. She has engaged with Dr. R. Sean Morrison, one of the nation's leading experts on the topic, to increase awareness among patients of the value of palliative care. Dr. Morrison is Director of the National Palliative Care Research Center, Director of Research at the Hertzberg Palliative Care Institute, and the Hermann Merkin Professor of Palliative Care at the Mount Sinai School of Medicine. Dr. Morrison met Elizabeth around 2005. She wanted to better understand what palliative care was all about, and she questioned him closely during a meeting at her office. That meeting was the start of a close relationship between Elizabeth and Dr. Morrison, and she has played a pivotal role in connecting him to the right people in philanthropy.

She also came to know Dr. Diane Meire, who heads the Center to Advance Palliative Care (CAPC). The fact that so many hospitals offer palliative care is due to her expertise and advocacy. "We're raising money for three things," says Dr. Morrison. "First, to let the public know what palliative care is and how to access it. Second so that health care professionals have an evidence base to provide it. And we want to do a national public relations and social marketing campaign. She is very quiet yet in complete control," says Morrison. "She has the presence of somebody who is six-feet-eight in less than a five-foot body!" Elizabeth has become so deeply involved that she founded and chairs the Partnership for Palliative Care.

.   .   .

She is frequently the object of adulation from people throughout the philanthropic world. Rarely, however, does she hear much in the way of praise for the work she did at Manhattanville. But in November of 2009, a reception was held in Elizabeth's honor at the elegant, old-world Cosmopolitan Club on East 66th Street in Manhattan. It was a touching event for Elizabeth since it was organized and hosted by Manhattanville's African American alumnae, many of whom took over Brownson Hall at Manhattanville forty years earlier. Deborrah Belcher Karim, Pamela Stewart Cassandra, Jeanette Michael, Cheryl Walton McNeil, Emily Belcher, Cheryl Hill, D/Oniece Shaw Dillard, Genevieve Shane Stanislaus, and Marsha Diggs formed a committee to host the event. They wrote in a program for the reception that while Elizabeth "presided over Manhattanville during challenging and turbulent times, many recall Elizabeth's compassionate leadership, her steadfast conviction and unswerving commitment to steer the school in an unprecedented historical direction. During Elizabeth's presidency, Manhattanville welcomed the largest African-American student population in the college's history."

They noted her "graciousness and compassion" and added that "while many years have passed since the '60s and '70s, some of us realize that we are forever connected to Elizabeth's legacy."

. . .

Elizabeth has many friends, and, somewhat unusual for a person of her years, they represent every imaginable age group. Her grandson, Nick Arons, for example, gets together with Elizabeth often for dinner or a movie or just to hang out. Nick has been close to Elizabeth his whole life, but even more so since Jerry's death. Nick finds that not only does he thoroughly enjoy her company, so does his wife, Vivien, and many of their friends—all in their early thirties.

"Our friends love her," says Nick. "They are always blown away by her. Most people aren't used to meeting someone that age so lucid who works every day. And her whole career—people are amazed by what she has done. And whatever the big issue of the day is she can talk about it intelligently—with anyone."

.　　　.　　　.

An article in David Patrick Columbia's New York Social Diary, an online source of information about the New York social scene, reported on an event marking the fortieth anniversary of the Asian Cultural Council (ACC), which Elizabeth chairs. Columbia was particularly interested in going because, some years earlier, when he had been in financial difficulty, Elizabeth's brother, George, had not only provided free care but also arranged for care and surgery at a major New York hospital. Columbia wrote that the event was

> in honor of ACC Chair Elizabeth J. McCormack, as well as paying tribute to the ACC's founder, the late John D. Rockefeller 3rd and his late wife, Blanchette Rockefeller. The evening was hosted by Bill Moyers and featured dance and music performances by leading Asian and American artists. . . . The concert was performed in the brand-new Jazz At Lincoln Center Allen Room with its back wall of glass framing Columbus Circle, Central Park South, the southern end of Central Park and in the distance the Upper East Side of Manhattan. There is no way to articulate the breadth and scope of the visual experience except to say that it reminded me of those movies and documentaries of the City moving at night, like a Gershwin rhapsody or the background to a jazz concerto. Brilliant.
>
> Bill Moyers told us that this evening, honoring this very remarkable woman, Elizabeth McCormack, was sold out six months before the invitations were even sent. There were more than 500 guests attending . . .
>
> From her brother's description in conversation, I had a picture

of a small woman with a very serious yet unstuffy personality, a woman of great character who despite her long devotion to piety was also well aware of the earthly realities of the day to day, and a woman armed with both wisdom and cleverness. Otherwise, she remained something of an enigma—a nun who becomes a financial adviser to the Rockefellers, abandons her habit, and marries a Jew . . . ?

She is a tiny woman. And white haired. . . . She was wearing a red silk blouse that had been provided by Josie Natori, who was a co-chair with Valerie Rockefeller of the evening. Dick Parsons, the CEO of Time-Warner, gave the toast, revering the woman whom he said he'd sought advice from hundreds of times and had never left without the satisfaction of hearing real common sense and real wisdom.

Bill Moyers, David Rockefeller Jr., and ACC President Richard Lanier talked about her with reverence, affection, and awe. Then presented her with a silk scarf, and a silver tray inscribed in English and several of the languages of Asia. The room was filled with distinguished people who were thrilled to be in the presence of this tiny humble woman who eschews long speeches and personal honors.

She gave a short speech telling us that there were many kinds of foundations and she had sat on many different boards (including Juilliard—some of whose board members were at my table). But the ACC foundation was different. It was simply about bringing together artists and creative people from the two cultures, America and Asia, to work together, to communicate and move through differences, to strengthen the bonds of humanity that exist in all of us.

The dinner and ceremony took place in the ballroom of the Mandarin Hotel on the 36th floor of the Time-Warner building with its glass walls affording the magnificent view of the Park and the city at night. Senator Jay Rockefeller got up to also say a few words about this woman—more words of admiration and respect but always with a flavor of reality, and humility and humor.

Someone said that the Rockefellers, whenever they hired someone to do something for them, had a knack for hiring the best. Elizabeth McCormack, someone else said, was the highest of the best. And the best of the highest, I should add. She reminded me of my former doctor, my friend, her brother George, and I was very moved to be in her presence. I was fully aware of my blessings and aware of the blessedness of which there is too little these days, maybe all days, for most of us, such as the blessedness of Elizabeth McCormack.

Index

Albany, NY, 15, 22
Allen, Woody, 168
Alliance for Justice, 213
American Jewish Committee, 118-119
Antarctica, 163-164
Aquinas, St. Thomas
  *Five Ways of Proving the Existence of
    God*, 45
Aron, Betsy (JA's daughter), 157, 170, 224
Aron, Jerome I.
  army service, 121-122
  birth (1917), 121
  burial of, 170-171
  as CFO of Manhattanville, 68, 79, 81,
    83-84, 108, 115, 122-124
  death of, 170, 224
  divorce of, 154-155, 159
  and EM's faith, 140, 145
  on EM's presidency, 116-117, 123-124
  first marriage of, 127-130, 154-155
  friendship with EM, 105, 123, 127-128, 132
  in garment business, 122
  and Haverford College, 121
  health of, 126-127, 155, 167-169
  humor of, 164, 168
  and languages, 121-122
  letter to children, 130-133
  marriage ceremonies to EM, 155-161
  on dying, 168
  parents of, 121
  proposal to EM, 154

  and Stanford University, 121
  and Yale Law School, 121
Aron, Joan Borgenicht (JA's first wife),
    122, 126-130, 164
  divorce of, 154-155, 159, 160
  and PhD, 129
Aron, Mark (JA's son), 224
Aron, Nan (JA's daughter), 126, 127, 128,
    129, 155, 157, 166, 224
  on JA's health, 168-169, 170
  on women in philanthropy, 212-213
Aron, Peter (JA's son), 224
Arons, Bernard (JA's son-in-law), 169
Arons, Nick (JA's grandson), 227-228
Asia Society, 188, 196
Asian Culture Council. *See* Asian Culture
    Exchange Program
Asian Cultural Exchange Program, 184,
    189-190, 228
Aspen Institute, 206
Atlantic Philanthropies, 201

Baker, S. J., Kenneth, 90-95, 97
Barat, Mother Madeleine Sophie, 17-18
  as Superior General, 18
Barry, Mother Agnes, 23, 26
Beinecke, Walter, 211
Belcher, Emily, 227
Bennett, Cynthia. *See* Cynthia Hettinger
Beowulf, 9
Berger, Cynthia. *See* Cynthia Hettinger

Berlitz immersion, 54
Bernstein, Bob & Helen, 148
Bieniek, Martin, 171, 224, 225
Blaine Amendment, 90, 99-100,
    102
Blue Book (Rockefeller), 179-180
Bodkin, Mother Superior Gertrude,
    15-16, 17, 43
Bourke, Mother Helen, 41, 42
Boyle, Mother Anna, 41
Bowen, William, 82, 200
Bradley, F. H., 50-51
Brady, Cora, 223
Bradshaw, Thornton, 194, 202, 206, 210
Brown, Larena, 83
Brownson Hall (Manhattanville)
    occupation of, 78-88, 105, 227
Buckley, Jr., William F., 89-103
    and *Firing Line*, 89
    and *New Yorker*, 99
Bulto, Mother Superior Josefa, 63-64
Bundy, McGeorge, 191

Caesar, 36
Cambodia, 106, 107
Cambridge College, 214, 216-217
Carovano, Martin, 212
Carter, Barbara, 29, 35
Cassandra, Pamela Stewart, 76, 227
Catholic Church, 223
    anger toward, 74
    arrogance of, 62
    on EM's marriage, 157, 160-161
    as infallible teacher, 97
Cavanagh, Sister Elizabeth "Betty", 14-16,
    17, 19, 23, 146-147
Center to Advance Palliative Care (CAPC),
    226
Chadayeva, Aset, 169-170
Cicero, 36
Coakley, Mother Margaret, 55, 145
Columbia, David Patrick, 228-230
Connecticut College for Women, 109
Conroy, Mother Ann, 82, 127

Convent of the Sacred Heart, Greenwich,
    CT, 35-37
    EM as Mistress General, 40-44
    feast day, 41
Corbally, John, 207, 220
Cosmopolitan Club, 227
Coughlin, Father Charles, 6
Cox, Harvey
    The Future of Faith, 222
    The Secular City, 222
Creel Committee, 185
Creel, Dana, 149-150, 185
Czech Republic, 194

Dammann, Mother Grace, 7-8, 47-48, 76
    "Principles vs. Prejudice," 48
De Chardin, Pierre Teilhard, 73
deValon, Mother General, 58-62
Dietel, William "Bill," 149-150, 174, 179,
    182, 186-187, 200, 202, 225
Diggs, Marsha, 227
Dillard, D/Oniece Shaw, 227
Dillon, C. Douglas, 199
Dole, Robert, 186
Dominican Order, 2, 45
Donovan, John, 14
Doyle, Rev. Jerald A., 160
Drake Hotel, 220
Dulany, Peggy (Rockefeller), 176, 182-183,
    214
du Lubac, Father, 57
Dudar, Helen, 114-115
Dunlop, Joan, 190

Ecclesiastical Court, 157
Einstein, Albert, 215, 222-223
Eliot, T. S., 50
Emma Willard School (Troy, NY),
    149-150

Fanton, Jonathan, 208-210
Ferry, Sandra. *See* Sandra Rockefeller
Filer Commission on Private Philanthropy
    and Public Needs, 199-200

Fitzgerald, Reverend Mother Helen, 40,
43, 55, 71, 74, 146
Fleishman, Joel L., 217
Ford, Gerald, 186
Ford Foundation, 216
Fordham University, 49

Garson, Mother Judy, 65
General Chapter (Sacred Heart
convocation), 54-66
and Cardinal Protector, 60-61
and deValon, Mother General, 58-62
membership of, 54-55
proposed changes, 55
General Foods, 205
Gilson, Etienne
The Mystical Theology of St. Bernard,
9-10
Goelz, Linda, 146, 163, 223, 225
Goldstein, Rabbi Herbert S., 222
Green, John T., 98
Greenhouse, Linda, 113
Growald, Eileen Rockefeller. *See* Eileen
Rockefeller

Halsey, McCormack and Helmer, 5, 6
Hamilton College, 211-212
Harrison, V. V.
Changing Habits, 48, 53, 142
Hettinger, Mother Cynthia, 72-73, 125,
157-158
Hill, Cheryl, 227
Hill, Superior Reverend Mother Theresa, 37
Howard, Herbert, 4
Howe, Sister Margaret, 26

IBM, 205
Indiana University Oral History Research
Project, 23
Institute for East West Policy Studies, 216

Japan Society, 184
JDR 3rd Fund, 188-190

Karim, Debbie Belcher, 76, 227
Kennedy, Joan Bennett, 48
Kennedy, Edward, 48
Kennedy, Ethel Skakel, 48
Kennedy, Robert, 48, 68
Kennedy, Rose, 48
Kent State University
shootings at, 106-107
Kenwood Sacred Heart Convent, Albany,
NY, 16, 18, 23-29
EM as teacher, 32
EM as Mistress of Discipline
(Surveillant General), 39-40
King, Jr., Martin Luther, 67
Kirkland College, 211-212
Kline, Ed, 159-160, 169
Kneedler, Frank 78-79, 113
Kohlberg, Jerome & Nancy, 220

Lake Placid, NY, 2, 12, 14, 18, 21
Club, 2, 12
LaMarche, Gara, 223
Lanier, Mary, 140, 164
Lanier, Richard, 140, 164, 175, 188-189,
196-197, 229
Larchmont, NY, 1, 5, 18
Lawrence-Lightfoot, Sara, 217-218
Linowitz, Sol M., 212
Literacy Volunteers, 167
Little Office of Our Lady, 25

MacArthur Foundation, John D. and
Catherine T., 194, 206-207, 208-211, 220
Mandarin Hotel, 229
Manhattanville Afro American Society, 77,
78
Manhattanville Alumnae Association, 87
Manhattanville College, 45, 141, 199, 227
applicants to, 75
as secular institution, 71-72, 110
Black Studies Program, 83
and coeducation, 109-111
crucifixes removed from, 72-74
diversity of, 53, 70, 75-77, 109

Manhattanville College *(cont.)*
    EM's first year, 9
    EM's legacy, 117
    EM's second choice, 7
    founding of, 47, 69, 71
    future of, 68-69
    integration of, 77
    and Kennedys, 48, 114
    legal charter of, 67-68, 71
    occupation of, 78-88
    and Project Share, 76
    salaries & benefits of, 68
    survival of, 108-109
Maplehurst School, 2-3
Maritain, Jacques
    Introduction to Philosophy, 7-8
Marlboro College, 216-217
Maryknoll sisters, 17
Mauzé, Abby Rockefeller. *See* Abby
    Rockefeller
McColough, Peter, 122-123
McCormack, Elizabeth,
    on abortion, 111-112
    as academic dean at Manhattanville, 52
    on afterlife, 135, 223
    as assistant at Manhattanville, 48-49
    birth (March 7, 1922), 2
    bride of Christ, 30-31, 115
    and Broadway theater, 11-12
    and Buckley, 89-103
    Catholicism, early influence, 1-2
    childhood, 1-3
    and Christian message, 112
    on complaining, 32
    conflict of faith and reason, 45-46, 135-
        139, 161
    at Convent of the Sacred Heart, 35-36
    on cross-country skiing, 14
    on dating, 13-14
    disillusionment with Chapter, 56-58,
        63, 136, 139
    early reader, 5
    falling in love, 125-128
    final vows, 38

finances of, 150-151, 219
as French speaker, 54
grandparents of, 5-6
hate mail to, 73-75, 81, 96-97
and holy water, 36-37
as Kenwood teacher, 33-34
Maplehurst School, 2-3
on marriage, 162
marriage ceremonies of, 155-161
master's degree of, 44-46
as Mistress of Discipline (Surveillant
    General, Kenwood), 39-40
as Mistress General (Greenwich), 40-44
as novice, 31-32
on nun's habit, 141-142
in Oxford, 51-52, 221
on palliative care, 226
PhD of, 49
on philanthropy, 200-201, 207-209,
    211, 213-215
as postulant, 24-29
on prayer, 28
as president of Manhattanville, 53-54,
    67-88, 105-119, 141, 144
on proselytizing, 93, 98-99
resignation from Society, 145, 148-149,
    153
and Rockefeller cousins, 177-178
"The Role of Love in the Liberation of
    the Will," 9-10
search for meaning, 222
spiritual calling, 15-19
on suburbia, 13
and summer theater, 12-13
on teaching, 34-36
on Thomistic Theology, 44-46
on treatment of nuns, 38
typing, 12-13
and Vietnam War protests, 107-108
on the wealthy, 195-196, 213
McCormack, George (EM's brother), 4, 12,
    119, 129, 151, 157, 168, 216, 219-220, 228
    on abortion, 112
    birth (January 24, 1925), 2

childhood, 1-2
Columbia Medical School, 21, 37
death of, 223
on EM's social life, 14
on EM becoming a nun, 21-22
tuberculosis of, 37
McCormack, George Henry (EM's father),
    2, 11
on drinking & smoking, 12
education of, 7-8
death of, 46
on EM becoming a nun, 22
on EM's boyfriends, 13-14
and golf, 5
and Halsey, McCormack and Helmer, 5
illness of, 38
marriages of, 135
on typing, 12-13
visiting EM, 29, 37-38
McCormack, Joy (GM's wife), 157, 162
McCormack, Natalie (EM's mother), 2, 4,
    130, 147
and Broadway theater, 11-12
parents of, 4-5
visiting EM, 29, 35-36, 37-38
McKinney and Doyle, 166-167
McLaughlin, Mother Iona, 83
McLaughlin, Morris, 75-76
McNeil, Cheryl Walton, 227
Meire, Diane, 226
Mellon Foundation, 200
Memorial Sloan-Kettering, 216
Merton College. *See* Oxford.
Michael, Jeanette, 227
Miller, Sister Mary Ann, 98
Morris, Nancy, 110
Morrison, R. Sean, 226
Mother House, Rome, 38, 54
Moyers, Bill, 228-229
Mroz, John, 216

Napoleon's tomb, 163
National Association for the Advancement
    of Colored People (NAACP), 187

National Association of Black Students, 78
National Palliative Care Research Center,
    226
National Review, 89
Natori, Josie, 229
Natural Resources Defense Council
    (NRDC), 181
Neier, Aryeh, 203
New York Civil Liberties Union, 203-204
New York Social Diary, 228-230
Niarchos Foundation, 222
Nicene Creed, 138
Nixon, Richard, 107-108
    petitioning of, 106

O'Byrne, Mother Eleanor, 49, 115
O'Clair, Robert, 141
O'Connor, Father Vincent, 155-156, 160,
    161
Ohio National Guard
    and Kent State, 107
Open Space Institute, 167
Oxford, England, 51-52, 221

Parsons, Richard "Dick," 229
Partnership for Palliative Care, 226
Pawling, NY, 165-167, 219
Pettit, Beth, 204-205, 217
Philip Morris, 205-206
Planned Parenthood, 112
Pocantico, NY, 177-178
Poland, 138
Pollock, Prof. Robert, 49-50
Pope John XXIII, 54
    Journal of a Soul, 143
Pope Paul VI, 158-159
Population Council, 184, 188, 190-192, 215,
    221
Port-au-Prince, Haiti, 154
Porter, Elizabeth, 74, 76, 125
Princeton
    and Institute for Advanced Studies,
        206
    and JDR 3rd Fund, 189

Providence College, 44-46
Purchase, NY, 67, 69

Radcliffe College, 6-7
Regents of the State of New York, 71
Reid, Whitelaw, 67, 113
Renard, S. J., Father Louis, 56
Rhodes, Frank, 139-140
Rockefeller, Abby, 174
Rockefeller, Alida, 184
Rockefeller, Blanchette, 196-197, 228
Rockefeller, David, 174, 185-186, 205
Rockefeller, Jr., David, 176, 229
Rockefeller, Eileen, 176, 193
Rockefeller, Hope, 184
Rockefeller, Jay, 176, 179, 184, 197, 230
Rockefeller, John D., 150, 173
Rockefeller, Jr., John D., 174
Rockefeller, 3rd, John D., 174, 184-191, 228
Rockefeller, Larry, 181
Rockefeller, Laurance, 174, 185-186, 192-194
Rockefeller, Nelson, 67, 174, 184-188
Rockefeller, Sandra, 184, 194-195
Rockefeller, Steven, 176, 177, 181-182, 183,
    187, 198, 203
Rockefeller, Valerie, 229
Rockefeller, Winthrop, 174, 185
Rockefeller Brothers Fund, 149, 174, 177,
    184-186, 208
  location of, 175
Rockefeller Family Philanthropic Office,
    180-184
  EM's retirement from, 197
Rockefeller University, 192
Romanov, Princess Nadia, 34
Rome, 38-39, 55, 57
Russell, Bertrand, 51
Rustin, Bayard, 175

Sacred Heart College, Tokyo, 196
St. Agnes Hospital, White Plains, 30
St. Aloysius Education Clinic, 204-205
St. Augustine's Academy, 2
St. Augustine parish, 18

St. Bernard, 10
Sales, Ruby, 81-82
Samuels, Dorothy, 164-165, 203-204, 217,
    220
San Diego College for Women, 110
Schrafft's, 11
Schreiber, Bill, 14, 21, 22
Schroen, Mother Marie Louise, 26
Schuman, Mother Miriam, 43
Schuster, George, 119
Scobey, Raphail, 118-119
Second Vatican Council. *See* Vatican II
Sheehan, Maggie, 22
Shawn, William, 99
Shultz, George P., 199
Simon, William E., 199
Skype, 224
Slaughter, Margaret, 30
Slavin, Father, 46
Social Security, 68
Society of the Sacred Heart, 144
  changes in, 64-65, 142-143, 221
  Father Varin, 18
  General Chapter of, 54-66, 221
  greater silence, 27
  history of, 17-18
  novices, 31-32
  postulants, 24-29
  and Manhattanville, 7, 9, 15
  and Maplehurst, 3
  and Mother House, Rome, 38, 54
  role of the Mistress General, 34
  uniforms of, 31
Somerville, S. J., Father James, 49
Soros, George, 201
Spellman Hall (Manhattanville), 72
Stanislaus, Genevieve Shane, 227
Stich, Katarzyna "Kate," 171, 224, 225
Sullivan, Father James Michael, 98
Survivor Corps, 221-222
Swarthmore College, 217-218

Theroux, Phyllis, 48
Thomistic Theology, 44-46

TIAA-CREF retirement plan, 68
transubstantiation, 138-139
Trinity College, 7
Tuohy, Jane, 114
Trust for Mutual Understanding, 194

Ursuline School, 2

Vatican II, 54, 61, 65, 73, 89, 112, 141
Vicariate House, Albany, NY, 36
Vietnam War, 57, 77, 84, 90, 105, 177
    antiwar movement, 106-107
Vincent, Sister Helen, 2

Wagner, Rodney, 192
Wallingford, Mother Peggy, 72-73
Weiss, Rabbi David, 156-157, 161
West Virginia Wesleyan University, 179
White, Jerry, 222
Williams, Paula, 78
Winged Foot Golf Club, Mamaroneck,
    NY, 5
wonderment, 158
Woodstock summer theater, 12-13
World Resources Institute, 211
World War II, 13

PublicAffairs is a publishing house founded in 1997. It is a tribute to the standards, values, and flair of three persons who have served as mentors to countless reporters, writers, editors, and book people of all kinds, including me.

I. F. Stone, proprietor of *I. F. Stone's Weekly,* combined a commitment to the First Amendment with entrepreneurial zeal and reporting skill and became one of the great independent journalists in American history. At the age of eighty, Izzy published *The Trial of Socrates,* which was a national bestseller. He wrote the book after he taught himself ancient Greek.

Benjamin C. Bradlee was for nearly thirty years the charismatic editorial leader of *The Washington Post.* It was Ben who gave the *Post* the range and courage to pursue such historic issues as Watergate. He supported his reporters with a tenacity that made them fearless, and it is no accident that so many became authors of influential, best-selling books.

Robert L. Bernstein, the chief executive of Random House for more than a quarter century, guided one of the nation's premier publishing houses. Bob was personally responsible for many books of political dissent and argument that challenged tyranny around the globe. He is also the founder and was the longtime chair of Human Rights Watch, one of the most respected human rights organizations in the world.

. . .

For fifty years, the banner of Public Affairs Press was carried by its owner Morris B. Schnapper, who published Gandhi, Nasser, Toynbee, Truman, and about 1,500 other authors. In 1983 Schnapper was described by *The Washington Post* as "a redoubtable gadfly." His legacy will endure in the books to come.

Peter Osnos, *Founder and Editor-at-Large*